D1200659

# WHAT
# I HAVE LEARNED

A collection of
twenty autobiographical essays
by great contemporaries
from the "Saturday Review"

A SATURDAY REVIEW BOOK

**SIMON AND SCHUSTER** · **NEW YORK**

# CONTENTS

preface
NORMAN COUSINS

## Adventures in Ideas and Learning

T HE IDEA for the series in "What I Have Learned" came from four short lines in *The Practical Cogitator*, edited by Charles Curtis and Ferris Greenslet. Originally published in 1945 and reissued in 1962, the *Cogitator* is one of the most compact, varied, and satisfying intellectual and literary feasts to appear in this country in the post-World War II years. The four sentences came from Charles Beard in response to a query by George Counts, now eminent professor at the University of Southern Illinois School of Education, once a professor of my own when I was a student at Columbia Teachers College: "How long would it take you to tell all you have learned from your lifetime's study of history?" Dr. Beard felt the great lessons of history could be summed up in just four lines:

1. Whom the gods would destroy, they first make mad with power.
2. The mills of God grind slowly, but they grind exceeding small.
3. The bee fertilizes the flower it robs.
4. When it is dark enough, you can see the stars.

Each of these sentences, of course, opens out on a universe of human thought and experience. Each seems enigmatic or paradoxical; all represent a challenge to the individual mind—not just to see fully into and beyond the separate statements but to relate them to personal experience.

Over the years, we have found Professor Beard's apothegms a most useful way of getting people to talk about themselves. There is a vivid recollection, for example, of a philosophical conversation with Jawaharlal Nehru in 1953. We were seated on the broad lawn in back of the prime minister's house in New Delhi. He was at the height of his popularity as leader of India's four hundred million newly independent people. Nehru relished reflective conversation and often complained that politics and contemplation didn't go well together. He said he regretted being so busy doing things he didn't have time to look into the meaning of them. Yet each man had the obligation, he supposed, to scrutinize his life and to ask whether it was teaching him anything—a paraphrase of Socrates' famous observation that the unexamined life isn't worth living. Nehru was just as much at home with the ideas of the ancient Greeks as he was with Eastern thought. He said he wondered how many people could penetrate their own experience in order to locate the essential lessons.

We mentioned Professor Beard's brief philosophical distillations. They delighted Nehru. Then we asked him how he would respond to the challenge put to Professor Beard by Professor Counts. He sat back in his lawn chair and slowly sniffed a tiny rose. Then he said: "I have often wondered whether I have learned anything at all in my life, really. It is possible the most important lessons are stored in the subconscious and that we act on them without identifying the source or even knowing they are there.

"One lesson I know I can identify. The teacher was Gandhiji. He taught me—he taught us all—the importance of making the means consistent with the ends. If you had worthwhile goals but pursued violent or evil means, the goals would change for the worse. Politicians are not philosophers—though I agree with Plato it would be nice if this were so. Anyway, it is somewhat out of tradition for a politician to make the means consistent with the ends. Few things are more typical of politics than the ease with which it degenerates into violence. Yet I have learned that it is worth trying to keep good ends from being diminished by poor means. Trying helps— at least a little.

"The second lesson I think I may have learned," he continued, "is that there is no natural conflict or contradiction between free will and determinism. Life is both. Life is like a game of cards. You have no control over the hand that is dealt you. The hand corresponds to determinism. The way you play the cards corresponds to free will. So I think I have perhaps learned it is better to make the most of what you are than to exhaust yourself in lamentation because you are not someone else."

Nehru's emphasis on the dominance of moral lessons over the practical ones was also clear in Albert Schweitzer's reaction to Beard's miniaturized formulations.

"All my life I have been asking myself not just what I have learned but what civilization has learned," Schweitzer said in our last conversation at the hospital in Lambaréné. "And I have come to feel that the greatest discoveries have to do with ethics. Man is still in search of an ethic which alone can give his life true meaning and beauty. For me, the greatest ethic is life-and-world affirmation. If we can develop true reverence for all life, we may be able to understand it. We cannot manifest it or be part of it without reverence. This, I think, is what I have most of all learned. There is also the need to understand the reality of the existence of God inside each man and to know how to make that inner kingdom manifest."

It is against this background that the "What I Have Learned" series was conceived and planned. Our hope had been that Nehru and Schweitzer would contribute to the series. Nehru said, characteristically, that he would only embarrass himself by revealing how little he had learned after all, but said he would try to find time to contribute. During the next year, he wrote us three long letters detailing his preoccupation with India's problems and world issues. Schweitzer, also characteristically, sent long handwritten letters, apologizing for the quality of the penmanship (he said he had inherited his arthritic fingers) and telling of his world concerns.

Though neither Nehru nor Schweitzer is represented in the "What I Have Learned" series or the book, their place in the development of the idea must be acknowledged. Their responses, as well as the original brief quotations from Charles Beard, were highly pertinent and useful in describing the project to possible contributors and in setting the stage for the book.

This volume of "What I Have Learned" consists of twenty essays. Publication of the book, however, will not mark the end of the series in SR. The editors intend to continue publishing the essays so long as reader interest in the series is sustained. It is possible that additional volumes may be brought together. All this, however, is for the future. Meanwhile, the editors hope the book will serve as a reminder that man can still preside over his experience. The perception of a better future must not be confined to soothsayers or astrologers. The proper assessors of human hopes are those who can comprehend the connection between cause and effect and who can extract governing principles from the multiplicity of events and forces. The learning experience is still the precarious and vital one.

The human race may not be able to generate as much conceptual thought as it can use, but it would be disastrous not to use as much as it has. Fortunately, thought does not have to be quantified—not even in an age obsessed with numbers. Even to promote respect for thought adds to the basic energy and quality of civilization.

NORMAN COUSINS

# WHAT I HAVE LEARNED

i

# AUGUSTINE CARDINAL BEA

## Paths to Ecumenism

---

W HEN MY nomination as cardinal was announced in November 1959, one of the first telegrams of congratulation came from Günther Dehn, emeritus professor of evangelical theology at Berlin University. In 1897 he had been my classmate in the high school at Constance (on the lake of the same name); indeed, I may be forgiven for saying that he was my partner at the head of the class. There were various Christian confessions and religious faiths represented in the class. All the same, we got on very well and worked harmoniously together. From that time I began to learn to have not merely a chilly respect but a genuine esteem for those of other confessions, and even to love them sincerely, while remaining loyal to my own faith. That was for me, who came from an entirely Catholic village, my first school of practical ecumenism.

In succeeding decades I continued in the same kind of "school." Besides studies done at schools within the order to which I belong, I had plenty of experience in training in distinctly pluralistic environments, in the universities of Freiburg in Breisgau, Innsbruck, Austria, and Berlin. Everywhere there was a mixture of students and professors of various confessions. I remember with deep veneration several of my teachers in Oriental sciences at Berlin University, all non-Catholics, each a real celebrity in his field. Eduard

Meyer, the historian of the ancient East; Hermann Strack, the Hebrew specialist; Jakob Barth, in Semitic languages; Joseph Mar-
quart, in other Oriental languages.

Such contacts continued during my teaching life, both at the
Jesuit college of Valkenburg, Holland, and at the Pontifical Biblical
Institute in Rome (1924–1959). The latter's great library was
known as the best library in Rome for Protestant scientific Biblical
literature. From the time of Pius X, when the index of prohibited
books was still in force and strictly enjoined, this Pope had, very
farsightedly, authorized the rector of the Institute to give his students permission to read non-Catholic books to the full extent required for their studies and research.

Soon there was a real exchange of contacts between the Institute and non-Catholic Biblical scholars and orientalists. Pius XI
personally made a decisive contribution in this direction. In 1935
the illustrious German scholars J. Hempel and P. Volz organized at
Göttingen the first International Congress of Old Testament
Studies. For the first time in its history the Pontifical Biblical Institute of Rome was invited to a gathering of the kind. This was so
novel that I felt I ought to put it directly to Pius XI himself. Now
he had been for most of his life a librarian by profession, first at the
Ambrosiana in Milan and then at the Vatican, and had considerable experience with scholars of all kinds. Hence he answered, with
his habitual assurance and energy, "Why shouldn't you accept? Go
by all means, and take with you some well-equipped men who
know their subject."

It was a brave decision for those days, and turned out to be
fruitful beyond expectation. In fact, the Institute delegation was so
well received at the Congress that its leader, the rector, was invited
to preside at the final session. In this way began frequent contacts
with the non-Catholic scholars of the world. These were further
intensified when the Institute acted as host in Rome to the International Congress of Studies on the Ancient East.

The total effect of these encounters was a steadily increasing collaboration of exegetes of various confessions in both Old and New Testament studies, expressed steadily in a large number of learned international congresses and reviews dealing with Biblical studies, ranging over the whole scriptural field. The latest initiative of this kind is the collaboration between Catholics and the non-Catholic Bible Societies in the translation and distribution of the Scriptures. In recent months this has taken still more definite shape and is richer than in mere promise, not only for Christians' getting to know the Bible better and drawing closer together, but also for their fulfilling their common duty and pledge of carrying the torch of the Word of God to all the peoples of the world.

What is the *interior attitude* which inspires a common life and activity of this sort among men belonging to various confessions and religious faiths? It is, obviously, somewhat complex and needs to be analyzed step by step. Clearly, I do not propose to tackle, much less exhaust, so exacting a theme, but only to illustrate some of its aspects in the light of my own experience. This example will illustrate a primary element.

One of my first studies in the field of Biblical science was two articles about German studies on the Pentateuch—i.e., the first five books of Holy Scripture. I concerned myself in particular with the theories of the illustrious German non-Catholic scholar Julius Wellhausen. The theme was an extensive one and, although I was only writing for the educated lay reader, it called for two articles. When the first appeared, the higher authorities of the Order in Rome let me know that I should not have eulogized a non-Catholic scholar, as I had done with Wellhausen, especially when he had done so much damage in the field of sacred Scripture. I answered laconically that they should wait for the second article. In fact, in the first article I had endeavored to explain Wellhausen's ingenious scientific construction, while in the next I showed its undeniable weaknesses and limits.

I did the same thing subsequently in my writings, in particular in the book I published fifteen years later on the same theme of the Pentateuch. This procedure started from the principle that there is not and cannot be an opinion, even if it be an erroneous one, which does not contain a kernel of truth. It was necessary first to grasp and frankly recognize this good element, this kernel of truth, when one found it. Only then, on this objective foundation, could one voice a constructive critical judgment.

The attitude I have described evidently presupposes a sincere and firm *will always to understand*, according to the motto of that well-known orientalist, Cardinal G. Mercati (1866–1957), prefect of the Vatican Library, *paratus semper doceri* ("always ready to learn"). The desire for a continual intellectual renewal is needed. In this sense I have more than once told my students, "What I teach you, I have learned in my activity as professor." I have told them, too, that I had always learned much from them. They, indeed, with their questions and difficulties, press—even force—the teacher to clarify and give greater precision to his thinking. A principle I always tried to follow in examinations was perhaps part of the same outlook and the same live relationship with my students. Alluding to the kind of examiner who tries to "trick" the candidate in order to discover what he has not studied, I used to tell my students, "I am not interested in what a candidate does not know but in what he does know."

This effort to understand what we have been talking about naturally calls for much attention and psychological insight regarding differences of mentality, language, ways of expression, etc. I remember in this connection that during my stay in Japan in 1929 an old European who had lived there many years told me, "For a Japanese, a syllogism is a cruelty," because with it one man tries to force another to recognize what he perhaps is unwilling to recognize. Now I believe that also in this field of sensitiveness to different mentalities recent progress in Biblical studies has made a notable contribution. The kind of interpretation, Catholic or not, of the

Bible which tended in one way or another to project the psychological and literary categories of Western Biblical scholars on it, doing violence to the sense, has been heavily challenged by the discovery of the riches of the various literatures of the ancient East, still far from being thoroughly explored today. This was a shock which brought us up against the great differences of outlook, language, and ways of expression between the modern Western mind and those literatures, the Bible not excepted.

It is interesting that from the Catholic side it was Pius XII (a canonist who as a young man had been secretary of the commission for the reform of the Code of Canon Law) who strongly drew the attention of Catholic exegetes to this problem. The fact that he was not only a canonist but also a diplomat of keen psychological insight enabled him to understand a field that was not his own. I can also add, from my personal experience, that from the time he was a young nuncio, Eugene Pacelli was deeply interested in Scripture. I knew him in Munich when, from 1921 to 1924, he was apostolic nuncio and I was superior of the southern province of my order. Even then he often sought my advice on the interpretation of this or that text of sacred Scripture. The same thing went on after he had returned to Rome in 1929 and become Secretary of State; in fact, it lasted until his death.

It was not without previous preparation that Pius XII could remind Catholic scholars in his well-known encyclical on the Bible, "What those ancient writers meant by their words is not determined only by the laws of grammar and philology, or argued from the context; the interpreter must also as it were go back in mind to those remote centuries in the East, and with the help of history, archeology, ethnology, and other sciences determine exactly what literary genres the writer of that distant time intended to make use of." A little farther on he added, "The exegete cannot decide a priori what they [the literary genres] are, but only after a careful study of the ancient literature of the East."

This spirit of respect for and openness toward the thinking of others is of fundamental importance for teamwork in any form. A well-known modern statesman is said to have declared that committees always work badly. Men of a similar outlook often refuse teamwork, thinking it leads inevitably to compromises which are signs of weak and servile giving way on principles. For my part I have often, especially during my forty years' work in Rome, had occasion to serve on a variety of committees. Naturally, I don't say that such work is easy or even that it is always agreeable. Obviously the result will depend on the choice of chairman and his collaborators, and on the harmony or lack of it between them. Nevertheless, even when I have very carefully studied and prepared the agenda, I have always realized afresh that the other members put their finger on things that escaped me, and in this way made their indispensable contribution which it was my business to recognize and accept candidly.

One of the chief problems posed by teamwork is *how to deal with divergences of view.* These are not merely inevitable, they are just what makes the work of a committee fruitful, bringing out the various points of view which must be taken into account. The problem lies in the way these divergent opinions are expounded on the one side and received on the other. Here is an example.

Years ago a well-known Catholic ecumenist gave a public lecture on the theme "The Council and the Union of Christians." After the lecture a non-Catholic speaker said, "The lecturer has said some rather hard things about us non-Catholics. All the same, he could have said more. Given the way in which he has said them, we are bound to accept them." One who had had a good deal of experience in committee work remarked that personally he always stuck to the principle, "If I have to express a difference of opinion with somebody I try to do it as courteously and amiably as I can. It seems to me that in this way I have managed for the most part to avoid unpleasantness."

Recently, in an address to the Secretariat for the Promoting of Christian Unity, Paul VI remarked very acutely how often difficulties of a psychological order tend to be represented as difficulties of principle. "Old positions hardened by bitter memories, mixed up with questions of prestige and subtle polemics, arouse reactions which tend to be represented as assertions of principle on which it would seem impossible to yield." Anyone who has worked in the difficult ecumenical field—and not only in this field—knows how often this is true, and how necessary it is to have uncommon clear-sightedness to understand and evaluate such situations.

So far, I have spoken of my experiences that bear on the way of traveling together toward a common goal. What are the *prospects* of arriving? In September 1961, while I was staying in Strasbourg, the mayor, M. Pflimlin, surprised me by asking, "Your Eminence, are you an optimist or a pessimist about the prospects for ecumenism?" "Mr. Mayor, I am neither an optimist nor a pessimist, but a realist," I answered promptly—and perhaps the promptness showed how much the answer reflected my deepest conviction and attitude.

If anyone, reading what I have said so far about respect for other opinions, the need for effort to understand, and so on, has thought that I am an optimist at any price, that I wrap myself in illusions that man is "by nature good" and disguise difficulties and obstacles, he is mistaken. In speeches and in my books I have always tried to guard against every illusion that ecumenical work is easy. When we are concerned with understanding and unity on the merely human level, difficulties increase immeasurably and the limits of human possibility are more restricted.

For the rest, I believe that much of my experience has educated me in this realistic view of life. During my life I have been able to feel the profound truth of the passage in the Book of Wisdom 9:14, "For the reasoning of mortals is worthless, and our designs are likely to fail."

When I was eleven, a doctor gave me only three months to live because of a pulmonary infection. In 1913 another doctor said, on the basis of an X-ray (that technique was then only beginning), that I should never be able to stand the climate of Rome—where I have lived for forty-three years. And my religious superiors—how many contrasting destinies they planned for me! In 1904 I was consigned to the study of ethnology; in 1910, to Greek and Latin philology at Innsbruck, which I was then to teach at the college of our order in Feldkirch, Austria.

Shortly afterward, at the end of my theology course, I was intended for a lectureship in theology, but in 1913 the superiors sent me to study Oriental languages at Berlin University as a preparation for teaching Holy Scripture. This I actually began to do in 1917. But four years later the higher authorities in Rome sent me to govern the South German province of my order; and in 1924 I was called to Rome, and here, too, the various tasks and offices and the teaching of various subjects followed one after another.

Why have I referred to these facts? Certainly not to deny the authority which, in my order as in the Church at large, guided me as I obeyed it. Nor do I intend to criticize my superiors who ruled me in this way. Superiors, of course, are not always free to do what they would like, and are dependent on many changeable circumstances. I have described these ups and downs rather to illustrate how experience has taught me a healthy realism—taught me to see clearly men's limits and the inadequacy of their work.

And there are worse things. Besides limits and powerlessness there are in this world the painful realities of evil and sin, with everything disorderly, unhealthy, and sometimes devilish that is involved. And, as if this were not enough, there are the invisible powers of evil—just as it was written that Christ came "to undo the work of the devil" (I John 3:8). For the same reason the apostle Paul wrote to the Ephesians, "For we are not contending against flesh and blood [against poor, weak creatures like men] but against the principalities, against the powers, against the world rulers of this present darkness, against the spiritual hosts of wickedness" (Eph. 6:12).

These, then, are the reasons on which a sober and authentic Christian realism is based. It is this that makes me profoundly convinced of what the Council solemnly declared at the end of the decree on Ecumenism, "This Holy objective—the reconciliation of all Christians in the unity of the one and only Church of Christ—transcends human powers and gifts" (Decree on Ecumenism, 24). But all this does not imply defeatism and discouragement.

It was no accident that good Pope John, nearly every time I met him, repeated with an affectionate smile this single word: *Coraggio*. I don't believe that the thought in the Pope's mind was that I lacked courage; rather, he wanted to underline how much courage was needed to face the obstacles that reared up, and are still rearing up, in the path of the Secretariat for the Promoting of Christian Unity—as, for that matter, they reared up in the path of Pope John himself, as I tried to make clear in a chapter of my book *Unity in Freedom*. Which is why I believe the Pope often had to repeat the word to himself.

What is the *foundation* of this courage? Here, too, I may be allowed, as when talking earlier about education for healthy realism, to point first and foremost to my own experience, especially that of recent years. Before the end of the Council I already was able to say publicly that what has happened in these last few years in the ecumenical field has surpassed the rosiest expectations we could have had a few years earlier. This judgment is even more valid today after the conclusion of the Council and after the latest developments in the field. The same could be said of the way the Council went, considered as a whole, of the most important documents it gave us, of the moral unanimity with which all, even the most difficult of them, were approved, and that in secret ballots.

But all these well-known facts are not more than episodes—indeed, relatively small episodes—in the immense work of God which is the redemption of humanity through His Son. The Christian faith witnesses to this, and gives us security. Full of wonder at this work, St. Paul was able to write, "If God is for us, who is against us? He who did not spare his own Son but gave Him up for us all, will He not give us all things with Him?" (Rom. 8:31–2).

It is in this light that we should view the prospects of our journey together toward the great goal which is *the full unity of the human family*. If I may be permitted yet once more to refer to my own life, it seems to me that the slightly tortuous path into which obedience has directed my life, as I have hinted above, is an image of the path of mankind through history. Certainly the path of humanity, seen merely through human eyes, is as tortuous as could be, full of failures and grave misadventures. It is nonetheless certain that it is guided, in a manner secret and unseen yet real and effective, toward the realization of God's plan with and for mankind. I believe that today I can be sure—so far as it is possible for man here below to be sure—that all those shuntings to and fro made up a preparation for the tasks which Divine Providence has gradually entrusted to me. Equally, I don't doubt that one day we shall be clear how the painful and wearisome groping of mankind through history was intended to educate man for his eternal destiny and guide him toward it—and has, in fact, done so.

Certainly, in marching toward the great goal set for humanity, we ought to engage ourselves very seriously, we ought to dwell on making plans, we ought to employ all our resources of mind and heart and collaborate assiduously with others, and, indeed, with the whole of creation ranged at man's disposal. But it is not said that all this will work out as we intend; it is not said that we shall be spared hard blows and even failures. Yet all this should not frighten us. "If God is with us, who is against us?" Who will succeed in overcoming us?

If Pope John solemnly declared his disagreement with the

"prophets of doom" he did not thereby deny that mankind's path is strewn with evils and misfortunes—he himself repeatedly and clearly denounced many of them—but he spoke thus to invite confidence in the safe guidance of Divine Providence. In the famous discourse—defined as prophetic by his successor—with which he opened the Council, he said, "At this moment of history, Providence is leading us toward a new order of human relations which, by the work of men and for the most part beyond their expectations, are developing toward the fulfillment of higher and unforeseen designs." It is in this light that we can safely and confidently march together toward the great goal of the unity of the human family.

## Augustine Cardinal Bea

*Augustine Cardinal Bea is a prominent figure in the remarkable ecumenical resurgence that has swept the Catholic Church within the past decade. Many of the far-reaching reforms enacted at the Second Vatican Council in 1962–3 directly reflect his eloquence and effective advocacy. The Cardinal was born in 1881 in Riedbohringen, Germany, was in 1912 ordained a priest in the Society of Jesus, and has served as rector of the Rome Biblical Institute, Confessor to Pope Pius XII, and editor of Biblica. He was ordained a cardinal in 1959 by Pope John XXIII and is head of the Secretariat for the Promotion of Christian Unity in Rome. His writings include* Unity in Freedom.

# DANILO DOLCI

## Tools for a New World

---

Until the age of fifteen, I made no particular effort to learn anything. I lived in a middle-class family and went to school year after year, paying rather more attention to the subjects taught by teachers I liked and less to the rest. I adored music, enjoyed reading, and was delighted when it began to snow and equally delighted when the weather turned warm and I could go swimming.

Since my father was a stationmaster, whenever he received a promotion we moved to another city; I thus had a store of different memories, and more than one avenue of communication with the world. Besides, though my father was Italian, I had a Slovenian mother and a German grandfather, so it was only natural for me, I think, to look to horizons beyond "the fatherland." During this entire period—that is, until 1939 or 1940—I amassed sensations and experiences which must have been those of most boys from traditional families in northern Italy, growing up without having to worry about such things as food, shelter, and clothes, and surrounded by smokestacks and factories.

After I turned sixteen, gradually—I still don't quite know why —the need to read, to acquaint myself through the printed word with the experience and thought of men who had lived before me, became so strong that if I had not found books in my immediate surroundings—on my father's modest shelves, in the libraries of friends, in shops when I could afford to buy—I would have stolen them. A normal day was now not long enough for me; every morning I got up at four (in winter I would put on my coat, to keep from shivering, and go sit beside the kitchen stove which, although unlit, still retained a modicum of warmth), and for three hours before beginning my regular school day, I silently communed with my kin, at first more or less at random, then more systematically. Every morning I was deep in one of Plato's dialogues—at least one of the shorter ones—or in a tragedy of Euripides, Shakespeare, Goethe, Schiller, Ibsen; then, going back to the beginning of things, in an effort to understand how men who had preceded me had interpreted the world and our life in it, I read the Bible, the Upanishads, the dialogues of Buddha, the Bhagavad-Gita, and on to Dante, Galileo, Tolstoy. I was truly happy.

Years passed, and the war came, and I emerged from a Fascist prison to cross front lines under fire; when the war ended and I had my first experience of working, my need to know kept growing, until at last, at the age of twenty-five, I had the feeling that I had absorbed what other men had learned and what the best among them had expressed. For several years I had felt a mounting need to take stock of what those different voices had told me, to distill the essence of what I had accumulated, and to compare it with my own experience of life, my own truth, my own intuition. But where was my own life? There was not much, and what there was had not been lived in accordance with what I had understood with my mind. What did I have that was truly valid that I could hold up against what I had learned? Was not all my learning secondhand? All around me, as I now saw, were people who thought in one way, spoke half the time in another, and often lived, disjointedly, in a third; they were at best disorganized, incoherent, superficial, apparently sure of themselves, but without any deep faith in the possibility of changing themselves or the world. They even used their knowledge of the Gospel as a means of personal affirmation. For me, too, "a new heaven and a new earth" was only an intellectual ideal. My dislike of violence was more passive than active. I would go to a concert, for example, and sense in Bach's music a striving toward a life harmoniously serene, and enjoy it; but on coming home I would be no closer to brotherhood than before, and if anyone annoyed me I would lose my temper. At home, the family called me "Let-me-finish-the-chapter."

It was coming in contact with Nomadelfia, a Christian community which gathered together in a vast family boys and girls left homeless by the war, that gave me my first opportunity to acquire knowledge through direct experience. Hoeing weeds, building latrines in the camps, living with orphans, former petty thieves, many of them sick, I discovered what it means to grow together; after several months of common endeavor, even abysmally stupid faces became more human, and sometimes beautiful. In the old Nazi-Fascist concentration camp at Fossoli, orphans found a new mother and father. Working together in the wild fens of the Maremma, we were able to transform the brush into orderly fields of grain, use the brushwood for bonfires to roast limestone from the nearby hills and make lime, take from the fields the big rocks dislodged by the plows and use them to build houses to receive new families. I became deeply aware that even as each man must take stock of himself and learn to live according to his convictions, so the life of the group, community life, is an indispensable instrument for stock-taking and for individual and collective maturation.

After a year and a half of this truly fundamental experience, through which I cleansed myself and, as it were, discovered my essential self, I began to see Nomadelfia as an island, as a warm nest that tended to breed complacency. Quite unexpectedly, almost as a flash of inspiration, I asked myself one day: And what about the rest of the world?

I am still not quite sure how or why, but one day, after bidding an affectionate farewell to Nomadelfia, I set out for Trappeto, Sicily, the most wretched piece of country I had ever seen. Ignorant as I was of the problems of the south and of the techniques of socioeconomic work (I had studied architecture at the university, but I had always been more interested in the structure of human relations than in the structural relationships of stones), I kept busy by working with peasants and fishermen and by participating in their life from within. From this time onward, I truly began to learn.

I found myself, while still in Europe, in one of the most miserable and blood-drenched areas in the world—with tremendous unemployment, widespread illiteracy, and Mafia violence reaching nearly everywhere, covertly or overtly. For the most part, the people were bitter and discontented, but they were not committed to bringing about a change in their situation. It was increasingly borne in upon me that as long as people have not discovered through their own experience that change is possible, that even profound and drastic changes are possible, they are all too ready to say, "It has always been like this and it always will be." I also saw that while this was true of the backward agricultural areas, it was no less true of the industrialized zones, where many people have no idea that development can proceed at a different pace or in a different direction from what they see around them. A man does not make an effort (toward what goal, since there is no goal where he is concerned?) unless he knows that he, too, can influence development in a given direction.

Thus I learned that one must work with the people to create new facts, at all levels, so that they can see through their own experience that things can be changed, and how this can be done, and to provide an opportunity for real communication between persons of many different backgrounds and walks of life.

Faced with the problem of a half-starving and desperate population, the state, instead of giving it the employment and the schools that it needed—actions which would have built up solid trust—responded by imprisoning or killing whoever uttered a protest, whether they were outlaws or those in peasant movements demanding possession of uncultivated feudal lands. Not infrequently, the police, with their brutality and their dirty tactics, behaved exactly like the outlaws—indeed, like the *mafiosi*, many of whom were intimate associates of highly placed politicians and policemen (in some cases, even at the highest levels, the police officers merely changed their uniforms).

These so-called remedies, which killed instead of curing, naturally had the worst possible effects on the region. Just how bad these effects were we attempted to present in an analysis published under the title *The Outlaws of Partinico*, the purpose being to provoke a searching of conscience, both in the region itself and elsewhere. It was becoming increasingly clear to me that this primitive evil, occurring the world over on a different scale and at different levels, must everywhere be identified, denounced, and stamped out.

How is it possible to transform a region when most of the local population can do nothing to help, being either unemployed or engaged in unproductive work? The attempt, in *Report from Palermo*, to lay bare to the people the tragedy of make-work helped us to understand a phenomenon which is also encountered on a large scale in other parts of the world. There can be no  true development unless men have an opportunity to work for it and take part in it according to their own needs and convictions.

The masses were beset by hunger and other evils; exploiters old and new were sucking their blood, worse than the lice. But these people, who in fact were idle or nearly idle for much of the year, would have been glad to work and bring progress to themselves and to others if only they had known what they could usefully do.

Water in winter runs down the hillside and is wasted in the sea, and in summer fields that might produce food for all lie parched and yellow; but how can you plan to build a dam if you have never heard of a dam? Manure is burned in heaps on the outskirts of many villages; how can you put it to good use if you do not know how to rot it and turn it into a valuable resource? Topsoil slides down from unplanted slopes, improperly cared-for crops and livestock produce low yields, while a large part of the population, often superstitiously regarding these evils as punishment from on high, stand around with their hands in their pockets. There is a living to be made here for all; but the people do not know it.

In an attempt to assess how great an obstacle to progress a low technical and cultural level represents in every part of the world, although in different forms, we carried out another study among the population, later published under the title *Waste*. Our questions: How can you solve problems of which you are unaware, which you are incapable of identifying? How can you develop natural resources when the very problem of resource development does not exist for you?

I had gone to Trappeto alone, led by my convictions. I did not find myself in a situation where *some* people were not succeeding and could have done so, given a hand. Rather, I found a mass of people who were in misery, in a situation from which the great majority could not extricate themselves.

It was essential to broaden contacts among individuals, to organize these largely isolated men and families into research-and-action groups increasingly aware of the need to develop resources by developing themselves, and to help the growth of those existing groups which were inclined to develop democratically.

A small but stable and competent group (some twenty persons working with the more advanced of the local people through four pilot centers in a great part of western Sicily), known as the Study and Action Center, was formed. I was no longer alone—a social laboratory, each member of which was in a state of creative symbiosis with the rest, was seeking and achieving. It was an open group of dedicated people. A group, one might say, of conscientious objectors who tended to establish an active relationship with other groups and individuals to give rise to the formation of new groups wherever they went, and to act as a stimulus for fresh undertakings.

To build a dam was important because the water would bring to the parched land, along with bread, the green shoots of experience, the proof that it is possible to change the face of the earth; but it was important also because the building of the dam meant a workers' union, a democratic management of the irrigation system, grape-growers' and other agricultural cooperatives. In other words, it meant the organization of chaos; it meant the beginnings of true democratic planning.

In order to build a new world, you must work with three basic tools—man, as the focal point of awareness and discovery; an open resource-developing group; and democratic planning of resource development. (In the first thirty pages of A New World in the Making, I have endeavored to state with precision the importance of these three basic elements—after having had direct experience with them and discussed them with my keenest collaborators and the most involved local people.)

But is it enough to become aware of a problem in order to solve it? Does it suffice to set up a few sensible targets, no matter how well documented, for the necessary solutions to be automatically brought about? Our experience on this point was consummately clear: When individuals or groups have a problem commensurate with their capacities, they can roll up their sleeves and go to work on it; but when, to go back to my earlier example, people are convinced that their region needs a large dam, the construction of which is a costly project within the jurisdiction of regional or state authorities, and when a mere request brings no results, the people must be prepared to engage in a struggle to get their dam.

The struggle must be nonviolent—taking the form of active or passive strikes; refusal to cooperate on what is deemed to be harmful; protests and public demonstrations in all the many forms that may be suggested by the circumstances, one's own conscience, and the particular need. The people should at the same time take advantage of any good laws that may be in existence and help to enact new ones if necessary—but the struggle must be carried on, peaceably but energetically, until common sense and the sense of responsibility have won the day.

Such struggle carries penalties with it, and the people must know it. Those who want things to remain as they are, to preserve the present "order," will try to put out of the running anyone who promotes change. That is how things are; and those of us who have been thrown into jail, labeled as criminals, denounced over and over again, know it well, as do all those who are striving toward a new life anywhere in the world. It is naïve to be surprised or shocked by it. Instead, responsible men must diligently look for those methods and strategies which can be used by the weak to bring about the triumph of reason, i.e., effective alternatives to violence. For the antithesis of peace is not conflict, but violence.

I no longer think it possible to dissociate the struggle for social and economic development from the struggle for peace; even as we cannot be satisfied with haphazard and inorganic growth, so we have learned that a pacifism which is not rooted in social and economic needs is generally so much verbiage.

The explosions of nuclear weapons have had their share in making us see how wrong it is to concentrate solely on the individual, or solely on a closed collectivity, or even solely on the human race as a whole; in other words, how essential it is to look for and discover, step by step, the best and most suitable forms of relations among individuals, among groups, and within the entire human community. Working in this direction from our laboratory in western Sicily, in recent years we thought it particularly useful to analyze the "client group" and the "Mafia-client group," to gain a better understanding of the region—a popular report on the subject was later published under the title *Chi gioca solo* ("He Who

Plays Alone"), taken from the skeptical Sicilian proverb, "He who plays alone never loses"—and of much that goes on elsewhere in the world.

I should like to digress long enough for a very brief analysis of the "client" system. Its basic components are:

• The crafty "politician," the public center of power in the group.

• The "clients," who control votes and who play a major part in determining the prestige and power of their politician. (*Clientes* in ancient Rome, according to the dictionary, were persons who, although enjoying *status libertatis*, i.e., not being legally slaves, stood in a relationship of dependence to a *patronus* who offered them protection; in other words, the institution of client was based on the premise that there was a substantive difference between the strong man, the patron—to whom the others pledged their allegiance—and those who submitted to him.)

• The "men in the street" who, being unable to recognize where their own vital interests lie, allow themselves to be deluded by the "politician" and his "clients," lending prestige and power to efforts which are nearly always opposed to their own interests.

Some of the characteristics evident in a group of this type, in its extreme form, are:

• No attempt is made to foster individual development.

• The relationship between the "politician" and the vote-controlling "client," as between the latter and his own "client" (and so on, in a veritable chain of clientship), is one of a systematic endeavor to obtain reciprocal benefits: "You scratch my back, and I'll scratch yours," "You give me a job and I'll get you votes."

• This system is often successfully palmed off on the people as a democratic one.

If we look at all closely at the Mafia-client system—whatever fine-sounding name it may bear—we shall see the following:

• The "politician" of this group uses his prestige to cover up criminal acts; if it were not for his ability to maneuver, his capacity to make what is now normally regarded as uncivilized appear civilized, his knowing how to paralyze the normal action of the organs of administration of justice, the Mafia system could not continue in existence.

• Some of the "clients," who can deliver votes in varying amounts, are actually *mafiosi* themselves; for that reason, their client chains, in addition to the usual parasitism of the client system, exhibit such typical features of the Mafia as the levying of tribute and resorting to extreme violence in order to procure something, with the consequent intimidation, secrecy, and often a total sealing off from the outside. (The word *procure* reminds me that at a very interesting trial in Rome which I attended, and indeed took part in, I heard an Under-Secretary of State—a Deputy-Minister—who was accused of being a man of the Mafia and of making election deals with Mafia groups, say candidly to the presiding judge, "No, it was not Tizio who *procured* votes for me in that town, it was Caio.")

The conditions which make this systematic network of parasitism possible are, primarily:

• The low economic level of the broad masses, for whom the search for their daily bread or for jobs is of such urgency that everything else is of secondary interest.

• The low cultural and political level of the great majority, resulting in shortsighted pursuit of their own selfish interests, without a minimum of realistic awareness of the common interest.

• The resultant incapacity for a new life of association and collaboration, which forms a fertile ground for authoritarianism, fascism, monopoly, and oligopoly of every conceivable variety.

Thus the client and the Mafia-client systems are made possible by the fact that the people, being isolated, do not know how to make their weight felt and resign themselves to inaction and to nonfurtherance of their own true interests. It is obvious, therefore, how necessary it is for the development of the human resources to form and interrelate new, open, democratic groups, and at the same time to attack and break up the old sclerotic groups, at every level of society.

Violence is not, of course, a phenomenon confined to western Sicily; in different forms, it reaches into every part of the world. I rather think that an understanding of the Mafia-client system is of great interest for all, precisely because it is an extreme form of organized violence, so that studying it is like examining organized violence under a magnifying glass. It has been demonstrated, for example, that in areas of advanced capitalist industrialization, with a higher literacy level—as in the north of Italy—power is concentrated not in the hands of the politician, but often, through a more complex and ingenious mechanism, in the hands of those with the most money (votes are not bought directly with a thousand lire, a couple of pounds of *pasta*, the right word in the right place, or intimidation, but primarily through heavy investment in the press and other instruments of molding public opinion, and only secondarily in such politicians as may be thought useful). But I do not believe it has been as clearly shown that on the international level the relations within and among groups fall into the same pattern as do the primitive relations between patron and client and those obtaining within the Mafia-client system. (I have found very useful confirmation of this idea in the studies of Johan Galtung and his Institute of the Sociology of Conflict at Oslo.)

Every morning, before daylight has effaced the stars, I continue to search in silence, before plunging into active occupations. I know that to accept being lost in the complexity of this world— where strenuous efforts to achieve understanding and growth are inextricably mixed with stubborn resistance and enormous waste— means to die a little; I know how reluctant is this world to emerge from the pre-atomic era into that post-atomic age in which your life will be my life, and my life cannot but also be yours; I know that we have barely begun to learn and that men cannot truly learn unless they are willing to search and can search together; and that on top of all this there is always the danger of forgetting what one does know.

## Danilo Dolci

In 1952, Danilo Dolci, the courageous writer and social reformer, journeyed to western Sicily and threw himself into a determined attack on the poverty, ignorance, corruption, and fear perpetuated by the island's brutal Mafia-client system and its traditional resistance to change. Despite enormous obstacles—including the wrath of the mafiosi and prominent officials who have repeatedly tried to halt his work—Signor Dolci has initiated many economic and social programs which have brought material progress and a new feeling of freedom and hope to Sicily. Born in Trieste in 1924, and graduate of the Faculty of Architecture of Milan Polytechnical School, Signor Dolci is an outspoken opponent of war and violence. He received the Lenin Peace Prize in 1958 and in 1967 was nominated for the Nobel Peace Prize.

His published works include The Outlaws of Partinico, Report from Palermo, Waste, and A New World in the Making.

# CONSTANTIN A. DOXIADIS

## Learning How to Learn

---

$\mathbf{M}$ANY YEARS AGO I was holding the tiller of a small boat in the Aegean Sea and listening to an old sailor telling me his story. I must have been quite absorbed, because he had to ask me to be more careful with my steering. "But the following wind is favorable," I told him. The old man smiled and said, "It is just for that reason that the danger of going off course is so great." How right he was! How many times in my life, seeing people veer off course at the moment of success, I have remembered him!

It was that night, I think, that I became convinced that one can learn from anyone at any moment, and that learning is a continuous process which starts when our own life starts and ends only when our life ends. I discover, for example, that I am learning even now, as I write. I am learning that we cannot make an inventory of our intellectual gains as easily as we can of our material ones—perhaps because there is no internal revenue department to keep track of them. Is it not time to think of an annual declaration of our gains in learning, not in order to pay tax on them, but so that we may know how far behind we are and that we need to catch up?

Humanity itself knows much more than we do as individuals, but it has not devised a system to assess what it has learned by trial and error over millions of years. Every time I visit a new land, a new city, and meet a new group of people, I am amazed at the things they know, things of which we others have no suspicion. It is then that I think of the many things that nobody yet knows. We may have systems to transmit certain types of specialized knowledge or certain ideas, but we have nothing that allows us to approach the total possible knowledge or even the total human knowledge and select in a practical way what we need.

Learning is a link that connects the individual with the totality of his surroundings—nature and art, men and animals, the atom, the earth, the cosmos. As long as we do not know about them, they do not exist for us. Man on this earth may therefore be viewed as the center of a world with which he is connected because he occupies a certain location and because he receives, processes, and transmits all sorts of material and nonmaterial goods. He breathes, drinks, eats, sees, feels, using what he needs and disposing of what he does not need or what others need. Man can thus be seen as the processor of solids, liquids, and gases and also as a processor of feelings and ideas.

Such a picture of man leads me to an egocentric view of what I have learned. I regard man not as Plato's thinking, feeling, and willing man, classified by the types of his actions, but as a man classified by the phases of his actions as the receiving, processing, and transmitting animal that he is.

I am interested in man and in the knowledge he acquires in his role as the conscious receiver, processor, and transmitter of senses, feelings, ideas, and actions. If we look at man in this way, there are these important points to remember—that man exists somewhere in the world; that he receives, that he processes, and that he transmits until his death; and that after his death the signs of his passage will be eliminated by evolving nature unless he has processed ideas and not only food and liquor.

One day I nearly fell asleep sitting in my bathtub. When I opened my eyes I saw, out of the open window, the sky below me and airplanes flying upside down. I was looking into the bathwater. It was then that I realized, although I had been taught about it earlier, that the sky is not up and man down, that God is not up or really anywhere. It was then that I realized that things are as they are, but that our images of them depend upon our position. Thus we are very often wrong, and we do wrong.

In this way I gradually came to understand that we are always both at the center of the world and in some other part of it, depending on whether we look at our situation from our point of view or from somebody else's. We belong not to one but to many spheres of which we are the center, from the personal sphere to the entire cosmos. We could, indeed, reach megalomaniac conclusions about ourselves if we did not realize how small our spheres are. When we speak, for example, of the sphere represented by the whole earth, we should bear in mind that we inhabit and use only a very thin crust of it.

While paddling for several days in the swamps of southern Iraq, and again when floating in the rivers of the delta of Bengal, I began to realize that we participate not only in many spheres of space but also in many spheres of time. When I first visited such areas I thought I was simply moving in space, only to realize that I was also moving in time, since some of the inhabitants live today as they did in prehistoric times. Thus some people belong to the present and some to various periods of the past (others belong also to the future). How many characteristics do I not have in common with those primitive people, how many of my features are not taken from my parents, and how many times have I not seen my eyes and my dreams in my children? Or as the Greek poet Palamas said:

How many times have we not seen in the child's tremor, the child's movements, the old father quivering and swaying in the depths of time.

It is necessary that we receive all possible information, ideas, feelings, sentiments; otherwise our system will starve in the same way we would starve and die if we ceased to eat and drink. Starvation from lack of information takes longer, but our world is full of living dead because we do not recognize this.

We must be prepared to receive from all sources and transmitters, whether they seem relevant to us or not. I cannot forget that I did not learn only about Arabia from Lawrence's *Seven Pillars of Wisdom*, but also about strategy and tactics, and about how to write of my impressions and keep a record of my knowledge. But we do not learn only from great minds; we learn from everyone, if only we observe and inquire. I received my greatest lesson in esthetics from an old man in an Athenian *taverna*. Night after night he sat alone at the same table, drinking his wine with precisely the same movements. I finally asked him why he did this, and he said, "Young man, I first look at my glass to please my eyes, then I take it in my hand to please my hand, then I bring it to my nose to please my nostrils, and I am just about to bring it to my lips when I hear a small voice in my ears, 'How about me?' So I tap my glass on the table before I drink from it. I thus please all five senses." That night, as I was walking home, I realized the wisdom of a popular saying that I learned from the mountain people: "Learning and knowledge are not sold in the same place." I decided to seek for knowledge everywhere and from everybody.

When should we learn? Here I cannot agree with those who answer, "Always." On the contrary, I am convinced that we must acquire the ability to close our receiving system when we have received too much or when we want to process or transmit information. It is imperative to know when we have had enough.

The importance of this is increasing as the amount of information that reaches us increases. Think only of the press, radio, and television and what they offer us, and think of the noises and the movement in a big city. How are we going to protect ourselves from the increasing radiation of information? I think we must build many shields around ourselves, and in a democratic society this has to be done by every individual for himself. But the system that permits one to do it must be provided by the society itself, and this is not currently provided at all. Our society has not managed to give us any protective system against either the quantities or the qualities of the information we receive. I do not refer only to bad information, but also to good information that reaches us in an uncoordinated way. Let us not forget that our knowledge almost always grows from the center outward and that there are no lines to connect our new findings with what we already know. This explains why so many great minds go wrong outside their own fields of thought, especially in politics.

It is essential that we learn how to learn. How wrong we now are in this respect can be shown by a single example. We are told by everyone how important it is to read at a high speed, but I have found many more people who read at a high speed going wrong than people who read slowly. Fast reading is like heavy rain that races to the sea, causing damage to the earth. It is the constant, slow rain that reaches deep into the earth. If we do not retain the knowledge we receive, it becomes an imitation of the ancient Romans who would vomit in order to continue eating. But if we learn to read at both a high speed and a low speed we will be able to choose the rate of our absorbing in every special case. This is what we need. If we manage to read slowly, listen slowly, and feel slowly, then and only then will we be able to enjoy receiving information. When he accomplishes this, man the receiver will have taken a big step toward achieving satisfaction.

I am often disappointed by people who try to learn only from others; they overlook the fact that we also have to learn from ourselves, by thinking, considering, and processing what information we have received and what we have already processed. Such people do not really learn anything, and they cannot create anything; they are not even able to select the best from what they have learned.

Processing is an important part of knowledge—processing in

order to do the right thing. Processing should not mean the creation of new things. I must emphasize how dangerous the people are who insist on being original, forgetting that they should be trying to create the right thing. If it happens to resemble the old, what does it matter? Do we not breathe air and drink water as we did in the past? It is time for us to understand that it is not our goal that should be changed, but only the degree of human satisfaction.

Processing is a natural ability, but it can certainly be further developed. For this, it is of the greatest importance to prepare the ground by forgetting many unimportant or distracting details. We cannot process properly unless we know what to forget—for example, those who have done us harm and those who do not express anything. They are just stones that can break or misdirect our processing mechanism.

In processing, we must also select and classify our subject matter on the basis of very specific criteria. This is where we are helped by our ability to locate ourselves in space and time. Between 1940 and 1945 my only criterion was survival, survival in spite of the enemy and in spite of starvation; this dictated my entire attitude. Now the criteria have changed and my mind is oriented in a completely different way—how to contribute to development.

The definition of criteria is not an easy job. But we must define them correctly if we wish to guarantee the best results from our processing mechanism. Last June I had the opportunity to present a long-term program for Rio de Janeiro. Among other things it provided for the elimination of the *favelas*, the traditional Rio slums. I was then asked the most important question of my professional career, "Who will write the sambas when the *favelas* are eliminated?" What this really meant was, how is the elimination of an unhealthy habitat going to avoid the elimination of the creative spirit of its inhabitants?

Processing requires patience. How many people jump to conclusions before they have the facts! Processing should not start before all necessary and possible information has been received. Even then our organism may not be prepared to process for decisions and action. In such cases we should not force it into processing; it might produce the wrong results. To all those who say, "Do it now," I want to answer, "Do not." The wise thing is not to do everything now but to know when to do each thing or whether to do it at all. Our organism has only a certain processing capacity. For those who doubt it, I must remind them of the telephone operators who, while they are taking your number, also talk to somebody else (it does not happen often in the U.S., but it does in other countries). Then they wonder why the connection is wrong. We often forget that even the best potato peeler can only peel one potato at a time.

Processing requires experience and the use of proper methods. Until the seventeenth century, historians and philosophers could describe their subjects solely on the basis of personal experience; the limited size of human phenomena permitted them to do so. Xenophon's description of a whole campaign was based on his personal experience. Aristotle did not need any surveys to understand politics; he could speak to virtually every citizen of Athens himself. Now the dimensions of our knowledge make necessary detailed surveys and the use of computers to get the same general conclusions. Processing also requires the proper use of conclusions. When statistics say that a certain operation will be successful in saving all but one per cent of the patients from death, we must not forget that for those who die, death is one hundred per cent.

It is difficult to process properly, but it is worthwhile because proper processing leads to an idea—"the idea-sword," as Palamas said, the idea that guides our action and can be expressed in an act of love, as it was in Michelangelo's Moses. Such an idea-sword has to be strong. It has to be produced after long forging in fire, and then it can cut deep into our lives.

When we enter the small port of the island of Ios in the southern Aegean Sea there is, on our right hand, the small, isolated church of St. Irene. Its unknown builder has managed to transmit a message of isolation and beauty, a message that prepares you to talk to yourself and, if you can, to God. Sitting on the wall of the small courtyard, unaware of the hails from the departing sailboat, I found myself envying this unknown builder who, in managing to build this church, perhaps fulfilled a lifetime dream. He did not have a tenth of the information possessed by any architectural student today, nor did he have any of the techniques that today's builders have, but he had the ability to transmit the right message in the right way—because his ideas, his processing, and his transmitting were in balance.

Transmitting is the final phase of our action; unless this phase is successful the cycle remains incomplete. It is well to remember Sir Robert Watson-Watt's comment, "The whole range of human error is essentially due to defective communication from mind to mind." We should try to transmit what we have to transmit properly. Transmitting properly means knowing when to refrain from the transmission of an action that might be harmful. It also means knowing what to transmit, because transmission is not for one person alone, but should connect him with others. Transmission presupposes an ability to find the connecting links.

Transmission should help people to form opinions, not to receive orders. How many people talk to us in terms of what they believe about a situation and forget to tell us the facts, substituting their personal interpretation for the world of facts. I believe the chief characteristic of good transmission is that it mobilizes the whole free organism of the receiver, leaving him the choice of action and not imposing anything on him. To achieve this we need a message not only with a certain content, but also with a proper expression by the use of proper symbols. Why are we today afraid of symbols when we know that civilization is based on language and writing? People—especially from the more educated classes—smile at every new word, not understanding that we cannot express the airplane by the word Icaros. They are reluctant to accept the right of others to express new ideas, a right that even primitive people have. Although they regard themselves as protectors of humanity's treasures, they are only protecting their minds from development.

I am glad that I discovered this need for proper symbols early in my life, but, perhaps because of my conservative environment, I was not as daring as I should have been. I was creating new words but not enough to transmit all the new ideas needed. For years I had been working on dynamic cities without thinking of giving them a name. One night I was working on a drawing of a geometric model of a dynamic city when my son, who was then five years old, came to sit on my knees. When he asked what I was drawing, I answered that it was a city. "What is its name?" he asked. Shamefully, I answered that it had no name, only to be told that there could not be a city without a name. That night "dynapolis" was born, and from then on the theory spread. The message had been there, but it was the symbol that gave it wings.

I came to the conclusion that what we need to be effective is the idea-sword, but it must be sharp, not only strong, to cut. Our chances are great if we know where and when to lift the sword and what to strike at—not at a stone, and not at a high-speed projectile, because the sword will break. I usually find fair and just people around me who are willing to receive messages. But I cannot forget the feudal owners of a certain country who wanted a housing program, provided that someone paid them ten times the real value of their land—land they were "offering" for the poor classes. I did not try my own sword of persuasion on them. What they needed was something quite different from an idea-sword.

When I speak of the city which, according to Aristotle's definition, should make man happy and secure, people politely look down or far away. But I have not lost my courage on this topic, and although I have no formula for total happiness I think I am under the obligation to work toward a city—the habitat of man—that will make man as happy as possible. And this means to satisfy as many as possible of man's needs in relation to space. In other words, to make space fit man.

I have found that, for me, learning about something is not important unless I can implement it. And, when we speak of implementation, what matters is not how much we learn but how deep it reaches. Such considerations explain why the builder of St. Irene transmitted far more important messages then many of us do; his learning was much deeper and could reach deep.

The question then arises, how does learning reach deep? The answer I found after many years of hard effort and failures had been already given by Aeschylus—learning through suffering. In this sense we return to the idea of Plato's thinking, feeling, and willing man. For learning to have a real meaning we must manage to reach all of his three selves. Make him think and suffer from his experience, and then the willing man is touched—and he acts. To achieve this we must participate in life, become an integrated part of the world, receive from all distances, at all speeds, and process and transmit. This will not show on our body as eating shows on our belly, but it will leave its marks deep enough to make our life worth living.

If man is only a good receiver, action has reached a dead end. If he is only a good receiver and processor, we have no benefit to the world surrounding him or to himself. There is one way that leads to a worthy life. Man must be a good receiver, a good processor, and a good transmitter. Only then does this temporary moving spot on the surface of the earth, the meeting place of a body and a spirit, have a meaning. It observes, it thinks, it acts in a reasonable way. For this whole process to be meaningful we must achieve a real balance of the input and output. The great mobile of which a man is the center must be in balance. It will be always a mobile, changing and never again being the same, but it must be in balance or it will be upset and overthrown. This balance should not be thought of as valid at every moment of our lives. We may receive for years and transmit only later, or even process later. But on the whole a useful life must achieve over reasonable periods a balance of input, process, and output.

If I want to understand what I am and where I am, I have to be aware of the great mobile of which I am the center. I must see that the input-process-output mobile or the receiver-processor-transmitter mobile is in balance, a balance that will satisfy us and lead us to happiness in this aspect of our lives.

This mobile, which keeps us in balance with time and space and defines our role in the world, is indispensable for our existence and evolution in this changing world. If we can see and understand it, if we can follow it as it expands into the unknown, if we can keep it under control so that it will not upset our balance, then we have learned something that can help us float in this vast unknown that surrounds us, that can help us float in a human way.

### Constantin A. Doxiadis

Constantin A. Doxiadis is an architect and planner whose central concern is human happiness and fulfillment. He is best known for his concept of "Dynapolis," the city planned for intelligent growth, as opposed to haphazard agglomeration and sprawl. In most cities, Doxiadis says, the central nucleus of business and civic buildings cannot grow. But the nucleus of Dynapolis is built along a projecting axis that widens as it advances. Mr. Doxiadis was born in 1913, in Athens, Greece, and was educated at the School of Architecture of Athens Technical University and Berlin-Charlottenburg University. He was the chief planner of reconstruction in Greece after World War II, and has been consultant to the United Nations, the Ford Foundation, and a large number of foreign governments. He lives in Athens, where he heads Doxiadis Associates. He has written Urban Renewal and the Future of the American City, and New World of Urban Man (co-author).

# iv
# ILYA EHRENBURG

## A Last Memoir

I HAVE been asked what life has taught me. Everything; I was born uneducated, like all babies. Everything and nothing, for I see every day how much there is that I do not know. For the past fifteen years or so, I have been learning how to be an old man. This is not nearly as easy as I thought when I was young. I used to think that desires die down along with the possibilities of satisfying them; but then I began to understand that the body ages before the spirit, and that one has to learn to live like an old man. One learns even in dying; to die in such a way that death is a fitting end to one's life is not an easy art.

A man who, like myself, has lingered on in this world must learn that experience, concepts, emotions are all relative. I do not approve of old people who grumble about the younger generation; instead of helping it to live in accordance with the requirements of the present era, they do nothing but carp on the era's mistakes. They are like old kerosene lamps that smoke instead of giving light —not a pastime to be recommended.

What I am about to say is not intended as a lesson for the young. Rather, it is the confession of a man who was born in the past century and whose mind was formed by many of its ideas. Such a confession may, perhaps, be of some use to the young. Of course,

47

I realize that people seldom learn from the mistakes of others—not because they deny the value of the past, but because they are faced with new problems. The tale of how their fathers and grandfathers got hurt cannot protect them from getting hurt in their turn, for they are beset by different dangers. At the same time, some of an old man's misadventures may give useful pointers to the young, and that is why for the past seven years I have been working on a book of reminiscences, *People, Years, Life.*

It is a familiar fact that objects seen in childhood are remembered as being very large. I used to think, for instance, that I lived in a great big house, and I was taken aback when I revisited the "big" house of my childhood—it turned out to be very small. When I was young, I thought history proceeded at a dizzying pace, although in those days there were no airplanes, and trains moved with slow dignity, like asthmatic old men. I did not know then that everything takes much longer than one would wish and that mankind is not speeding down a freeway in a racing car but painfully groping along winding paths which sometimes turn right around, so that pessimists take them for circles, although in fact they are spirals. When I was fifteen, I became obsessed with politics, joined an underground Bolshevik organization, and even spent six months in a Czarist jail. At the age of eighteen, I had to flee to Paris to escape prosecution. There I began to write poetry, fell in love with art, and forgot politics—but politics soon caught up with me, as it did with everyone else in Europe. The First World War broke out, and hard on its heels came the Russian Revolution.

What did I learn in the decades that followed? First of all, that it is far more difficult to change the mentality of the people than it is to change a country's political order or even its economy. The second of these changes may be effected in a few hours, the third in several decades, but the first can take centuries. Let me take nationalism and racism as examples. When I was a child I knew that if I wanted to be admitted to school I had to do better than everyone else in the entrance examinations—at that time there was a three per cent quota for Jews in Moscow. When I went to visit my grandfather in Kiev I heard that there had been a pogrom and that there would surely be another. My father read the *Frankfurter Zeitung* and the liberal Russian newspaper *Russkie vedomosti*. He used to say that anti-Semitism was unthinkable in such a culturally advanced country as Germany. Thirty-five years later the Nazis had their *Kristallnacht* in Berlin—that is what they called their pogrom.

When traveling in America, I toured the Southern states— Alabama, Mississippi, Louisiana. This was in the spring of 1946, one year after the collapse of German racism. I saw racism in another form. The whites have for too long insulted national and human dignity in America, in Africa, and in Asia; there has been an accumulation of hatred, and accounts are often being settled in the same currency. I understand now that one must see the world as it really is and not mistake one's wishes for reality. Naturally, I continue to think that solidarity among men will overcome intolerance, racial and national arrogance, and brutality, but now I know that the road is long and that strenuous efforts and great sacrifices will be required.

I have lived through two world wars (I am not counting the Russian and Spanish civil wars). I have come to hate war not only because it kills off the flower of every nation, but because it destroys spiritual as well as material values, and sets people and nations far back in their development. I see no other way out for mankind than complete disarmament, especially now that the greatest discoveries of physics are being used to manufacture weapons capable of wiping out all life on our planet. And yet this urgent need to save mankind from a final disaster has been turned into a subject for endless bickering, which may go on until there is no one left to study the records of ten-year-long conferences. Yet, despite all this, I remain an optimist. I believe that the will to live of people who are not interested in the growth of the munitions industry, who are not obsessed with the desire to prove that the order they are used to is morally right, and who are neither hair-splitters, politicians, nor diplomats, will end by forcing everyone to agree to general disarmament.

Why do I cling to my optimism? Certainly not because of any fidelity to Cartesianism. True, I am too accustomed to logic to renounce it lightly. Once, when I was talking to Einstein, he asked me, smiling, how much is two times two. Startled, I said that I had been taught that the answer was four. "But what do you think yourself?" he asked. "Four," I replied timidly. He smiled again. "As for me, I don't know. It might be five. . . ." Nevertheless, when he protested against nuclear weapons, Einstein based his arguments on logic.

I refuse to relinquish my hopes. In the early days of the Russian Revolution, the young poet Nikolai Tikhonov wrote a poem ending with the words:

> Nails should be forged out of people like these—
> They'd be the strongest nails in the world.

Many of my contemporaries have been done away with, many others have succumbed to their trials, but the survivors have been forged by their experience—we have truly become nails. And we have also become incorrigible optimists. Where Pascal called man a "thinking reed," we have earned the right to call ourselves thinking nails. We have developed the characteristic which literary historians call "romantic irony"; the nails have learned to make fun both of one another and of the various hammers and mallets with which they have come in contact. They are a very special breed.

Why did I believe that Nazism would be crushed when, on a cold day in January 1939, I crossed the Franco-Spanish border? Why, when the Nazis had occupied Kiev and were approaching

Leningrad and Moscow, did I continue to hold that man would overcome Nazism? Why do I believe today that general disarmament is going to take place? Is this mere obduracy? Is there something in human nature that preserves man from despair? I do not know; I am simply recording, in all sincerity, what I think and feel.

Dual lighting—as when electric lamps are turned on in daytime—is very hard on the eyes. I have lived my entire life in the dual light of two different and unlike centuries. It seems to me that while there is much that divides them, we must do something to unify them.

Even as an adolescent, I loved justice. A man—unless he is rich or drunk with power—tends to relate his personal happiness to that of his neighbors, his people, the whole of humanity. This is not rhetoric; those are the natural feelings of any man who has not grown spiritually fat and is not blinded by megalomania.

As for spiritual beauty, I think it fills as vital a need as does the green of the grass or the smile of a child. I would not for the life of me renounce any of the ideals that captured my imagination when I was fifteen years old. I am as convinced as I ever was that interest on capital must not be equated with personal welfare and happiness, and that the socialist system of economy is not only more rational but more ethical than the capitalist system. But we must add beauty to justice, breathe human warmth into the commandments of the new society.

When I was young, the moon's main function was to shed its light on lovers. Now it is being photographed and studied and will soon become the first stage in man's conquest of the universe. Will that make young love any less romantic? I hardly think so.

I said earlier that in 1933 Germany was a "culturally advanced" country. That is what I thought at the time, when "culture" was associated in people's minds with certain external indicators. Germany had long since wiped out illiteracy, it had good roads, many cars for those days, many specialized institutes, excellent hospitals, a highly developed printing industry. But all this was only one component of culture, and in the mentality of a young Nazi the learning he had acquired readily coexisted with complete savagery. In telling me about German soldiers who threw a baby into the well because it had been crying and disturbing their sleep, a Russian peasant woman said, "They have no conscience. . . ." I have long ago revised my idea of culture; it is a complex concept, requiring a high degree of development of critical thinking, emotional sensitivity, and moral controls.

Our mentality has greatly changed in the past half-century. The natural sciences have made enormous progress. We are beginning our conquest of the universe, and the concept of infinity, which in the early years of the century was abstract if not metaphysical, is becoming a reality. The thinking of the astrophysicist reaches far out, while the thought of the contemporary philosopher stays on the ground.

When I was young, I believed that progress was possible in all spheres of human activity. I have now come to think that there is undeniable progress in the exact sciences, social structures, and living conditions, but that in the sphere with which, because of my work, I am particularly concerned—the arts—there is never any progress, but only changes in form which give expression to what men are like in any particular epoch.

There is no comparing the sum total of knowledge of modern man with the knowledge of the Cretans who lived three thousand years before our era. The Cretans knew very little, and we know even less about them. Undoubtedly there was slavery in Chios, and men peopled the heavens with benign and malevolent gods. But their art was decorative and rather festive. Their frescoes show us men and women who remind us of nothing so much as Toulouse-Lautrec.

The frescoes in Ajanta, India, are painted with great skill and are close to the canvases of Botticelli.

There is no progress in art, and it would be madness to assert that modern sculpture is better than the sculpture of Ellora or Mycenae. Man is apt to be more moved by the art of his own period, not because it is more perfect, but because it is organically related to him. At the same time, I must confess that in my youth literature and art occupied a far more important place in people's lives than they do today. Art now reaches a greater number of people than it used to, in the capitalist as well as in the socialist countries, owing in part to cheap editions of modern writers and poets, the new reproduction techniques, radio, and sometimes even television; but in the daily life of the individual, art has become cake where it used to be bread.

Some say that this is the result of the extraordinary leap forward of the natural sciences. This is partly true. Half a century ago, the movement for peace was headed by Romain Rolland, and then by Barbusse, but during the last war it was headed by Joliot-Curie. The Pugwash Conferences deal with matters of far greater concern to the average man than do the meetings of PEN Clubs. But that is hardly an adequate explanation. Chekhov wrote seventy years ago, "The natural sciences are doing wonders now and they can march like Mamai on the general public and conquer it by sheer mass enormousness. . . ." But in another letter he rightly argued with those who held that the progress of science must mean the decline of art.

I would like people not to see a conflict where there is none. There has always been knowledge in the world. Anatomy and belles-lettres are of equally noble descent; they both have the same purposes and the same enemy—the devil—and there is absolutely no reason for them to fight each other. There is no struggle for survival here. If a man understands the system of blood circulation, he is rich; if in addition he studies the history of religion and learns by heart the poem, "I recall the miraculous moment," he will be richer and not poorer; consequently, we are dealing only with positives. That is why geniuses have never fought, and in Goethe the scientist got along beautifully with the poet.

When educated people engage in fisticuffs, we can take it that their deepest emotions have been aroused. Before World War I, I saw fistfights twice at performances of Diaghilev's Russian ballet —once at *The Rite of Spring*, over Stravinsky's music, and the other time at *Parade*, over Picasso's costumes. Nowadays such fights occur only at football matches. Shostakovich is an ardent football fan, but I doubt if many football players are devotees of music.

The popularity of sports has nothing to do with the point I am making. The real causes are more deep-rooted and serious; knowledge has outstripped character development, and the young today are given an education rather than an upbringing. People develop lopsidedly, and on every hand one sees a surprising accumulation of knowledge coupled with an utter lack of emotional refinement. The Russian writers of the last century were remarkable for one attribute which I believe has not lost its validity—a conscience. Mankind will not survive without it.

The automation of production and the emergence of some new branch of physics or chemistry narrow our horizons; they can turn man into a piece of electronic machinery. Moreover, leisure now serves a different purpose. When I was a boy, people worked fourteen hours a day, came home exhausted, ate, and went to bed. Now people work six or seven hours a day. They come home without being physically tired, but in a sort of stupor, induced by repeating the same movements or dealing with similar problems over and over again. No potter or carpenter today can put a little bit of himself into the pot or table he produces. There cannot be a Goethe today—the sum total of knowledge has increased too much. What is to be done to cultivate the mind and refine the emotions?

In art, I am primarily a consumer. Not only when I look at the canvases of Picasso or Matisse, but also when reading books I like, I do not stop to consider how they were fashioned. Like any art lover or reader, I give myself to the work and let my imagination build upon it. To my way of thinking, responding to art is a creative process which can broaden and enrich a person's inner life. What is your idea of Don Quixote? What was Hamlet like? Each individual will give his own answer to these questions; he will add something of himself, of his character, of his experience, to the texts of Cervantes and Shakespeare. That is why in the past ten years there has grown up a mass art appreciation movement among the young in the Soviet Union. Its initiators, in nearly all cases, were college girls and young women workers. Their instinct of self-preservation prompted them to introduce young men to poetry, music, and painting; they did not want to spend the rest of their lives with pieces of electronic machinery.

But I am digressing. True, I have been talking all along of what I have learned in my lifetime, but I may have sounded didactic. When I was sixteen, I used to go around repeating the words of one of Ibsen's heroes, "All or nothing!" But I soon realized that the world does not offer a choice between everything and nothing, that life is complex, and that neither white nor black may be used in a painting. I began to learn to read the hearts of other people, and I am still learning.

Men of many professions should teach the young. An instructor does more than teach; he learns at the same time. I am thinking not only of the development of science, I am thinking also of enrichment of the spiritual life of the young people to whom the instructor is to impart knowledge. Every master knows that the material teaches the artist, and Picasso once said to me that he learned a great deal at the age of eighty—for instance, when he began to work in tole and to make linoleum cuts in color. But human material is far more demanding.

My trade requires a knowledge of human beings, and whereas I have some insight into the mental and emotional reactions of my contemporaries, I have to keep on studying every day in order to decipher the feelings of the young.

I am old in years, but now I know with certainty that I know little. One must go on learning as long as there is breath in one's body, and a student's bench becomes even an old man far better than the preacher's pulpit or the academician's chair. That is my conviction.


### Ilya Ehrenburg

*Ilya Ehrenburg, who died in 1967 at the age of seventy-six, was one of the Soviet Union's best-known writers and public personalities. Both before and after the Communist revolution in Russia, he was a forthright, controversial, influential figure. Born in Kiev in 1891, he had by 1908 already been expelled from school and had gone to Paris, where he stayed for nine years before returning to Russia. This was the first of many long sojourns in Paris. In World War II, his scathing, moving accounts of Nazi atrocities won him fame as a news correspondent. After the war he became deputy of the Supreme Soviet of the U.S.S.R. but nevertheless championed various peace initiatives. In later years, he outspokenly called for more freedom of expression for writers and other creative people, drawing much criticism upon himself from the Soviet government. His influence, personal and artistic, was considerable abroad, as well as within the Soviet Union. His titles include A Street in Moscow. The Storm, The Thaw, and Memoirs.*

▼
# DWIGHT D. EISENHOWER

## "What I Have Learned" *

D

WIGHT DAVID EISENHOWER, thirty-fourth President of the United States and General of the Army, lives most of each year in a sleepy little town in southern Pennsylvania made famous long before his birth by the most ferocious and bloodiest battle ever fought on American soil. The Eisenhower farm at the edge of Gettysburg lies near waving fields and gentle slopes where Pickett led the disastrous "charge," which wasn't a charge at all, his twelve thousand men all but slaughtered in Union crossfire before they turned and fled at the highwater mark of Confederate arms. General Eisenhower's office is not, however, near the hallowed ground, where he and Mamie live contentedly in their comfortable rambling farmhouse home, but in a red brick building at the north end of Carlisle

* When the editors of Saturday Review invited Dwight D. Eisenhower to contribute to its series "What I Have Learned," General Eisenhower replied that he would be willing to submit to a paraphrased interview at Gettysburg. SR's managing editor, Richard L. Tobin, was assigned to the interview because he had covered General Eisenhower at Supreme Headquarters in London for the New York Herald Tribune before, during, and after D-Day in 1944, and had been in and out of the White House several times a week as a newspaperman in 1955 and 1956. The interview took place in General Eisenhower's town office at Gettysburg, Pennsylvania, on the campus of Gettysburg College.

Street, on the corner of the Gettysburg College campus. General Eisenhower goes to this office each weekday morning and his schedule is still unbelievably full. It was in this office that the interview took place. After an exchange of letters outlining the ground rules, the General fixed the interview date (the hottest day of a hot summer), and he was sitting erect behind a leather-upholstered desk in front of his five-star flag in an air-conditioned office when I was admitted at precisely 9:30 A.M.

Dwight Eisenhower is now nearly seventy-six years old, a survivor of substantial pressures—Commander-in-Chief of the Allied forces, D-Day, Columbia University, NATO, and eight years in the White House, not to mention a serious heart attack, an ileitis operation, a stroke, and, in recent months, nagging arthritis. But he seems much his old blue-eyed, optimistic, confident self, if a bit on the thin side. He weighs 161 pounds, thirteen pounds less than when he played halfback at West Point fifty-four years ago. The doctors keep him on an anticholesterol regime. He feels well, despite the arthritis in his hands that prevents him from playing golf. When he was President there were gibes about his golf-playing, but of one thing he's sure—his rounds of golf made the demanding life of the Presidency and its problems easier to sustain. Did he still paint? Not much any more. There didn't seem to be enough daylight time to do all the things one wants to do and he's trying to put down in articles and other writings some of the lessons he thinks he's learned, and that takes a lot of time.

I asked what he considered his greatest achievement. He thought the greatest accomplishment in which he had had a significant influence was probably the defeat of Nazi Germany within eleven months of the invasion at Normandy. When one considered the forecasts that victory in such an invasion of Hitler-held Europe would not come for several years at the least, he believed the eleven-month conquest by the Free World an undertaking that justified a measure of pride. He also believed that the greatest peacetime achievement in which he participated was eight peaceful and secure years as President of the United States.

What was his greatest failure? He was sure that it was our inability to bring about a trustworthy accord with the Soviet Union. He tried everything he could think of, he said, including bringing Khrushchev to this country for private talks. But for reasons of their own they didn't want to open their doors to real peace and cooperation. His disappointment was not one of mere incident. He had hoped the eight years of his Presidency would bring us to a place where we could say definitely that a just and permanent peace was really in sight.

Didn't the President think he was being too negative about his accomplishments vis-à-vis the Soviets, since many people feel that his peace efforts with Khrushchev opened up an American-Soviet dialogue out of which substantial benefits have already come? There had been some progress, he felt. Though the immediate response from the Kremlin to the Atoms for Peace speech was hardly encouraging, out of it eventually came the International Atomic Energy Commission. That was one break in the Iron Curtain that would have been very likely impossible a few years earlier. Another was Soviet-American cooperation in the International Geophysical Year projects. Later, the Antarctic Treaty, guaranteeing that the southern Polar regions would be used only for peaceful purposes, assured by a system of inspection, was an international milestone. Never before had nations of conflicting interests and ideologies voluntarily committed themselves to partnership use of an immense and unoccupied area. The proposal for such partnership was made by General Eisenhower in May 1958. Eighteen months later the treaty was signed by twelve governments. By the end of 1960, at least within the scientific communities of the two nations, we had achieved a reasonable measure of communication and cooperation. Moreover, beneficial by-products of the Khrushchev visit to the United States were numerous. At the very least,

Khrushchev and his entourage saw at first hand both the strength of the American nation and the natural friendliness of its people; their estimates of us underwent a lot of revision. At second hand, because the visit was publicized throughout Russia, every newspaper reader and radio listener there got some proof that we were not a nation of warmongers bending all our energies toward their destruction and they learned a lot about us that they could not have learned had the invitation never been extended and accepted. Any lessening of Soviet ignorance about us was a strong plus because it lessened irrational hatred and fear of us. In that light, failure has to be measured in perspective. But we did not reach anything like the fullness of American purposes he had hoped for.

Because my earlier experience with General Eisenhower revealed he had plenty of iron in his soul, I asked him whether he had found it difficult to make decisions in such actions as Little Rock on the domestic scene; Lebanon, Iran, Suez, Guatemala, and Formosa on the foreign. In such incidents, the Constitution that he had sworn to uphold, he replied, was the standard which had to rule his conduct, regardless of personal feeling or public pressures. To be sure, the eighteenth-century writers of the basic document could not have foreseen the mid-twentieth-century role of the United States or the domestic and foreign problems then confronting its President. Of him, consequently, in such instances, were required earnest study and a search in conscience so that both the letter and the spirit of the Constitution be observed with the sole purpose of advancing the welfare and the security of the Republic. Once the action most effectively contributing to that purpose became apparent, he promptly made his decision to put it into effect.

What, in General Eisenhower's opinion, was the future of the United Nations? It is the only thing we have, he replied, and he believes we must make it work. We cannot rush ahead, each nation for itself, and expect peace to last very long. He does not believe,

however, that the UN is as effective as it should be. He would like to
see a real effort to revise the charter. How did he think the United
Nations could do a better job and in what way can the world become more peaceful? If the people of Russia and China could only
talk with the people of Western Europe, Japan, and the United
States, talk with them face to face and without interference from
political bosses and their propaganda, he believes, he *knows* that
the United Nations could do a better job and we'd have no fear of a
war among the great nations. That's the thing he believes most. It's
a simple matter of communication. If we could talk directly with
them and if they could talk with us, he knows we'd find answers to
our major problems. He hates war—its stupidity, its brutality, its
futility—as only a soldier who has lived it can. Yet there's one thing
to say on the credit side—victory over Hitler required of the Allies a
manifestation of the most ennobling virtues of man—sacrifice,
faith, courage, fortitude. If we can put these virtues together in
peacetime and remember that the international cooperation so
generously displayed during war points a sure way to the success of
the United Nations, then that war simply cannot be regarded as
totally futile. He once said in Moscow that he would die for the
freedom of the press, even for the freedom of newspapers that were
calling him everything that was a good deal less than being a gentleman. He was afraid the Soviets didn't understand this; and he was
sad that they didn't. He thought if they had we might have achieved
that people-to-people understanding he had been talking about.

Did he have any personal philosophy or principle that he had
followed throughout his life? He replied that he was born optimistic. He believes in enthusiasm and the confidence that one can do a
job. He has never in his life gone into any fight to lose it. This
includes the fight for peace. It isn't enough that we provide international machinery through the UN to keep the peace, but we must
also be strong and optimistic and wise ourselves. Weakness never
cooperates with anything, only strength can cooperate. In any case,

he was not pessimistic about the future for he is sufficiently old-fashioned to believe that in the end right must triumph, though he knows it is also true that no worthwhile goal is ever reached without hard work. He never criticizes others. He just tries to tell the story. And speaking of trying to tell the story, he said that when he had been criticized for his bad grammar and syntax in Presidential press conferences, he paid little attention. The way ideas are presented is not nearly as important as the ideas themselves, even though he admired the abilities of those who had both accuracy in speech and worth in ideas.

If he had his life to live over, would he live it differently? To answer such a question, said the General, was an adventure into the impossible. It is difficult for one to reconstruct, even in imagination, a lifetime already lived. He didn't think he would depart very far from the basic principles he grew up with but he'd try harder to keep them always in the front of his mind. The older he got, the wiser he found the ancient rule of taking first things first, which is a process that often reduces the most complex human problems to manageable proportions. That's the way he tried to live his life and if he had to do it over that's one rule he'd never abandon. But of course everyone would want to avoid past blunders, and do better in every task he ever undertook.

I then asked General Eisenhower who were his heroes in American history. He said he kept on the wall of every office he had ever had pictures of four men, and he told why he thought they were the greatest men in American history. For him, George Washington was the greatest, the classic American example of fortitude. His devotion and his conviction were so great that he pledged his entire fortune, which was not inconsiderable, to the cost of freedom and independence. He never even considered final defeat. He turned his back on any suggestion that he become a king and insisted instead that this be a democratic nation. He had thought over many times who may have been the man of greatest stature in this country's history and he always came back to Washington, without whom there would have been no country at all. Then there was Lincoln. What could anyone say about Abraham Lincoln that has not already been said? He preserved the Union of the states and sometimes when you look at his face in a few of the saddest of the photographs you see a man bearing almost intolerable burdens and sorrows. Yet, like Washington, he persevered, and he never thought of quitting or giving up. He sometimes wished the meaning and eloquence of the Gettysburg Address could be taught with the glowing patriotism that it was when he was in school. General Lee was one of the truly outstanding military leaders, a man of enormous intuition and professional talent, as well as character. Robert E. Lee was to him practically a perfect character, a person of sensitivity and kindness, a gentleman through and through. If Lee had any of the human flaws he had never heard of them. And as for Benjamin Franklin, he didn't know exactly why he took to him as he did, but the fact is that in his wisdom, his homey eloquence, and his ability to bring two sides together in the early conventions that formed the Constitution and the guiding principles of our nation, he was without peer, in his opinion. It seems that he had his personal weaknesses, but he still classed him as a truly great man.

Who, in his opinion, were the best field officers in his Overlord command in World War II? General Eisenhower placed General Bradley first among ground commanders. Generals William Simpson of the 9th Army and Courtney Hodges of the 1st Army were two men who knew precisely what they were trying to do and how to get it done. They did it with that selflessness he talked to General Marshall about one day. Patton excelled in pursuit and wide-open situations. Incidentally, he thinks an atmosphere of serenity and confidence touched with a bit of humor is absolutely essential in commanding officers. If the men under you see that you are worried and tense, nervous and fearful, this will be contagious all down through the ranks. But when you create an atmosphere of confidence and good-humored serenity, even during the worst crises, this also seems to be contagious and more conducive to victory.

What did he think of Franklin D. Roosevelt and General Marshall? He replied that Franklin Roosevelt was an inspiring war leader, a man of high humor and sometimes frightening casualness. He'd tell General Eisenhower to do things with a wave of his hand, a sort of general sweep, without much, if any, regard for the logistics of the case, but he was an inspiring man who seemed absolutely certain of victory.

General Marshall and Winston Churchill were for him the greatest figures in World War II. In many ways General Marshall was the finest man he ever knew. Marshall asked him casually one day in 1944—he believed it was D-Day plus six—when they were sitting in a jeep together on the Normandy beachhead, "What qualification do you place above all others in selecting and recommending men for the combat commanders of your division, corps, and other principal units?" Without taking even a moment for reflection he popped out with "selflessness," which he thought of at that moment because he was thinking of Marshall himself. He could never claim a close or intimate personal friendship with General Marshall but he knew him well and saw him often from the week after Pearl Harbor. Yet Marshall never hinted, then or later, whether or not he actually wanted the Overlord command. He didn't know of any man in our time who embodied this quality of selflessness to a greater degree than George C. Marshall. Any leader worth his salt must, naturally, possess a certain amount of justifiable pride and ego. But if he is a truly great leader, the cause must predominate over self. A commander of his used to say to him, "Always take your job seriously, never yourself," and that, he believed, defined General Marshall. All competent men should have some ambition, said the President, for ambition is like the temper in steel. If there's too much the product is brittle, if there's too little the steel is soft, and without a certain amount of hardness a man cannot achieve what he sets out to do.

I then asked the General about his religious beliefs. He said he didn't think anyone could look up into the heavens and contemplate the vast areas of space and the myriad stars and not believe in a universal plan. Every man has some evidence of human frailty in him and knows he is not omnipotent. So we pray to God for guidance, though it is on our shoulders that the responsibility rests to reach mundane objectives. His mother, who was highly religious and a student of the Bible, taught him his belief in a higher being. She also loved the game of solitaire—he thought it was her favorite recreation—and out of it and her religion grew a phrase she often repeated to him with a twinkle in her eye, "The Lord deals the cards; you play them." He thought it was her way of saying that human beings are given tolerance and ability in greatly varying degrees with full freedom of decision, and it's up to each one to make the best of what he has been given. He often thought that his mother's homely little epigram also applied to nations. In any case, there was imbedded in him from his boyhood a deep faith in the beneficence of the Almighty. When it came to his first inaugural address he didn't want it to be a sermon, not by any means, for he was not a man of the cloth. But he wanted to make this faith clear and at the same time not create the impression that as the political leader of the United States he was going to avoid his own responsibilities and pass them on to the Deity.

What advice would President Eisenhower give young people today? He thought he expressed it best at the Exeter commencement in June. He told the boys up there that the career of an individual was was like a house—a lifetime home, built for one's own deeds, words, mistakes, and accomplishments, growing continuously through the years until the day comes when the final piece is fixed firmly in place and the occupant lies down at last to rest. He told them that if the house was to be strong rather than weak, beautiful instead of mean, useful instead of worthless, its foundation must be sturdy and solid, and he recalled the Biblical parable of the two houses, one built upon the sand and the other upon durable rock. When the winds and floods struck them both, the one was demolished and swept away—the other, built on rock, withstood every shock of wind and wave. He told them that the core of the rock foundation they were building was "character," a word that defies exact definition.

Then he tried to explain some of the elements of character. First, there was integrity and your own inner concern for it to ensure its permanence and bright visibility. Then he said ambition was another necessary stone, and he likened ambition to salt in the food—too little and the food lacks appeal and savor, too much and the whole dish becomes inedible. Then he thought there is the capacity for hard work, and it is no exaggeration to say that whoever loves his work and tries to do his duty is a happy and constructive man. And another stone in the foundation is loyalty. Without it one can have no deep friendships, and if the house of life is to be devoid of friends it will be a sorry structure indeed. Loyalty to the nation is patriotism, a proud word to any true American. Further, he thought, there is common sense—the ability to place facts in perspective and even in crisis to make a calm appraisal of the overall meaning of these facts. And then there are several closely related stones in the foundation of character—conscience, decency, self-respect. And finally, moral courage has to be there—the readiness to stand up for what you believe to be right, after determining what is right through study, reflection, and common sense. This includes self-reliance and self-confidence but never arrogance, egotism, or self-righteousness. That's the advice he would give to young people now.

How did the President feel about giving the vote to eighteen-year-olds? He had several times suggested that states lower the voting age because he believes that anyone old enough to fight is old enough to vote. He would like to see the minimum age fixed at nineteen.

•    •

What were some of the books General Eisenhower had liked in his lifetime of reading and which had influenced him most? He had always loved ancient history and historical novels, including the splendid books of the other Winston Churchill—*The Crisis* and others. He read and liked Conan Doyle's stories of the Middle Ages and he read a great many Civil War novels. His mother made him read the Bible and memorize large passages of it. When it came to the "begats" she told him he didn't have to study them because, she said, it was too difficult to memorize them and he wouldn't get much out of it anyway. He was not sure that many young people today even read the Bible, and he thought it was a shame. One book he knew backwards and forwards was *Pilgrim's Progress*, which he read from cover to cover in his youth several times. He had, of course, read a great deal in the field of the military history written by both American and foreign authors. The most profound of these was Clausewitz on war. He said that he would have to say that he had read those three volumes more than once because he didn't understand much the first time. He read often in Tacitus, Plato, Cicero. He started seriously to read Nietzsche but he did not like it—and quit. He read the *Federalist Papers* twice. As to his reading of Westerns, this has been greatly exaggerated; when he did read them it was normally at night to help him go to sleep.

Did the President have any afterthoughts about the 1960 Presidential campaign, the one in which Richard M. Nixon ran on the Republican ticket against John F. Kennedy? He answered that throughout the campaign he conformed to the plans made by the Vice President and his political advisers, doing everything proper he was asked to do. Understandably, they were reluctant to impose on him. Once, in fact, discussing an appearance and speech in Illinois the week before election—urged on General Eisenhower by the White House staff—the Vice President argued against it. Consequently, the President decided to go no farther west than Cleveland. Years later he learned the reason for Mr. Nixon's position.

What happened was that before the President's luncheon with the Vice President on Monday, October 31, Major General Howard McC. Snyder, the President's physician, talked to Vice President Richard Nixon and Secretary of the Interior Fred Seaton in the Cabinet Room. He told them that the President had just had a restless night; that he (General Snyder) and Mrs. Eisenhower were worried that General Eisenhower might now take on too heavy a load in the campaign windup. General Snyder ended with a strong expression of hope that the Vice President would be a restraining influence and would do his best to hold down on the schedule. As the Vice President and Secretary walked to the White House, the former said, in substance (this, of course, is not an exact quote), "Fred, if anything should happen to President Eisenhower while he is out campaigning, a wave of sympathy for my candidacy might easily sweep the country. I could even be President before Election Day with all the advantage of already possessing the office. I don't want to become President of the United States in that way or in any way that endangers Dwight Eisenhower. When we discuss the schedule after lunch, I'm going to insist that it be restricted to the engagements already decided on—Cleveland and Pittsburgh and the election eve broadcast." He held to that position. To every argument in favor of President Eisenhower's trip to Illinois, he had a counterargument. And the matter was settled when the President, not knowing the real reason for the Vice President's attitude, finally agreed with him that Illinois was out.

Could General Eisenhower think of especially amusing or important incidents during his presidency of Columbia University? He replied that predictably there were plenty of humorous incidents, if only such faux pas as lighting a cigarette in the Board of Trustees room where never in the long history of Columbia had smoking been permitted, with an instant rush by deans and trustees to find an ashtray. (It turned out to be a metal wastebasket discovered by Dean Leopold Arnaud of the School of Architecture.) He found the post intensely interesting; practically every day, at least in the first year and a half or so, had its important decision.

But, to him, the job was much larger than the sum of all its incidents. An early priority had to be given to ending the annual deficit—something in the neighborhood of $1,000,000 and $1,500,-000 a year. This gap between income and expenditures made difficult any physical expansion, program development, increases in faculty salaries—all the things that mark a dynamic institution. But in two years or so this problem was pretty well solved.

It was more important from the very beginning, however, to arouse within the entire Columbia family—students, faculty, staff, trustees, friends—a spirit of teamwork, a realization that the increasing greatness of Columbia was dependent on their enthusiastic support of it in talent, in time, in money. For too many years, the faculty and administration had left the raising of money, the development of projects, to President Nicholas Murray Butler. Consequently, through the whole time at Columbia, General Eisenhower was forever making speeches in New York and around the country, writing letters, holding conferences that were aimed at building, particularly among the alumni, a sense of the role a great number of people should play in Columbia's progress.

For him, the best part of Columbia life was the number and the variety of challenges that he encountered there. For some of them he had absolutely no preparation. He never dreamed they existed. But the longer he was at it, the more he loved the job; and the more outright fun he had in discharging it.

If President Eisenhower could have any one wish, if he could wave a magic wand and make one thing come true, what would it be? He would, he said, wish for full and free communication between the two sides of the Iron Curtain. He was as sure as he was sitting there that if the people of Russia could talk face to face with the people of the United States there would soon be no more cold war or world tension and the United States would come into its rightful inheritance as a keeper of the peace. He believes it is wholly a matter of communicating people to people and avoiding the prejudices and propaganda angles of the leaders. He thinks that the prosperous nations have to be ready to operate their own economies so that less fortunate nations can also live in something other than privation. No principal section of the earth should become so continually impoverished that the people who live there reach the conclusion that any catastrophe, even war, would be better than what they now have.

# RICHARD BUCKMINSTER FULLER

## How Little I Know

---

"Tell me—
In five thousand
Written words"—
(Equivalent, at my oral rate,
To three-quarters of an hour's discourse)
"What you have learned—
In your lifetime,"
Said Norman Cousins.
"That ought to be easy" said I.


Three weeks have gone by—


I recall that
Thirty-eight years ago
I invented a routine
Somewhat similar to
Muscle development
Accomplished through
A day-by-day lifting
Of progressively heavier weights.

But my new
Intellectual routine
Dealt with the weightless process
Of human thought development
Which subject is
Known to scholars
As *epistemology*.

And I have learned
That such words as Epistemology
Stop most of humanity
From pursuing
Such important considerations
As the development
Of the thought processes.

So my new discipline
Was invented for dealing
Even with the ephemeral
Which word means
*Conceptual but weightless*—
As is for instance
The *concept of circularity*.

My new strategy required
That on successive days
I ask myself
A progressively larger
And more inclusive question
Which must be answered
Only in the terms of
Experience.

Hearsaids, beliefs, axioms,

Superstitions, guesses, opinions
Were and are
All excluded
As answer resources
For playing my particular
Intellectual development game.

However, when lacking
Any possible experience clues
I saw that it was ineffectual
To attempt to answer
Such questions as for instance
"Why I?"
Or
"Why . . .
Anything?"

And because it was my experience
That some individuals
Proved as persistently faithful
In reporting their experiences to me
As were my own senses
The rules of my game permitted
My inclusion of such individuals'
Directly reported experiences
In my inventory of experiences
For use in my progressively
Great and greater
Self-questioned answering.

In playing that game
I soon came
To what I assumed to be both

The largest askable and
The largest answerable
Question:
"What do you mean,"
I asked myself,
"By the word
Universe?
If you can't answer
In terms of
Direct experience
*You must desist*
*From the further use*
*Of the word UNIVERSE*
*For, to you*
*It will have become*
*Meaningless!"*

The twentieth century physicists,
In defining the physical universe
As consisting only of energy,
Deliberately excluded the metaphysical universe—
Because the metaphysical
Consists only of imponderables,
Whereas the physical scientists
Deal only with ponderables—
Wherefore their physical universe
Excluded for instance
All our thoughts,—
Because thoughts are weightless—

But thoughts are experiences—
Wherefore I saw
That to be adequate

To the intuitively formulated
And experience-founded controls
Of my ever bigger
Question and answer routine,
My answering definition
Of UNIVERSE
Must be one which
*Embraced the combined*
*Metaphysical and physical*
*Components of UNIVERSE.*

Thus my self-formulating answer emerged,
And has persisted unshattered
By any subsequent challenges
From myself or others
As:
"By universe I mean:
The aggregate of all humanity's
Consciously apprehended
And communicated
(To self or others)
*Experiences.*"

And later I discovered that
Eddington had said "*Science* is:
The conscientious attempt
To set in order
The facts of *Experience.*"

And I also discovered
That Ernst Mach—
The great Viennese physicist,
Whose name is used

To designate flight velocity
In *speed of sound* increments,
Known as Mach numbers—
Said:
"*Physics* is:
Experience
Arranged in
*Most economical order.*"

So I realized that
Both Eddington and Mach
Were seeking to put in order
The same "raw materials"—
I.e. *Experiences*—
With which to identify
Their special subsystems
Of UNIVERSE.

Wherefore I realized that
All the words in all dictionaries
Are the consequent tools
Of all men's conscious
And conscientious attempts
To communicate
All their experiences—
Which is of course
To communicate
Universe.

There are forty-three thousand current words
In the Concise Oxford Dictionary.
We don't know who invented them!
What an enormous, anonymous inheritance!

Shakespeare used ten thousand of them
With which to formulate
His complete "works."
It would take many more volumes
Than Shakespeare's to employ
The forty-three thousand—
Logically and cogently.

In a five thousand word article
I would probably have use for
Only one thousand.
Are forty-two thousand
Of these words
Superficial and extraneous
In reporting on
*What I have learned?*
I have learned that
You would think so
If you ever saw a magazine's
Space rewrite editor
At work on my work!

"What's stopping you?" said Norman
"I'm not stopping—
I've never started.
I can't find the self starter
Or, more truthfully,
The self starter can't find me
Oh—there it goes"

Womb days—
Womb days—
Dear old tummy tomb days—

I can't consciously recall
Those busy elementary assembly days
But post-graduate activity in
Experimental biology
By me and you (one and two)
Which surprisingly produced
Wee thee (we three)
And more (four)
Suggests to us
That our subconscious reflexing
Can never forget
The satisfactory routines of our 273
Undergraduate days.
Probably no billionaire
Out here in the air
"Ever had it so good."

It is understood
That if you know that I know
How to say it "correctly"
(The exact meaning of which
I have not yet learned)
Then I am entitled to say it
All incorrectly
Which once in a rare while
Will make you laugh.
And I love you so much
Whenever you laugh.
But I haven't learned yet
What love may be
But I love to love
And love being loved
And that is a whole lot
Of unlearnedness.

I haven't learnt yet
What laughter is
But a mother told me
How surprised was she
When an undergraduate first
Belly laughed in her
Alma mater
Dormitory.


I haven't learned
How or why
Universe contrived to implode
And intellectually code
The myriadly unique
Chromosomically orchestrated
DNA–RNA,
Quadripartite moleculed,
Binary paired,
Helically extended
And unzippingly dichotomied
Regenerative symphonic
Jazz, as
A one and two,
Three and four
Me – – – You,
Thee – – – they
And more
Thine and mine,
Sweet citizen.
\*   \*   \*   \*   \*   \*   \*   \*
THYMINE–CYTOSINE
GUANINE–ADENINE
\*   \*   \*   \*   \*   \*   \*   \*

That tetracouplet
Won the Nobel prize

The Wilkins, Crick and Watson Waltz

C · G    T · A    A · T    G · C    A-T    G · C

And that GC–TA jazz
All synced into
The non-simultaneous aggregate
Of complex frequency integrated,
Multi-degrees of freedom permitted,
Individualized sequences,
Of experience evolutions,
Which we wave-modulatingly identify,
In the subconsciously formulated,
Tongue and lips shaped,
Omni-directionally propagated,
Air wave patterning—
Sound
WORLD
—Whirled into the world
Of positive and negative
Of—

| | | |
|---|---|---|
| MALE | and | FEMALE |
| Singular | and | Plural |
| Discontinuous | and | Continuous (has ovaries) |
| Compression | and | Tension |
| Hunter | and | Consolidator |
| Differentiator | and | Integrator |

```
    I                        O
    I n          and         O u t
   l I v e        and        l O v e
  e v I l         and       e v O l
 e v I l u t i o n  and    e v O l u t i o n
d e v I l          and       l O v e d
```

The Devil lived
But never loved
Which is lonely—
L — one — only
As are all
Self Isolations

So let's withdraw
From exclusivity,
Into world music
Where—
As yet dancing to
The DNA waltz—
I am now seventy years, or
Approximately 600,000 hours old.

I have slept away 200,000 of those hours.
While another 200,000—
Which is half of
My 400,000 awake hours—
Have gone into routine work which has been
Prescribed, imposed or induced by other men—
Such as being "educated," earning a living,
Paying taxes, obtaining licenses,
Answering telephones and questionnaires.

And another 100,000—
Half of the remaining 200,000 awake hours—
Have gone also into routine work
But this time prescribed
In the by-laws of membership
In the non-simultaneous invention Universe—
As one of its impressively independent,
Variable functions—
A *human* member.

Each such member is
A metabolically regenerative
Ninety-nine per cent automated,
Individually unique,
Abstract, pattern integrity system,
Whose input-output energy involvement
And control capability
Must continually expand, extend, relay, rebuild
And maintain, as "operative,"
An interior-exterior, bi-partite tool complex
Beginning with an integrally centralized organic set
Which is subsequently extended into
An extra-corporeally decentralized organic set.

Both of which interior and exterior sets consist of
Progressively interchangeable and intertransformable
Chemical, hydraulic, pneumatic,
Electro-magnetic, thermodynamic,
Molecular and anatomical,
Structural patterning processes.

All of which complex
Regenerative processes

Are compounded as a unitary,
Invisibly minute,
Abstract pattern marriage operation,
Inaugurating a new individual life
Which like a telephone message
Has some of the thoughts of both parties
Yet weighs nothing in itself
But makes its compounded
Pattern self known
By a complex pattern of orderly and local
Physical environment displacements,
Which—as the circular wave
Emanating in any liquid
Such as water, milk or kerosene,
From the impact of an object
Dropped in the liquid—
Grows or expands regeneratively.

But as with the circularly expanding
Weightless wave emanation
There occurs also at outset
A momentary displacement exchange
As a centralized splash-back
Dissipated against gravity
To balance the local accounts.

And thus there is propagated
An abstract and weightless
Horizontally flowing
Wave impulse pattern integrity
Which though visibly apprehended
By its succession of local displacements
Does not consist of an horizontally moving

And ever increasing aggregate
Of water molecules.

There is another experiment
Which discloses the pattern integrity
Which can be demonstrated
By taking three different
Pieces of rope of equal diameter
One of manila
One of nylon
One of cotton
And making a beautiful running splice
Of one end of the manila rope
Into the end of the nylon rope
And the other end of the manila rope
Into the end of the cotton rope.

Next we make a simple back loop knot
In the end of the cotton rope
And slide it along the cotton rope
Until it slides along over the splice
Into the manila rope and along the manila
Until it slides past the splice
Onto the nylon
And makes it clear
That the knot is neither
Cotton, manila, nor nylon
But a pattern integrity
Made visible to us
By its temporary local displacement
Of the electro-magnetic frequencies
Visible to us as colors
Within the frequency range
Tuneable by our human optic system.

Neither water nor rope
"Went" anywhere
Only the weightless pattern integrity
Moved from here to there.


So too does the complex wave package
Of *human being* pattern integrity
Begin to compound and
Expand regeneratively
The local environment's chemical association
And disassociation events;
Continually shunting more
And more chemical event patterns
Into its local disturbance—
Like a tornado gaining twist,
Power and *visible presence* on Earth
By inhibiting ever
Greater quantities of
Local-ly available dust, fibers,
Water droplets and larger objects—
Until the new human being
Nine months later emerges
From its mother's womb
As a seven-pound, placid
Pink tornado.


And this tomato tinted tornado—me—
Swollen 24 fold to approximately 160 pounds—
Each day takes in and compoundingly processes
Approximately three pounds of foods,
Six pounds of water and
Sixty-four pounds of air—
From which it extracts six pounds of oxygen:—

Amounting at my seventy years
To a cumulative total
Of approximately 1,000 tons—
The weight of one United States Navy's
World War Two destroyer,
Or 300,000 fold my arrival weight.

But the thousand tons
Is in effect the weight
Of a seventy years long
Thirty-six inch girthed "rope"
Twisted of imaginary strands
Of food, water and air molecules
Drawn randomly from all around Earth,
And twisted temporarily together.

Into the molecular rope
A complex slip knot has been "tied"
Which complex knot
Is both internally and externally
In the exact pattern
Of the complex, pattern integrity:—
Me,—
Which has been slipped
Along the rope
By time.

And as the knot passed,
The rope behind it
Disintegrated and
Its atoms dispersed
And deployed into
Other biosphere function patternings.

Concurrently with "slipping" of corporeal "me"
The extra-corporeally decentralized
Originally integral functions of "me"
Are externalized into a complex of tools
Averaging ten tons of steel,
Twenty-nine tons of concrete
Plus one mixed ton
Of all the other metals
Per each industrialized man.

And man's tool extensions
Process universe energies,
Occurring only external to man, and
Provide each 1965
North American type industrialized human
With 200, 24 hour serving, energy slaves;
Each slave being capable
Of doing as much physical work as
A human can do;
But at a ten millionfold
Finer degree of precision;
While working tirelessly
Under conditions of heat
And cold which would destroy man.

All of this combined internal and external
Metabolically regenerative man package
Arrives without any instruction manual
Covering either its own operation
Or that of the non-simultaneous Universe
Within which man must function
As an independent variable.

But the human package

Of integral and deployed tooling
Has fortunately
The built-in subconscious capability
Of self-discovery which in turn
Has discovered its conscious ability
To discover experimentally and progressively
The ability to formulate concepts and words
And thereby to relay to other contemporaries,
And to subsequent generations of man,
The apprehended data and
Comprehended principles
Apparently governing
Some of the Operations
Of Universe
Including man.

Of my remaining 100,000 hours
60,000 have been used
In getting from here to there;
And that has left me
A bonus of 40,000 hours
Or 6⅔ per cent of my life's total hours
To invest at compound interest
In whatever way the
"Conscious" I
Wishes.

It is hard therefore to explain
Why conscious I
Should have behaved so perversely
As to have concentrated on producing
Explosives equivalent in destructive capability
To fourteen tons of T.N.T.
Per each and every human on Earth.

And how perverse I have been
Is only to be comprehended
When it is realized
That the 14 tons per capita
Of self annihilating explosives
Represent an energy harvest
Which if properly cultivated
Could have been made to support
At high standard of living
All human life on earth
For all the rest
Of this century
While thus providing the opportunity
To invest the gained time
In providing for all
Human generations to come.


I'm not inclined to use
The word "Creativity"
In respect to human beings,
What is usually spoken of as creativity
Is really a unique and unprecedented
Human employment of *principles*
Which exist a *priori* in the universe.


I think man is a very extra-ordinary
Part of the universe
For he demonstrates unique capability
In the discovery and intellectual identification
Of the operative principles of universe
—Which though unconsciously employed
Have not been hitherto differentiated,
Isolated out and understood

As being principles,
By other biological species.

Rejecting the word "creativity"
For use by any other than
The great intellectual integrity
Progressively disclosed as conceiving
Both comprehensively and anticipatorily
The complex interpatternings
Of reciprocal and transformative freedoms
In pure principle
Which apparently govern universe
And constitute the verb god,
I go along with the 5,000 year old
Philosophy of the Bhagavad-Gita
Which says "Action is the product
Of the qualities inherent in nature.
It is only the ignorant man,
Who, misled by personal egotism,
Says 'I am the doer.' "
I am most impressed
With the earliest recorded philosophic statements
By unknown individuals of India and China.
Through millenniums the philosophies
Have become progressively
Compromised and complicated.

I am an explorer, however,
Of the generalized design science principles
Which seemingly differentiate
Man from animal
And *mind* from *brain*.
The word "generalization"

As used in the *literary* sense,
Means "a very broad statement."
It suggests covering too much territory
—Too thinly to be sound.
The literary men say
"This is too general."

In the mathematical sense,
The meaning of generalization
Is quite different.
The mathematician or the physicist
Looks for principles which are
Persistently operative in nature,
Which will hold true in every special case.
If you can find principles
That hold true in every case,
Then you have discovered
What the scientist calls
A *generalized principle.*
The conscious detection of
Generalized principles which hold true
Under all conditions
And their abstraction from any and all
Special case experiences of the principles
—Is probably unique to humans.

By abstraction, I mean an idealized,
"Empty set" statement
Such as, for instance, one of my own!,
—"Tension and compression are only coexistent"
—E.g., when you tense a rope
Its girth contracts—ergo compresses.
When you compress a sphere's polar axis,

Its equatorial girth expands and tenses.
It is inconceivable that a dog
Tugging at its leash at one time
And, compressing its teeth
On a bone at another time,
Should formulate consciously
The generalized
"Only coexistence of tension and compression,"
Though the dog is subconsciously coordinate
In tension-compression tactics.

To generalize further than
"Tension and compression are only coexistent,"
We may say that "plus and minus
Only coexist"
And generalize even further
By saying "Functions only coexist."
Then there is an even more powerful
And intellectually more exalted stage
Of generalization of principles
And that is the generalization
Of a complex of generalizations
—Such as—unity is plural and at minimum two
—Which combines the generalized law
Of the coexistence only of functions
With the theory of number.
In turn we discover the generalizations
Governing the associative powers
Of the nucleus and of the weak interactions
For the unity is two
Of the congruent, convex and concave spheres
As evidenceable in the generalized laws
Disclosed conceptually, arithmetically, and geometrically
In synergetics.

I am certain that what we speak of
As human morality
Is a form of tentative generalization
Of principles underlying
Special case experiences of human potentials,
Behaviors, actions, reactions and resultants.
Man has also the unique ability
To *employ* generalized principles
—Once recognized—
In a consciously selective variety
Of special case interrelationships.
The whole regenerative process
Of intellectual discovery
And specialized use of generalized principles
Is known as teleology.


Teleology embraces
The theory of communication,
Though as yet having special case limitations.
It is an hypothetical
Approach to a pure, abstract generalization
To say that *teleology*
*Is only intuitively initiated by humans.*


Intuition alerts brain
To first apprehend
And then recognize
Each special case experience
Within some minimum number
Of special case recognitions.
Intuition alerts mind
To comprehend, and
Formulate conceptually

The abstract generalization
Of a principle recognized
As operative in all the special cases.
Intuition alerts brain to
The objectively employable generalized principle
In hitherto unexperienced special case
Circumstances inexplicably remote
From the earlier set of
Special case experiences within which
The generalized principles were first experienced
Before their generalization
Occurred in the mind.


Teleology—as part
Of communications theory
Relates to the pursuit of truth
As entropy and anti-entropy.
It may be that
Communications theory
May be mathematically equated
With electrical
Transmission theory
Whereby the higher
The meaning or voltage
The more efficient
And longer distance
Communication attainable.


Based on experiments
With any and all systems,
The second law of thermodynamics
Predicts the inexorable energy loss
Known as ENTROPY.

Because the escaping energy
Does so diffusely,
In all directions,
Entropy is also known
Mathematically
As "The Law of Increase
Of the Random Element."

Before it had been discovered
By rigorous experimentation
That light has a *velocity*
It was erroneously assumed
To be "self-evident"
That light was instantaneous—
That all stars in the sky
Were "right there now"
In exact geometrical pattern,
Being seen instantaneously
And simultaneously
By all who looked their way.

But since Michelson's measurement
Of light's speed
We have learned that
The light from the sun,
Our nearest star,
Takes eight minutes
To reach us here on Earth.
From our next nearest star
Light takes two years
To reach our planet Earth.
And other stars
Are so far away
Their light takes millions

Of years and more
To reach us.

Assuming instant-universe
Classical Newtonian Science
Also assumed that universe
Must be an instant system—
A simultaneous unit machine,
In which every part
Must be affecting
Every other part,
In varying degrees
But in simultaneous unity.
They assumed also that the
Unit and simultaneous universe
Must of course obey
The great Second Law
Of Thermodynamics
Whose, inexorable,
Entropic energy loss
Required self-dissipation
And ultimately utter
Self-annihilation
Of universe.
"Running down" they called it
Wherever "down" may be.

Though light's speed
Of seven hundred million miles per hour
Is *fast*
It isn't anywhere nearly as fast
As "instant"—
Which means reaching anywhere
"In no time at all."

Ergo, the Einsteinians
Instituted experiments
To ascertain the behavioral characteristics
Of a physical universe comprised
Of only partially overlapping,
Progressively intertransforming,
Non-simultaneous, energy events.


The Einsteinian Era scientists' experiments
Showed that entropic energies
Accomplished their disassociations *here*
Only through associations *there*—
That is by regroupings elsewhere.
Thus early twentieth-century scientists
Found the intertransformative
Energy quanta transactions,—
To be eventually,
But not always immediately,—
One hundred per cent accountable.


As a consequence of
The Einsteinians' experiments
The eighteenth and nineteenth centuries'
Concept of a continually
Self-dissipating universe
Had to be abandoned
And in its place was established
The, experimentally required,
Law of Conservation of Energy
Which states that energy
May be neither created nor lost;
Ergo the energetic universe
Is the minimum,

But non-simultaneously realized,
Energy exchanging system,
Which is to say
That physical universe,
As experimentally demonstrated
Is the minimum and only
Perpetual motion process,
Which as an aggregate of finite,
Dissimilar and non-simultaneous
Energy events
Is in itself
Sum totally finite.

All the foregoing
Dissipates the foundations
Of the Newtonian world's
Cosmogony and economics
Which assumed
That a "running down world"
Suggested the prudence
Of saving, conserving and hoarding;
And that those who spent
Were fools who would perish
As resources dwindled.

Though entropically irreversible
Every action
Has its reaction and resultant,
And every nuclear component
Has its positive or negative
Behavioral opposite
Which is however
Not its mirror image.

And the irreversible situations
Give an evolutionary direction
To otherwise stalemated
Conditions of physical universe.

For instance it is discovered
That wealth, whatever else it may be,
Cannot alter an iota of yesterday
And can alter only
The present and forward
Metabolic regeneration
Conditions of humanity.

Song of the Dead
And the Quick—
Newton was a noun
And Einstein is a verb.
Einstein's norm makes Newton's norm
INSTANT UNIVERSE,
Absurd.
"A body persists
In a state of rest
Or—
Except as affected—"
Thus grave stones are erected!

Non-simultaneous, physical universe
Is Energy; and
"Energy equals mass
Times the second power
Of the speed of light."
No exceptions!
Fission verified Einstein's hypothesis—

Change is normal
Thank you Albert!

Irreversible verse.
Einstein's intellect
Defined *energy* as $E = MC^2$
*Energy* cannot define *intellect*.
Intellect the *metaphysical*
Is comprehensive to
Energy the *physical*.
While Universe is *finite*
Energy is *definite*
Because definable.
Energy is XY.
Intellect is 0.
The wealth of Earthians
Is irreversible.
Wealth cannot alter yesterday's experience.
It can only alter today's and tomorrow's experiences.
It can buy
Forward time in which intellect
May scientifically explore for
The orderly interrelationships
Disclosed in yesterday's experiences
Which can be employed by intellect
To forecast
Anticipatory and orderly rearrangements of tomorrow
By technological transformations
Of the physical energy environments,
Events and circumstances.

Wealth is the organized and operative
Tool and energy capability

To sustain man's forward metabolic regeneration;
To physically protect him;
To increase his knowledge
And degrees of freedom
While decreasing his interfrustrations.
Solo wealth is to commonwealth
As X is to $X^4$.
Wealth is: *Energy compounded*
*With intellect's know-how.*

Every time man uses his *know-how*
His experience increases
And his intellectual advantage
Automatically increases.
Because of its *conservation*
Energy cannot decrease.
Know-how can only increase.
It is therefore scientifically clear
That:—wealth which combines
Energy and intellect
Can *only increase,* and that wealth can
Increase *only with use*
And that wealth increases
As fast as it is used.
The faster—the more!

Wealth is accountable as
The inanimate energies shunted
Onto the ends of industrial levers
Whose physical capability is
Stateable in forward, automated,
Man days of travel miles
With first class comprehensive services

Including food, lodging, clothing,
Amusements, communication, information
And medical services
Based on the average physical experiences
Of a top civil service rating's
World travel involvements.


Has man a function
In Universe?


In dynamical balance
With the inside-outing,
*Expanding universe*
Of radiant stars,
Man witnesses
Radiantly dormant Earth as
A collecting or outside-inning,
*Contracting phase,* of universe.
Earth receives and stores,
A continually increasing inventory
Of sun and star emanating radiation
In its lethal-energy-concentrates
Sifting, sorting and accumulating
Spherical Van Allen belts.


In addition to the Van Allen belts
The succession of Earth's concentric
Spherical mantles, e.g.,
The ionosphere, troposphere *et al.,*
Constitute an extraordinary series
Of discrete filters for
The random-to-orderly sorting,
Shunting, partially accumulating

And final inwardly forwarding
Of the benign radiation residues
To the biosphere stage
Of Earth's continual and orderly
Processing of its discrete share
Of the expanding universe propagated
Energy income receipts.
Earth also receives daily
Additional thousands of tons
Of expanding Universe dispatched
Stardust.

This concentration around Earth's surface
Of the universe deposited dust
Apparently consists of 91 of the
92 regeneratively patterning
Chemical elements
In approximately the same systematic order
Of relative abundance of those elements
As the relative abundance
Of those same elements
As they are found to occur
In the thus far inventoried
Reaches of universe.
The biological life on earth
Is inherently anti-entropic
For it negotiates the chemical sorting
Out of the Earth's crust's
Chemical element inventory
And rearranges the atoms
In elegantly ordered
Molecular compound patternings.

Of all the biological anti-entropics,

I.e., random-to-orderly arrangers,
Man's intellect is by much
The most active, exquisite and effective agent
Thus far in evidence in universe.
Through intellect, man constantly succeeds
In inventing technological means
Of doing ever more orderly
I.e., more efficient,
"Better sorted-out,"
Local universe, energy tasks
With ever less units of investments
Of the (what may be only apparently),
"randomly" occurring
Resources of energy,
As atomic matter,
Or energy, as channeled electro-magnetics.


To guarantee
All of life's
Anti-entropic functioning
The intellectual integrity universe,
That has designedly arranged the great game
Has also arranged that mankind
Like all the other living species,
Has its ultra-shortsighted,
Built-in, "desire" drives,
Its romantic conception ambitions
And protectively colored self deceits,
As well as its longer distance "needs,"
All of which cause each specie
To pursue its particular "honey"
With its particular rose-colored glasses,
As does the bumblebee

Which at the same time
Inadvertently and unconsciously performs
Myriads of other tasks,
Designed with fabulous
Scientific capability by nature,
Which inadvertent inco-ordinate tasks
Unknown to the separate creature species
Are all essential to realization
Of the regenerative continuance
Of the much larger
Survival support conditions
For the generalized
Ecological system of "all life."

It is part of
The comprehensively anticipating,
Design science of life
That the bumblebee's self-unviewed,
Unwitting, bumbling tail
Bumps into and knocks off male pollen,
Which it later
And again inadvertently,
Knocks off upon the female botanical organs,
Thus unconsciously participating in
A vastly complex ecological interaction
Of the many energy processing
Bio-chemical "gears"
Of the total life system
Dynamically constituted by
All the living species.

The myriad inadvertencies
Of all the living species
Have sum totally provided

A metabolically sustaining
And regenerative topsoil process
Which—it is realized now,
But only by
Our retrospectively gained knowledge—
Has kept man
Regeneratively alive on Earth
For at least two million years,
While ever improving
His physical survival advantages
And increasing his longevity.

This vast "game playing" of life
Has also indirectly occasioned,
Not only the regenerative multiplication
Of human beings,
But also a progressively increasing
Percentage who survive in conditions
Of ever improving
Physical advantage.

I think man is very properly concerned
About that which he does not understand.
I don't think that it is the machine per se
That bothers man;
It is just not understanding
Anything
That disturbs him.
When an accident bares
Portions of human organs
Familiar only to doctors,
Those organs look foreign
And frightening to people.

Stick your tongue way out
Before a mirror.
It is a strange looking device.

If existing originally and
Transcendentally as psyches only,
Individuals had to choose,
And assemble their own sets
Of organic parts,
Having been assured of mortal incarnation
And of mortal "honey chasing" experiences
But only after successful selection
And completion of the assembly—
And were endowed—as psyches—
Only with an aesthetic
Sense of selectivity,
Being devoid of any understanding
Of either the separate or integrated
Functions of those parts—
No humans would merger
Those co-operatively functioning parts
Into Mortal beings
For no part of the "guts"
Would be chosen.
Nature had to skin over the regenerative
Chemistry and physics controls,
With an aesthetically intriguing,
Pseudo-static, sculptural Baby doll unity
In order to trick the immortal psyches
Into the problem beset,
Temporary occupation
Of such humid process regenerative machines
As those of the humans.

I have learned
That man knows little
And thinks he knows a lot.
When any man can tell us
Just how and why he is handling and disposing
The energies of his breakfast;
How he breaks down his chemical energy and
To which glands is he routing
The diversified energies of his ham and eggs;
Or when any man can tell us
That he is deliberately
Pushing each of his million
Head hairs
Out through his scalp
At specifically preferred rates
And in specifically controlled shapes
For specific purposes
We may say that this man
Knows a little,
But I don't know of any man
Who can tell me
So little even as
Why we have hair.

I am the most unlearned man I know.
I don't know anyone
Who has learned
How little one knows
As have I.
But that does not belittle
The little I seem to know,
And I have confidence
In the importance of remembering

How little we know
And of the possible significance
Of the fact that we prosper,
And at some times even enjoy
Life in Universe
Despite the designed in littleness
That we have to "get by with."

I like algebra

        Positives more powerful than negatives
$$(+) \times (-) = (-) \quad \text{minus wins}$$
$$(+) \times (+) = (+) \quad \text{plus wins only by default}$$
$$(-) \times (-) = (+) \quad \text{plus wins}$$

The game is over—
Plus wins two to one.

What the astronomers rank as
The nearest "bright" star to Earth
Is "Rigel Kent"
Which is three hundred thousand times
Further away from Earth than is the Sun.
It is easy to see a man
One third of a mile away and
We were surprised when young
To see a man
At that distance
Swinging a sledge
To drive a post into the ground
And to realize
That the sound of his maul
Hitting the post top

Registered in our brain
As reported through our ears
Four seconds later
Than had the visual news
Which "long since" had told us
That he had once more
Hit the post.
Through physical experiments
Performed by our scientists
We have learned that
The highest known velocity
Among physical phenomena
Is the speed of light and all radiation
Relayingly scanned by nerve lines
To our brains' television conceptualizing
Through the optics of our eyes.

Because the speed of light
Is approximately 186,000 miles per second,
And the Moon is
About twice that distance
Away from Earth.
If we had a large mirror on the Moon,
And we flashed a powerful
Light toward the Moon
It would take four seconds
For the light to be reflected back
To our eyes.
That is, the light takes
Two seconds to get to the Moon
And two more seconds
To return to Earth.
And the overall four seconds lag

Of the visual report
Is the same time lag as that in
Our childhood realized lag
Of the *sound report*
Behind the *visual report*
Of the post-sledging event.
Because the light coming to Earth
From the Moon
Takes two seconds to make the trip,
And because the light
Coming to Earth from the Sun
Takes eight and one-half minutes,
And because the light
Coming to us from Rigel Kent
Takes four and one-half years,
We all see a live show
Taking place in the sky
Four and one-half
Years ago.

And as we gaze around
The starry heavens
We see right now
Live shows of "yesterdays"
Ranging from millions to sextillions of years ago,
As we look at the stars
We see all of history
Now alive.

It took only two million years and
Four and one-half billion human babies
To establish a human survival beachhead
Aboard the little

Eight thousand mile diameter
Spherical Spaceship EARTH.
Whereby life could successfully realize
Its highest known potential life span
Possibly to continue indefinitely
As one self-rejuvenating generation.
Few of the stars we look at,
Live starring out there,
Are young enough
To witness
Those first human events
Taking place on Earth
Only two millions of years ago.

Since all the vital parts
Of human organisms
Have now become interchangeable,
And many of them
Have also become interchangeable
With inanimate mechanical parts,
And since human longevity
Is continually increasing
There is a good possibility
That humanity is developing
A continuous man
Who will persist in prime health
And youthful vigor.

With the lessening of need
To replenish the population,
With fresh baby starts
The built-in drives to procreate
Will lessen and be manifest in a proclivity

Of females to camouflage as male
And male to camouflage as female
Thus suppressing the procreative urge
By superficial antipathetic illusions,
While permitting and promoting
Procreatively innocuous sex companionships.

Despite their billionfold numbers
Babies and very young children
Soon after their arrival on Earth
Have uttered and continue to utter
Spontaneous comments and questions—
Concerning life on Earth
And in Universe—
Which are so economical
And uniquely fresh
In viewpoint and formulation
As to be pure poetry
Proving, apparently, that
Poetry is inexhaustible;
To which their sophisticated
And surprised off-guard adult audience
Cliché unpoetically
"Oh how cute."

In the year 1964
The one hundred largest
Industrial giant corporations,
Born and reared
In the United States of America
Invested four out of five
Of their new plant and equipment
Expansion dollars

In production and service facilities
In world lands outside the U.S.A.
This trending to World identity only
Of the industrial giants
Held true also not only with thousands
Of lesser magnitude
U.S.A. and European born
Limited liability industrial organizations
But also with the Communist countries'
Giant industrial organizations.
Wherefore world industrialization trends swiftly—
And altogether transcendentally
To man's conscious planning—
Into an unitarily co-ordinate
World giant
With built-in automated,
Research fed,
Computer analyzed and selected,
Evolutionary self-improving
And self-transforming
Through alternatingly regenerated
Competitive precessioning
Of all the variable functions
Of general systems theory.

TRUTH
I have learned that truth
Is an omni-present, omni-directional,
Evolutionary awareness,
One of whose myriadly multiplying facets
Discloses that there are no "absolutes"
—No "ends," in themselves—no "things"
—Only transitionally transformative verbing.

It seems possible to me
That God may be recognizable
In man's limited intellection
Only as the weightless passion drive
Which inspires our progressive searching
For the—momentarily only—
And only most-truthful-thus-far-possible—
Comprehension of all the interconnections
Of all experiences.
It seems then to me
That the nearer we come to understanding,
The nearer we come to the
Orderly omni-interrelationships
Of all the weightless complex
Of all generalized principles
Which seem to be disclosed to us
As so important
As to be tentatively identified as God.
For it is the integratable interrelationships
Of all the generalized laws
Which apparently govern
The great verb "universe"
Or the vastly greater
—Because comprehensively anticipatory—
Verb *intellecting*
Which verb of optimum understanding
May be "God."

It seems that Truth
Is progressive approximation
In which the relative fraction
Of our spontaneously tolerated *residual* error
*Constantly diminishes.*

This is a typical
Anti-entropy proclivity of man
—Entropy being the law
Of *increase of the random element.*

Heisenberg's indeterminism,
In which the act of measuring
Always alters the measured,
Would seem entropic were it not
For the experimentally realized knowledge
That the successive alterations
Of the observed,
Diminish
As both our tooling and instrumentation
Continually improve;
Ergo intellection's effect
Upon measurement and the measured
Is a gap closing,
And the pursuit of more truthful comprehension
Is successfully anti-entropic.

Before Heisenberg, T. S. Eliot said,
"Examination of history alters history"
And Ezra Pound,
And even earlier poets,
Reported their discoveries
That in one way or another
The act of thinking alters thought itself.

When we ask ourself
"What have we learned?"
We feel at first
That the answer is "nothing."

But as soon as we say so
We recall exceptions.
For instance we have learned
To test experimentally
The axioms given to us
As "educational" springboards, and
We have found
That most of the "springboards"
Do not spring
And some never existed.
As for instance
Points, holes,
Solids, surfaces,
Straight lines, planes,
"Instantaneous," "simultaneous,"
Things, nouns,
"Congruence," "at rest"
The words "artificial" and "failure"
Are all meaningless.

For what they aver
Is experimentally "non-existent."
If nature permits a formulation
It is natural.
If nature's laws of behavior
Do not permit the formulation
The latter does not occur.
Whatever can be done
Is natural,
No matter how grotesque, boring,
Unfamiliar or unprecedented.
In the same way
Nature never "fails."

Nature complies with her own laws.
Nature *is the law.*
When man lacks understanding
Of nature's laws
And a man-contrived structure
Buckles unexpectedly,
It does not fail.
It only demonstrates that man
Did not understand
Nature's laws and behaviors.
Nothing failed.
Man's knowledge or estimating
Was inadequate.

Step to the blackboard.
Write out a number so lengthy
It has never been written before.
The pattern of numbers
Constitutes a new form.
The number is a doodle.
And I cannot accredit novel form
As creativity of man.
The number of relationships between items
Is always $\dfrac{N^2 - N}{2}$.

The relationships between four or more items
Are always greater in number
Than the number of items.
Ergo, there are always more chords than notes
And chords by themselves are not music.
It takes two to make a baby
But it takes God to make two.

God is twoing
God is threeing
God is multiplying
By dividing
The second law of thermodynamics—
Entropy—is also as we have learned
The law of increase of the Random Element
I.e., every system looses energy—but
Synergy means
Behavior of whole systems
Unpredicted by
The behavior of their parts.

EN–ergy behaves entropically.
SYN–ergy behaves anti-entropically.
God is entropy
And God is also anti-entropy,
God is synergy
God is energy.
And God is always
A verb—
The verbing of
Integrity.

I assume that the *physical universe is definite*
And the *metaphysical universe is finite.*
What men have called infinite
I call finite
And what men called finite
I call definite—i.e., definitive.
By my philosophy
The finite, but imponderable
Metaphysical universe

Embraces the definite,
Ponderable, physical universe.
*Finite* is not conceptual.
*Definite* is conceptual.
I have mathematical proof
That the difference between the sums
Of all the angles around all the surface vertices
Of any conceptual, definitive physical system
And the finite but non-conceptual metaphysical universe
Is always 720°
Or a difference of only one
*Definitive tetrahedron,*
Therefore, the combined
Physical and metaphysical universe is finite.

You can't buy anything worthwhile
Like spontaneous *love* or *understanding.*
Though metaphysically finite
These are imponderables.

The absolute would be
Non-transformable, static and weighable.
Ergo, experimentally meaningless.
Infinity is only local
And occurs within definite systems,
As for instance
Following a great circle
Around a sphere
Which because of the fact
That lines,—
Which occur experimentally
Only as energy vectors—
Cannot go through

The same point
At the same time—
Due to interference,
Which means also that lines
As curves
Cannot re-enter, or
"Join back into themselves,"
Therefore, the circling line
Can only wrap around
And over its earlier part—
As the knot-making
Sailor says it,
The circle when followed
Around and around
Results in a coil
Which is
An assymetric spiral,
Which may be followed experimentally
Only as long as intellect follows.

Not being simultaneous
Universe cannot consist of one function.
Functions only co-exist.
Universe while finite is not definable.
I can define many of its parts
But I cannot define
The non-simultaneously occurring
Aggregate of experiences
Whose total set of relationships
Constitutes the whole universe
Though the latter as an aggregate of finites
Is finite.
All the words

In all the dictionaries, as noted before,
Represent all of humanity's attempts
To express Universe.
And while the dictionaries are finite
All the words
In all the dictionaries
Cannot be read simultaneously
And there is not one
Simultaneous sentence
Inherent and readable
In all the words.
In the same way
All the non-simultaneous experiences
May not be conceived
And expressed as
A simultaneous system.
Ergo, there is no thinkable and logical
Simultaneous conception
Of non-simultaneous Universe.

There is strong awareness
That we have been overproducing
The army of rigorously disciplined
Scientific, game playing, academic specialists
Who through hard work
And suppressed imagination
Earn their Ph.D.'s
And automatic contracts
With prime contractors
At fifteen thousand dollars
Per year—and more—
Only to have their specialized field
Become obsolete and by-passed in five years,

By severely altered techniques, instruments
And exploratory stratagems.
Despite their honor grades
They prove not to be
The Natural Philosophers
And scientist-artists, inferred by their Ph.D.'s
But just deluxe quality
Technicians or mechanics.
And a myriad
Of emergency committees—
Multiplying swiftly
From one or two
Emergency Committees
Appointed by the President,
Have altogether discovered
That what the
Ph.D. scientists lack—
To adapt themselves to change
Has been officially pronounced to be
"Creativity,"
But to my thinking
They lack the unique capability of mind—
Which is the ability not only to generalize
And to integrate a complex
Of pure generalizations
But also to project teleologically—
With fundamental understanding—
In any special case, direction.
Fundamental wisdom
Can readily identify any and all
Special case aspects within
The generalized whole
When listening

Sensitively to one's intuitions
By which alone
The generalized sub-subconscious integration
Of pattern cognition feed-backs
Are articulated.


Philip Morrison—Cornell's Head
Of the Department of Nuclear Physics—
Talks about what he calls
"Left-hand" and "right-hand" sciences.
Right-hand science deals in all the proven
Scientific formulas and experiments.
Left-hand science deals in
All of the as yet *unknown* or *unproven*—
That is: With all it is going to take
Intellectually, intuitively, speculatively, imaginatively
And even mystically
By inspired persistence
To open up the as yet unknown.
The great scientists were great
Because they were the ones
Who dealt successfully with the unknown.
All the "great" were left-hand scientists.
Despite this historical patterning of the "greats"
We have government underwriting
Only the right-hand science,
Making it bigger and sharper,
Rather than *more inclusive* and *understanding!*—
For how could Congress justify
Appropriations of billions for dreams?
So the billions went only
For the swiftly obsoleting
Bigger, faster and more incisive

Modifications of yesterday's certainties,
By Ph.D. specialists
Guaranteed by the great
Institutes of Technology
To which the Congress
Allocated the training funds
As obviously "safe"
And exempt from political criticism;
Despite that scientific investigation
Had shown beyond doubt
That almost all of America's
Top performance scientists
Had been educated
In small, liberal arts colleges,
And that almost all
Of those top scientists
Attributed their success
To their good fortune
In having studied intimately
With a great inspiring teacher.
It would be considered
Political madness
To risk charges of corruption
Through voting government funds
To any individual
Especially to "Great inspiring teachers"—
"Crack-pot, longhairs!"
So it goes—
To Hell with the facts
When re-election
To political office is at stake.

Everything that constitutes science
Is unteachable.

And we recall that
Eddington said: "Science
Is the earnest attempt
Of *individual initiative*
To set in order
The facts of experience."
Scientific routines for specialized technicians
And scientific formulas for their reference
Alone are teachable.

Because we have been governmentally fostering
Only right-hand science and
Right-hand science to excess
The U.S.A. President's science advisor
Instituted last year
A new direction of search
For sources of so-called "creativity."
Financed by the National Academy of Sciences,
He asked New York University's Art Department
To bring together a representative group of
America's leading art educators and artists.
It was felt by the National Academy
That the art educators—
As those who dealt with
Most of the almost drop-outs
Who had been switched into art
As a "last resort"—
Were probably intimate
With the type of emerging youth
Who were allowed to remain
In a freer state of mind
—In the world of art—
Than would they have been

If disciplined rigorously
In sharp specialization by the sciences.
That meeting, I thought fascinating
For it disclosed the artists as being
Individuals who develop powerful self-protection
Of their innate intellectual
And conceptual capability inheritance.
They often protect their innate capabilities
Through intuitively triggered poker-faced silence
Which in the elementary or high schools
Is interpreted as non-cooperative, mental inferiority,
Often causing early termination
Of their formal education.
I think the consensus
Of the New York University meeting
Was that individuals
Of original conceptual brilliance
Were most frequently
Detected, protected, and made to grow
By equally sensitive art teachers.
"Great teachers."
Which agrees elegantly
With the statements
Of the proven scientists
Regarding their own experiences.
Congressional appropriations committees
Please take notice!

To see the whole world picture of science
As a part of a complete creative need—
As an artist's need to articulate—
Kepes at Massachusetts Institute of Technology
Made a beautiful demonstration.

He took hundreds of 8″ × 10″
Black-and-white photographs
Of modern paintings and mixed them thoroughly
Like shuffled cards
With photographs taken by scientists
Through microscopes or telescopes
Of all manner of natural phenomena
Sound waves, chromosomes and such.
The only way you can classify
Photographs with nothing recognizable in them
Is by your own spontaneous
Pattern classifications.
Group the mealy, the blotchy, the striped,
The swirly, the polka-dotted, and their sub-combinations.
The pattern classified groups
Of photographs were displayed.
The artists' work and the scientists'
Were indistinguishable.
Checking the back-mounted data, it was found
That the artist had frequently conceived
His imagined pattern before
The scientist found it in nature.
Science began to take
A new view of artists.

Loving mothers
Prohibit here and promote there—
Often in ways irrelevant or frustrating
To brain-coordinated genetic evolution,
Often suppressing
A child's profound contribution
Trying to emerge.
We have to look on our society

As we look on the biological world in general
Recognizing, for instance,
The extraordinary contributions
Of the fungi, the manures, the worms, et al.—
In the chemical reprocessing—
And fertility up-grading of the earth.
We must learn to think
Of the functions of the trees' roots
As being of equal importance
To the leaves' functions.
We tend to applaud
Only the flower and the fruit
Just as we applaud only the football player
Who makes the touchdown
And not the lineman
Who opened the way.

What society applauds as "creative"
Is often isolated
Out of an extraordinary set
Of co-equal evolutionary events,
Most of which are invisible.
Evolutionary "touch-downs" are unpredictable—
Sometimes centuries apart.
Who knows which child is to make the next breakthrough?
In the next decade society
Is going to be preoccupied with the child
Because through the behavioral sciences
And electrical exploration of the brain
We find that given the right environment
And thoughtful answers to its questions
*The child has everything it needs educationally*
*Right from birth.*

We have thought erroneously of education
As the mature wisdom
And over-brimming knowledge of the grownups
Injected by the discipline pump
Into the otherwise "empty" child's head.
Sometimes parents say "don't"
Because they want to protect the child
From getting into trouble.
At other times when they fail to say "no"
The child gets into trouble.
The child, frustrated, stops exploring.
It is possible to design environments
Within which the child will be
Neither frustrated nor hurt
Yet free to develop spontaneously and fully
Without trespassing on others.
I have learned to undertake
Reform of the environment
And not to try to reform man.
*If we design the environment properly*
It will permit child and man to develop safely
And to behave logically.


Order is achieved through—positive and negative
Magnitude and frequency controlled alteration
Of the successive steering angles.
We move by zig-zagging control
From one phase of physical universe evolution to another.
The rudder concept of social law is most apt.
The late Norbert Wiener chose the word *cybernetics*
Derived from Greek roots of "rudder"
Because Wiener, Shannon and others in communication
     theory

Were exploring human behaviors
And their brain-controlled "feed-back," etc.,
As a basis for the design of computers—
And it became evident
That the human brain
Steers man through constant change.

No sharp cleavage is found
Which identifies the boundary between life and non-life
Between the heretofore so-called "animate" and "inanimate."

Viruses,
The smallest organized structures
Exhibiting "life"
May be classified either—
As inanimate or animate—
As crystalline or "cellular" forms.
This is the level also at which
The DNA/RNA genetic code is essentially
A structural pattern integrity.
Such pattern integrities
Are strictly accountable
Only as mathematical principles
Pattern integrities are found
At all levels of structural organization in universe.
The DNA/RNA is a specialized case
Of the generalized principle of pattern integrity
Found throughout life and non-life.
All pattern integrity design
Is controlled by
Angle and frequency modulation.
The biological corpus
Is not strictly "animate" at any point.
Given that the "ordering"

Of the corpus design
Is accomplished through such codings as DNA/RNA
Which are essentially angle and frequency modulation.

Then we may go on to suggest
That "life," as we customarily define it
Could be effected at a distance—
Precession is the effect
Of one moving system
Upon another.
Precession always produces
Angular changes of the movements
Of the effected bodies and
At angles other than 180 degrees,
That is, the results are never
Continuance in a straight line.
Ergo all bodies of universe
Are effecting the other bodies
In varying degrees
And all the inter-gravitational effects
Are precessional angular modulations
And all the inter-radiation effects
Are frequency modulations.

The gravitational and radiation effects
Could modulate the DNA/RNA
Angle and frequency instructions
At astronomical remoteness—
Life could be "sent on."

Within the order of evolution as usually drawn
Life "occurred" as a series
Of fortuituous probabilities in the primeval sea.

It could have been sent or "radiated" there.
That is, the prime code
Or angle and frequency modulated signal
Could have been transmitted
From a remote stellar location.
It seems more likely
(In view of the continuous rediscovery of man
As a fully organized being
Back to ever more remote periods)
That the inanimate structural pattern integrity,
Which we call human being,
Was a frequency modulation code message
Beamed at earth from remote location.
Man as prime organizing
"Principle" construct
Was radiated here from the stars—
Not as primal cell, but as
A fully articulated high order being.
Possibly as the synergetic totality
Of all the gravitation
And radiation effects
Of all the stars
In our galaxy
And from all the adjacent galaxies
With some weak effects
And some strong effects
And from all time.
And pattern itself being weightless
The life integrities are apparently
Inherently immortal.

You and I
Are essential functions

Of universe
We are exquisite anti-entropy.

I'll be seeing you!
Forever.


## Richard Buckminster Fuller

Architect/engineer R. Buckminster Fuller first gained prominence in 1927 with the invention of the Dymaxion House, a spacious, low-cost, high-strength dwelling uniquely suspended from a central mast. In the early 1930s he introduced the three-wheeled Dymaxion car, which had a top speed of 120 miles an hour, went forty miles on a gallon of gasoline, and could turn in its own length. Of his many other inventions perhaps the most famous is his geodesic dome, whose design is based on a mathematical formula he himself developed and named "energetic synergetic geometry." Born in Massachusetts in 1895, Mr. Fuller is a graduate of Harvard University and U.S. Naval Academy. He has founded several design and manufacturing firms and served as a consultant to industry, the U.S. Government, the Ford Foundation, and most recently to the government of Japan. He has been a visiting professor, lecturer, and critic abroad and on many American campuses, including Harvard, Yale, Cornell, Princeton, the Massachusetts Institute of Technology, and the University of California at Berkeley. He now holds a professorship with life tenure at Southern Illinois University. His books include No More Second Hand God, Education Automation, and The Unfinished Epic of Industrialization.

# JAMES M. GAVIN

LIEUTENANT GENERAL, USA (RET.)

## Military Power:
## The Limits of Persuasion

---

$S$INCE THE beginning of time, power has been used to persuade. Yet, paradoxically, at a time when we possess more power than any nation on earth, we are not very persuasive. It is frustrating and baffling, and public debate on the use of power in Vietnam rages throughout the land. Perhaps it would be well to examine the nature of our power and, more important, its changing character since World War II.

Usually we think of power in terms of military power—military weapons systems—and most of us have long considered these to be the primary source of power in world affairs. Of course, to exist, military power must have a base of economic support. In all past experience only a society that had the natural resources and, in addition, the inventiveness and industries to produce modern weapons systems could bring them to combat and thus gain a decision in international conflict. Hence, from history we are inclined to think of military power as the dominant force, and the economic power which supports it as a *secondary* source of military strength.

History is replete with examples of aggressor nations' adding to their total power by taking from others. In an excellent and comprehensive volume, *Power*, written in the 1930s, Bertrand Russell expressed it this way, "Economic power, unlike military power, is not primary but derivative." He then went on to illustrate how military power had been used to seize vast colonial empires from which great wealth could be extracted—wealth in minerals, oils, and arable lands, for example. Hence, the nation that could seize the most resources could, in the long run, develop the most powerful military forces.

I believe that there is a fundamental change taking place, and indeed it has taken place, in this relationship between military and economic power. Fundamentally, today technology can, if wisely directed, provide adequate resources for humans to live comfortably on this earth. At the same time, technology can, if so exploited, provide the weapons systems to destroy a major portion of the human race. Finally, technology is having, and will continue to have, such a tremendous impact on world affairs that it is changing the balance between economics and military power significantly. It is this change that I would like to examine.

First, let me call attention to the talk given by our Secretary of Defense in Montreal on May 18 [1967]. He referred to the sources of unrest and discontent around the world, and emphasized that security is not military hardware; security means economic development. In fact, he stated flatly that, in his opinion, the concept that military hardware is the exclusive or even the primary ingredient of permanent peace in the mid-twentieth century is absurd.

During the past twenty years I have been closely associated with the use of military power, the planning and execution of national military policy, and, to a lesser extent, the conduct of foreign policy. To say that it has been an extremely active environment is an understatement, for we never have had such amounts of power available nor have we had so many problems associated with its use. And never has there been such widespread interest in our many commitments and involvements abroad, nor so much social turbulence at home.

Having been in the vortex of much of the discussion, I find it deeply disturbing that we have yet to get to the heart of the matter. To do so we must understand, and articulate, in much clearer terms than we have so far, our total *diplomatic* and *political* power, for this is the power that persuades—the economic, technological, and military components of such power. Part of this examination will be a consideration of the role that each of these will play in our national strategy.

Actually, we have been doing very well in the realm of economics and technology, especially during the past decade. It is in the area of applied military power, tactical military power, that most of the misunderstandings and frustrations seem to exist. In order to understand their cause, therefore, I believe that we should begin with an examination of the meaning of the most significant military event of our time—the detonation of the first nuclear weapon.

The shock waves from the Hiroshima blast went far beyond those predicted by the nuclear physicists. Nothing in our country's history has had a comparable impact upon foreign policy and military affairs. Governments have fallen, coalitions of nations have been formed and reformed to cope with the problems caused by the bomb's existence. The bomb was at the heart of de Gaulle's rejection of Great Britain's desire to join the European Common Market. The bomb was ever present in the mind of President Kennedy and his advisers at the time of the Cuban missile crisis. The bomb today casts a long shadow over all discussions on the future of NATO. For the fundamental nature of military power changed significantly with the advent of the bomb.

Few realized in 1945 that the bomb was the beginning of the end, if not indeed the very end, of man's search for energy to be used as military force. The more prevalent view was that a new era was born—the age of atomic force. Now, twenty years later, we understand better the place of the bomb in the spectrum of history. It was the end, not the beginning, of an era. It was the end of man's search for force and it marked a beginning of a new quest—the search to find new ways and means of influencing the behavior of other humans. It was to be the age when the earth would shrink rapidly due to high-speed air travel, space exploration, satellite communications, and rapid data processing systems, for example. More and more the nations of the earth were to consider themselves part of one large world community—the logical end of an evolutionary process that began many thousands of years ago with the family, tribal, and city-state, and later, national groupings.

Furthermore, in the armed forces the physical effects of the bomb alone made plain for all to see that all the boundaries between the traditional arenas of combat—land, sea, and air—were wiped out. The earth was soon to become one theater of operations, shrunken to such small size that no area was immune from attack from any other point on the globe. And when, in the traditional manner, our military recalled its own experience for answers to deal with the new problems of the day, it did not find them. For the answers were not to be found in a remembrance of things past, they could be found only in a thoughtful analysis of the future, in a profound search for the meaning of the period that we were about to enter. The classical military formula of escalating power until total victory would be achieved was to become absolutely meaningless. For wars, if there were to be wars, and the means that would resolve them, were going to be many orders of magnitude different from what they had been in the past.

In 1950, five years after the end of World War II and Hiroshima, Soviet-equipped North Koreans invaded South Korea. It was a costly experience for us. Possessing the most powerful military establishment in the world, well equipped with nuclear weapons, we suffered more than 140,000 casualties and had to accept terms less than victory. Yet, despite the Korean experience, our national strategic policy in the mid-fifties was still based on massive retaliation. Admittedly there was much argument and discussion about the validity of this view. Indeed, our Promethean achievement seemed to have left us in intellectual disarray.

But from the mid-fifties on, our total power seemed to paralyze our intellectual processes, and our response to challenges of lesser magnitude than total war were of a diminishing degree of credibility. This was because a number of myths prevailed in our thinking, and they stemmed from a tendency to look inward to our experience rather than to postulate technology and political trends into the rather clouded and hazardous unknown of the future.

The first myth is that war is a continuation of politics by other means. This Clausewitzian orthodoxy holds that wars will be fought and won, and sufficient power will be applied until they are won. Then war will be followed by peace, a period in which politics as usual will be the preoccupation of the world powers. This, in turn, very likely will be followed by a period of war, and the difference between the two will be quite discernible. I believe that by now most of us realize that this no longer is true.

In his recent Montreal speech, our Secretary of Defense discussed conflicts of recent years and pointed out that in the past eight years "there have been no less than one hundred sixty-four internationally significant outbreaks of violence, each of them specifically designed as a serious challenge to the authority, or the very existence, of the government in question. . . . And not a single one of the one hundred sixty-four conflicts has been a formally declared war." From this experience, realistically, we must conclude that wars will not always be declared and that nations will not always commit their total resources to win in every confrontation. There will be wars that are not wars, if defined in terms of our experience before Hiroshima. In fact, for some nations it may be wiser to keep a shooting war limited and undeclared while pursuing national goals by other means, never admitting the existence of a war nor indeed a desire to bring it to an end.

The second myth is that if you destroy enough people and enough property you will overcome an enemy's will to resist. A corollary to this is that a nation should use as much force as necessary to win, since in war there is no substitute for victory. Actually, the nature of conflict being what it is, and the danger of a nuclear holocaust being ever present, it is compelling that solutions less than total war be found. The indiscriminate use of power has been further complicated by modern communications media that now bring more and more detailed information about the conduct of war into every home. The inevitable, and needless, loss of civilian lives has become the subject of concern to more than just the contending military forces. Thus, sensitivity to public opinion has made it necessary to consider restricting attacks to military targets whenever this is possible. Unless, of course, the nation's goal is to seek total war.

A third aspect of existing military thinking deserves mention. The thought still persists in many minds that the ultimate in sophistication and usefulness in weapons systems is the high-yield megaton bomb delivered by missile or aircraft. By its very nature it is believed that it should be able to cope with almost any threat to our survival. The fact is that it is the very effectiveness of our strategic air force, and the overwhelming, devastating potential of H-weapons, that prevents their employment in a conflict other than total war. And again, it is the devastation that would be caused by the use of these weapons by the strategic air arm that has given tremendous emphasis to the role of the other services—those that have it in their ability to apply power with discrimination, flexibility, and restraint. It is this possibility of devastation that gives great emphasis to the need to find and understand the uses of other forms of power stemming from our science and technological programs and our great economic strength.

The changing nature of conflict today makes it imperative that we develop better means of dealing with limited wars, guerrilla wars, and other types of conflicts that we cannot yet anticipate with accuracy but which will not be total war. Studies in these areas will require great effort not only in anticipation and planning but in research and development as well.

Until World War II, we were protected by a shield of time and space. And while we were enjoying that protection, Hitler's forces ravaged Europe and, more important, his scientists developed the first surface-to-surface rockets, surface-to-air rockets, air-to-air rockets, the snorkel submarine, the first jet plane and the first rocket plane, nerve gas, etc. And he came close to developing the atomic bomb. After we entered the war, and finally overran his concentration camps, we found the gas ovens being enlarged—and he had already destroyed more than six million human beings. Today we no longer enjoy the advantage of time and space. Our armed forces must be ready for every challenge that confronts our nation regardless of how sophisticated the weapon or the technology from which it springs. This will require a continuing expenditure of our national resources if we are to achieve an adequate state of readiness for every reasonable challenge. And this, in turn, necessitates a dynamic, imaginative, productive economy.

How good is our economy?

Most people will remember that after World War II the Soviets anticipated an economic collapse of the West, believing that our economy was entirely a war-based one. What we have accomplished has been truly remarkable, and during the past twenty years our economy at home has expanded at a tremendous rate. It is vital that we sustain this growth.

In 1966 our Gross National Product will be in excess of $700 billion. Our industry is doing very well. During the decade beginning in 1955 combined annual sales of the five hundred largest industrial corporations increased by $100 billion (from $161 billion to $266 billion). Corporate profits last year before taxes were $73 billion, an increase of $9 billion over the previous year. Per-capita income reached $2,700 last year, a six per cent increase over 1964 income. Personal income was a record high of $528 billion, up $35 billion over the previous year.

These are impressive statistics. We should have no apprehension whatsoever about the outcome of any competition with the Communist countries in the realm of economics. Our apprehension, if any, should be concerned with whether or not we use our resources wisely and well—to provide a good society at home, to aid the emerging young nations abroad, while at the same time we provide our armed forces with weapons systems adequate to meet the broad spectrum of challenges that will confront us. We must give serious attention to the problems of exporting our economy abroad.

One of the most remarkable and farsighted programs ever undertaken by any country was the inauguration of our foreign assistance program in 1949. Through it we were able to provide economic assistance, wherever it could be properly used, to the newly emerging nations as well as to many of the older powers. In 1949, this program amounted to a little over $4.5 billion and was 1.75 per cent of our Gross National Product. It has been overwhelmingly successful, and today South Korea, Taiwan, and Indonesia, for example, all are monuments to the achievements of this program. In addition, a country geographically almost a part of the Eastern bloc, Yugoslavia, was able to achieve economic prosperity and retain its political independence from Moscow.

Our foreign aid program has been overwhelmingly successful in areas where the Communists can least afford to have us succeed. In areas where they would like to accuse us of colonialism and, indeed, do accuse us of economic colonialism today, we have been able in many countries to help achieve an unpredecented standard of living, far superior to anything that the Communists could offer. This has been accomplished despite the fact that we have steadily reduced the amount of foreign aid until today, in 1966, it is but .48 per cent of our Gross National Product, compared to 1.75 per cent at its inception in the late 1940s.

There is an old combat maxim that one should reinforce success; this we are not doing. In speaking at the Boston University commencement exercises in June of this year, Lady Barbara Ward Jackson recommended that the "have" nations, such as the United States, contribute one per cent of their Gross National Product to help the underprivileged and underdeveloped countries. Some attribute our unwillingness to do so to the cost of the Vietnam war. If so, this at least raises the question of whether or not we may now be following a course inimical to our long-term strategic interests.

Another area in which Americans have achieved great success has been in the exportation of products and business know-how. Our exports, which amounted to approximately $37 billion in 1950, have grown to well in excess of $100 billion in the mid-sixties. Our direct investment abroad has increased from $25 billion to $50 billion in the same period of time. In addition to this direct investment, we have indirectly invested $20 billion through stocks and portfolio holdings. Our direct investment abroad is now increasing at an average of more than $10,000,000 a day. With this investment we have exported entrepreneurial skills and management techniques that have proven to be very attractive to the Western world. So successful has this been that the return on our investments abroad today amounts to $4 billion annually.

This has all been possible because of a burgeoning economy at home and the aggressive drive of our businessmen to find markets and business opportunities abroad. At the same time, businessmen have sought to raise the standards of living wherever they have marketed their products and services. In this they have been, by and large, very successful. There is nothing that the Communists have done, or so far can do, that can compare with this. It is with great uneasiness, therefore, that thoughtful businessmen consider restrictions on the flow of dollars overseas. For the export of our entrepreneurial skills and products has been one of the most successful undertakings of foreign affairs in the history of our country, and the most productive of good in our confrontation with the Communist bloc. No tactical conflict, whether it be undeclared war or not, should be allowed to expand at their expense.

Maintenance of our position in the world community is based not only on those programs that we export abroad, but also on the kind of a society we have at home. World opinion will be formed by not only the prosperity and higher standard of living that we can help other nations achieve, but also by what the world knows that we are able to do in our own society. Through our ability to manage our own internal affairs, we export an image of America and of our way of life. And in this area there is much to be done.

We have made progress in dealing with some of the problems of the aged and of the very young, but, in my opinion, we have not yet begun to deal adequately with the problems of the teen-agers and the near teen-agers. We must completely revitalize our educational system by bringing together the vast industrial, scientific, and technological resources of this country with our educators, to the end that we can significantly improve the education and technical training of our young. In addition, we must provide opportunities for those out of school for some time to return to educational centers to update their knowledge and to learn new skills.

Equally as important as directing the intellectual energies of our young people into useful channels is the problem of helping them to develop their physical talents. Very few countries do not have national amateur sports programs assisted and guided by a national council; the United States is one of them. It was the hope of our late President, John F. Kennedy, that some day every boy and girl, regardless of race or economic background, would be given an opportunity to achieve excellence in competitive amateur sports.

President Johnson directed a study to this end some time ago, and, it is hoped, a program will be under way this year. The solution of this problem is intimately related to the problems typified by Watts.

Now, what does this discussion on the relationship between military power and economic programs mean when applied to problems of today? What, for example, does it mean in terms of Vietnam?

I think that we would all agree that we should not be in the predicament that we are in in Vietnam, but the fact is that we are there. The problem now is to handle our resources—men, weapons, aircraft, etc.—in such a manner as to neither impair our strategic efforts in other areas nor our tactical prospects in future conflicts. The cost of the Vietnamese involvement now is on the order of $16 to $18 billion a year. This has already made it necessary for us to curtail the flow of dollars overseas. We have also continued to cut back on our foreign aid programs. Our domestic economy is beginning to show the impact of the Vietnam struggle.

Obviously, we have reached the point where further escalation could seriously impair our strategic commitments—our exportation of capital and management skills, our foreign aid programs, and our science and technology programs—and our social programs at home. Perhaps we have passed this point. Furthermore, we should anticipate and be ready for a very serious struggle for Thailand and the Kra Peninsula. And if our involvement plunges us deeper into war in Southeast Asia, we should be prepared for a reopening of the Korean front. It is important, therefore, that we accelerate the measures to bring the Vietnam situation under control. Certainly, we should not willingly allow it to escalate.

For example, our present position in Vietnam is based upon the need to defeat the North Vietnamese aggressors who have carried their attack into South Vietnam. What is the nature of the aggressor's forces coming from North Vietnam, in weapons, size of forces, and current rate of buildup? Are they as numerous and as well equipped as we allege? It seems to me that answers to these questions should be obtained as a matter of highest priority.

One of the outcomes of the 1954 Geneva Conference was the establishment of an International Control Commission. This Commission should be abundantly equipped with helicopters, fixed-wing aircraft, and up-to-date communications equipment if it is to do its job. The staff supporting it should also be increased until it is capable of carrying out its intended task. It is not capable of doing this today. If we were to spend but a small part of what we are expending in combatting the North Vietnamese to determine with accuracy the nature and composition of their forces, we could probably make a significant contribution to the ultimate resolution of the problem. Concurrently with this improvement in the capability of the International Control Commission, we should ask for a reopening of the 1954 Geneva meeting to determine if other measures can be taken to bring the situation under control, and hopefully find a formula for resolving the conflict.

High on the list of national priorities must be the restoration of stability within the Atlantic Alliance. We have insisted for too long on maintaining the status quo in NATO, ignoring the powerful trend toward Europeanism and the towering strength of the European Common Market. Profound changes have taken place in Europe since NATO was originally established, and our policy does not reflect an awareness of these changes. At times we seem more preoccupied with isolating de Gaulle than with making positive proposals to which our European allies could adhere.

The most significant change that has taken place has been the growth of the European Common Market. Although conceived as an economic organization, it is rapidly assuming all aspects of a powerful military and political bloc. Purists will argue this point, pointing out that the Fouchet Mission to Brussels of five years ago failed in its efforts to have the members of the Common Market agree on a commonality of political, military, and cultural objectives. But the fact is that the European Common Market represents growing political and military strength. The need, therefore, is for a recognition of this within the structure of the Atlantic Alliance.

There are those who fear such a Europe as a third power, but now is not the time for such fear; it is a time for an understanding of Europe as a strong partner. Furthermore, Great Britain is part of Europe and must play a significant role in the affairs of Europe. Our reaction to de Gaulle's withdrawal of his armed forces from NATO has been to orient our attention more toward Germany as the leading power on the Continent. This policy has in it the seeds of disaster, for a German-dominated Europe would never be accepted by our allies and would be bitterly opposed by the U.S.S.R. and its satellites. A Europe without Great Britain's participation in its economic and political affairs will be an unending source of irritation and trouble for us. It is imperative, therefore, that we assist in any way that we can Great Britain's entry into the Common Market.

This should begin with an understanding on our part of the need for Great Britain to sever her special nuclear relationship with us, and for her to enter into frank discussions on the problems of nuclear weapons and the Common Market area. Based upon numerous conversations that I have had with responsible members of the de Gaulle government, including the General himself, I am convinced that Great Britain would be welcomed into the Common Market if she were willing to come in, bombs and all, and meet all the provisions of the Rome Treaty. Among other things, this will require a minimum period for the transition of the Commonwealth nations out of their special relationship to the U.K. economy.

As the strength of Europe increases, the need for U.S. military forces on the Continent will diminish. Our present commitment is based more on diplomatic than military need. A significant reduction of our troop strength, in my opinion, would improve our economic situation worldwide and thus add to our global strategic strength without increasing the military risk in Europe.

General de Gaulle's recent visit to the U.S.S.R. was a remarkable tour de force. Although generally denigrated in the American press, the General's achievements were noteworthy. There were many who remembered that the General had written in his memoirs, published in 1959, that it was his intent to insure the security of France by making arrangements with either the East or the West; hence, there was concern lest he enter into a conventional military pact following the withdrawal of French forces from NATO. On the other hand, many recalled how bitterly he opposed negotiations with the Soviets following Khrushchev's threat to the Berlin Corridor in late 1961. He had said at that time that he would refuse to enter into any "negotiations" since we were there by right and to agree to negotiate would suggest to the Soviets an intent on our part to give something away that was rightfully ours.

The remarkable thing about his trip, therefore, was that he so skillfully avoided leaving any impressions that he was negotiating over West Germany, despite the desire of the Soviets to talk about European "security." At the same time he was able also to finesse Soviet suggestions of the need to discuss recognition of East Germany. On the positive side, agreements were reached on technological, cultural, and scientific exchanges. Since current French economic trade with the Soviet bloc is going quite well, the total package represents significant achievement. The ultimate outcome of his visit, therefore, could have profound military significance.

For some years the United States has exchanged visits of artists, athletes, and academicians as part of a program that had as its goal the relaxation of tension between the United States and the

U.S.S.R. The time now has come to encourage the visits of business-men between both countries, and to encourage our trade with the U.S.S.R. and its satellites. To an increasing extent, the profit mo-tive is playing a significant role in the Soviet economy, and the So-viets are trading extensively with our allies. Our President, in his State of the Union message this year [1967], urged Congress to pass the necessary legislation to enable us to get on with an in-creased trade. This should be done without delay, for increased trade will not only reduce tension, but will increase the standard of living and improve the social and economic prospects of people wherever the trading is done.

Conspicuous by its absence from this discussion is the problem of the unification of Germany. It should be absent, for until eco-nomic and political relations between western Europe and the So-viet bloc are improved, there is little prospect of finding an accepta-ble reunification formula.

In the past two decades, the world has changed from a com-munity of many independent nations, frequently remote from one another, to one small world community. It will look with great ap-prehension on any indiscriminate use of military power. In the meantime, from an unprecedented abundance of scientific and technological knowledge, man has acquired the potential for tre-mendous good and tremendous harm. This new knowledge must be channeled into the areas where the greatest good for the most can be realized—to help our Great Society at home and to help the emerging nations abroad. The most influential force in world affairs today is the economy of the United States. It should be sustained and enriched as a matter of sound strategic policy.

Tactical engagements that do occur should not be permitted to grow as uncontrollably as a malignant cancer. Fighting will cer-tainly occur, from time to time, at any point along the abrasive interface between the Communist nations and the free world. Our power must be used to persuade those who seek to improve their position through aggressive attacks upon their neighbors that they will be deterred and cannot possibly succeed. Concurrently, we should make clear our intention and ability to maintain a dominant position in global affairs. Our global power must be exercised with restraint and wisdom. At a time of Great Britain's greatness, Disraeli said, "All power is a trust—and we are accountable for its exercise." Now, we too are accountable, not only to the American people but to people of the world community of nations.

## James M. Gavin

General James M. Gavin, retired U.S. Army officer, diplomat, and corporation executive, is widely known for his critical comments on the conduct of the war in Vietnam and for his eloquent opposition to the spread of nuclear weapons. He was born in 1907, went to West Point, and rose to the rank of Lieutenant General during World War II. Retiring from the Army in 1958, he joined the firm of Arthur D. Little, in Boston, where he is now chairman of the board and chief executive officer. In 1961–62 he was U.S. Ambassador to France. During the mid-sixties, he strongly advocated that U.S. forces in Vietnam be concentrated in coastal enclaves, or strongpoints, which could be defended indefinitely, pending a negotiated settlement of the war. His books include Airborne Warfare, War and Peace in the Space Age, and Civil War Album (co-author).

**HARRY GOLDEN**

## How to Live with a Chair You Hate

---

**H**AVING RECENTLY undergone a serious gall bladder operation coupled with a respiratory failure, I know what I *should* have learned: Keep your weight down and your medical insurance up. The gall bladder, at least, puts me in distinguished political company. And the recuperation gives me plenty of time to mull over anything else I may have learned.

I am glad SR wrote me when it did. For ordinarily, I would be quick to leap to my typewriter and divest myself to interested readers of the sum of my learning. I think this is true of all journalists. Used to daily writing, most of us come to feel no topic is hard, or intractable, or delicate. One who constantly editorializes deals with the world practically, and with every event therein as a self-completed unit. He lives in the world at its basic linear and chronological levels; or, as I once expressed it more metaphorically, writing a story one day and another the next makes it difficult sometimes to realize we are all on the same ball of yarn.

Let us take an example. In North Carolina, the State Supreme Court ruled that brown-bagging was illegal. Brown-bagging is the genteel disguise adopted by a patron to furnish his own liquor when he dines at the local restaurant. In all the years I've lived in Charlotte I never saw the bare whiskey bottle exposed anywhere. Liquor was always sheathed in an obvious if opaque brown bag, as though there were some minister on the CIA payroll eating nearby. The Court ruled this practice was illegal, that the law specifically allowed a man could drink in North Carolina, but he could drink only at home.

Every newspaperman in the state rejoiced. Not because any of us are prohibitionists. Indeed, the contrary is probably true. We rejoiced because we had a ready-made story not only for today and tomorrow but for weeks and months to come, for as long as the state legislature—once divided into Republicans and Democrats, now into "wets" and "drys"—haggled about what the Bible said about drinking and what the constituency wanted.

In my columns I was able to point out the terrible damage the Carolina Supreme Court had done the average digestive system. Many a pal of mine by-lined a story about the economic deprivation Charlotte was sure to suffer as the conventions canceled.

The court ruling came just before the state election. We Tarheels listened to candidates haranguing the public pro and con. In one of our eastern counties, always dry, on Election Day the church bells rang every hour on the hour just to remind the folks, in the words of the local editor, "there was a candidate amongst us who would change the law like the Supreme Court was doing, distressing our way of life." One brown-bagger down the drain.

Despite the gallons of ink devoted to the subject, despite the forests reduced to pulp for newsprint, despite the sermons, I doubt anyone *learned* anything. No one who read my stuff learned anything about the nature of alcoholic addiction or about the nature of the judicial and legislative process. All anyone learned really was that there was a new excitement throughout the state and the excitement was there because, literally, people feel one way or another about liquor. That's human interest. Human interest is hardly learning. A man can spend money without the least knowledge of economic principles.

In practical terms, I know that readers will follow a story about whiskey because they know whiskey induces drunkenness. I've learned that people will read about anything that relates to the body—heat, cold, sex, health, beauty, ugliness. The body is an object, an idea, easy to relate to. As I say, however, this knowledge is practical, so basically practical that any cub reporter who doesn't learn it on his first story had better turn in his Smith-Corona and his press card. When a fire wipes out a family, you write about tears, not antiquated fire laws.

As a man gets older, he tends to confuse what he has learned with what he has experienced. I have in my time been a son, a husband, and a father. For the life of me I cannot discourse on any of the three. But I tried. I asked my oldest son, "Was I a good father?"

"Sure," he said.

"You didn't waste any time thinking. Just because I'm in the hospital doesn't mean you have to be nice. What makes you so positive?"

He shrugged. "Hell," he said, "I'm forty years old. What difference does it make now?"

"You don't get my meaning," I persevered. "Did I teach you anything? Anything besides chess, that is?"

"Sure," he said.

"What? Precisely what?"

This time he thought. "I guess you taught me what it's like to be the son of a celebrity."

I think of my own father, who wore a Prince Albert coat and a high silk hat, and before we walked out of the house he automatically put his foot up on a chair, and my mother ran with a cloth to polish his shoes. As my mother polished, my father always said, "Oy, de krizshes" ("Oh, my aching back"). She was polishing and his back hurt.

I learned early that my father was a failure. I even memorial-

ized his failure years ago in an essay which I called "The Status
Wanderer." We have had stories of the Horatio Alger immigrant
who went from cloaks operator to peddler to manufacturer and re-
tail merchant. We know, too, the story of the immigrant involved
in the class war, the fellow who worked all his life in a sweatshop,
contracted tuberculosis, and died, or was killed on a picket line. But
only I told the story of the immigrant who failed because he refused
to enter the American milieu on its terms—to start accruing status
on the basis of money. My father was this status wanderer. He went
down with the ship, or, I should say, he went down with his high
silk hat.

My father came to America in 1900 from the Galician town of
Mikulince in the Austro-Hungarian Empire. He was an immigrant
when there were Jews who, though poor, still had status. My father
was a learned man, and this made him something of a snob. He
could never understand how it was that the son of a coal dealer or
the son of a tailor could go to City College as an equal with me. He
felt that no matter how much money those other fellows made,
they did not dare wear a high silk hat. If the peddler made a million
dollars he would still wear a cap, or at best he might toy with the
idea of a fedora and a derby.

Out of these two experiences, mine and my son's, I find I can
distill one element common to both. I think that element is that
the people who are not expendable are fathers and mothers and
sons and brothers. It is incorrect to say life goes on without them. It
is not a substantive statement. It is much too thin. When fathers
and mothers die the world is qualitatively a different world, just as
it is a different world because they are in it. It's an old truth. For my
money, it's learning; learning is that which it takes the generations
to discover.

One wishes it didn't take the generations. One wishes wisdom
or learning were ready-made, immediate.

Communicating this has little practical value. Any writer can tell you of the letters which come across his desk from time to time, the letters pleading for advice. I have come to the conclusion that the Advice to the Lovelorn is not journalistic invention but a deep-rooted emotional institution.

The editors of SR are not the only people who have asked me what I've learned. Perfect strangers ask me because they think what I've learned will help them. Some of these questions I have no objection to but rather a delight in answering. The young people, the college boys and girls, write to ask, "How can I become a writer?" I think they should ask and I think writers should answer because it is only by questions that these young people begin to see there is an answer they might find.

I am aware that many writers turn a deaf ear to these naïve pleas. There is an apocryphal story about Mozart, of whom a young man asked, "Shall I become a musical prodigy?" to which Mozart replied, "No."

"But you were a prodigy!" the young fellow returned.

"But I didn't ask anyone," Mozart replied.

This is not my way, principally because I'm too old to be clever at youth's expense. I advise everyone who asks about the career of writing to get himself all the books he can carry before he buys a typewriter. Library cards are more important than pencils. Read everything, I say. Good books, bad books, hard books, easy books, underground books, popular books, square books, hip books—never stop reading and you will become a fortiori a writer.

Sometimes these kids balk. "Writers are supposed to live! To live with a vengeance! To tell the world about their living!"

Nonsense. Nonsense. Writing is a sedentary and lonely profession, hardly adventurous in any physical sense. And journalism is worse because journalists are writers who have no education and disdain looking up words in dictionaries or subjects in encyclopedias, relying on their memories. Certainly none of it is romantic. If it were, policemen and nurses and cab drivers would compose all the novels. A writer is supposed to read and write. I remind the would-be writers that Pascal said every man carries around his own precipice, and Melville believed no one had to sail in whaleboats to find sharks.

But what advice can I offer the woman who writes of her fear that her children want to institutionalize her? What advice can I offer the young girl who asks, "Shall I marry out of my religion?"; the young boy who wants to change his name? What advice can I give to the retired teacher who wants to know how to live with a terminal cancer?

By nature, I am physically and emotionally unable to succumb to the temptations which lure on the would-be and the real saints. But sainthood is perennially one of the underpopulated professions.

What shocks me is why I receive the questions at all. I don't deny these are pleas for help but why should the afflicted suspect that a celebrity can offer better answers than someone else, especially a celebrity who is totally unknowing of the situation and its prospects?

I suspect that a celebrity, even if only a modest celebrity who makes his living as a journalist, is associated with money, and money is associated with wisdom; anyone with money is supposed to have vanquished the frenzy of modern life. But celebrities have their own problem, which is keeping up their image, refurbishing it daily. I rather doubt that the powerful receive these pleas—the Lyndon Johnsons, the Robert Kennedys, the George Romneys—but I will bet that on occasion the Norman Mailers and Norman Podhoretzes get them.

Do not think I spend my morning in profound depression. I do not. I send these petitioners a sample copy of my newspaper, the *Carolina Israelite*, and I send it not in the hopes they will become subscribers, nor in the hopes the paper will provide the way and the light, as we say down heah, but in the hopes the pleaders may get a laugh or two out of some of the editorials.

It is much easier to answer the hate mail, which continues unabated, lo! these twenty-five years. Some of it is anonymous, in which case it goes straight into the wastebasket. Curiously, a lot of the folks sign their willfully malicious missives.

Our station in life, our education, our religion, our upbringing often prove insufficient in subduing our basic arrogance. People vent their spleen on me, feeling perfectly justified in their violence because I am a "Jew nigger-lover."

I used to answer these with the simple statement, "Your last letter has been referred to the postal authorities." After a while I felt the postal authorities had all they could do to deliver first-class mail for a nickel, so now I write, "Thank you for your last letter which we have referred to our hate file." Or sometimes I say, "Thank you for your hate letter." No sample copies of the *Carolina Israelite*, either.

The calls at night are something different. They come in spasms. If a civil rights bill is signed into law you can bet that every liberal editor who urged its passage is beset evenings, at midnight, and at dawn with sibilant whispers over the phone. I tried every gambit which came to mind, from explaining my position to stating unequivocally, "Every word you say is being monitored by the FBI and will be used against you." You'd be surprised how little either logic or the FBI frightens most people.

What proved most successful was suffering the inconvenience of turning the telephone off at night. Simple sacrifice to the rescue. I comfort myself with the idea of sacrifice. After all, I haven't suffered the pillory of many of the civil rights workers; nor the contempt suffered by noble Christian men and women like Martin Luther King, Norman Thomas, Roy Wilkins, or Lillian Smith, nor the despair of embattled social workers in Harlem and Watts. Still, I hate giving up the telephone when I can pay the bill on the tenth of the month.

What I like best are the letters of disagreement. The most successful column I ever wrote was a virulent attack on the eggplant, which, I noted, was invariably the main course of the bad cook. I also said the only use I could see for this clumsy vegetable was that it was a handy weapon to throw at Neapolitan tenors who sang flat. I had some other nasty observations to make, like preferring an oleomargarine sandwich on stale white bread to rat-a-tat-touey. I say the eggplant column was successful because the day it saw syndication was the very day John Glenn became the first American to complete an orbit in space.

We have put billions of dollars into the space program, little into the eggplant subsidy. Yet I was inundated by mail. Folks pushed on me recipes for eggplant pizzas, for eggplant foo yung, for baked eggplant, for fried eggplant, for boiled eggplant. Complaints of every size and measure roared from envelopes. Eggplant and Shakespeare were all a man needed to survive on a deserted island; what was I trying to do to the Eggplant Club of Downtown Pensacola? One lady said she had tried blintzes, why couldn't I give eggplant a fair shake? My secretary had to establish a separate eggplant file and we had to compose a special eggplant letter. It said, "Don't worry, dear, he'll still love you if you can't boil eggs."

Were I not true to my principles, which include a detestation of eggplant, I could publish the Harry Golden Eggplant Cookbook. But I did serve my purpose—haven't had to eat eggplant since. Someone even suggested I grow eggplant in the half-acre lot behind my house. As a matter of fact, I was glad for the suggestion. I thought eggplant just happened, not that it was cultivated.

Which returns us to the subject proper: What have I learned? You see, I have no intention of leaving unsettled what learning is that is the property, sole and unmortgaged, of one Harry Golden, editor, publisher, son, father, and celebrity.

Ask me directly, and I shall reply that I have learned the things we were told when we were children are really true. First among which is the maxim that there is really only one woman in the world who will do.

By no means do I insist that that woman will make you happy. She may make you unhappy. But it is also true subsequent women make you no more comfortable. If you can't get along with the first one, you're not going to get along much with her successors—unless at heart you're a compromiser—and you're going to pay a lot of alimony to discover this. No one has yet formulated any substitute for monogamy for the raising of a family. If we all lived in Plato's Republic and the state collected all of the newborn and shuffled them off to a work farm—and we all accepted this as part of the natural order of things—then I think we should all marry one woman when we're twenty, another when we're thirty, still a third at forty, and another at each turn of the decades. Fathers and mothers so far have proved bound and determined that they and not the state will raise their offspring.

It is true that many men and women feel divorce is not so much a selfish as a sanitary matter, that without divorce they will lose their equilibrium. I feel sorry for them. My heart always welled with pity for Tommy Manville. Tommy never understood the furniture of life.

I remember an easy chair I hated. It was new and it had usurped an older, more comfortable chair. I learned to live around that chair. I never sat in it, I never commented about how ugly I thought it, how it wrenched my back to read the front page while I was seated there, how it partially blocked passage from the living room to the kitchen and hall. That chair was there! I imagine personal unhappiness much in the shape and substance of that chair: You must learn to live around it, not to sit in it, nor declaim its hideous features, not to notice it. Unhappiness is a cobra which will not strike unless you startle it.

God, insists the Talmud, is a maker of marriages. For every abrasive personality, there's a matching personality. I thought early on I would let Him figure it out and He has. And if I hadn't let Him, I would have wound up just as unhappy as poor Thorstein

Veblen, the American thinker who made the singular contribution to economics by outlining the theory of conspicuous consumption. Veblen wound up teaching at a California college with a wife at one end of the campus and a girl friend at the other.

"I'm not happy with your marital situation," the school's president told him.

"Neither am I," sighed poor Veblen.

Truth No. 2 is that hard work and only hard work pays off. Hard work, in fact, is the only thing that *does* pay off.

The social revolution of the American Negro would never have come about had the Negro left it to humanitarian whites. Humanitarian whites had succeeded in abolishing slavery, but then they ran out of gas. When the Negro, sadly reviewing his long empirical history of failure, decided he himself would undertake hard work, that was when he began to make headway. And the revolution is by no means complete. And it will not be complete until more hard work and sweat have been invested.

Those of us who are, for want of a better word, co-revolutionists see now that the road toward absolute equality is longer and more treacherous than we thought. We cannot traverse it with song and enthusiasm; we have to hack our way through prejudice, distortion, ignorance, and plain intransigence. Hard work and patience are the only blades we have. Millennia are not something which we see happen; they are something we usually just passed.

Sometimes I hear disturbing rumors about youth, that the young folks today cannot bring themselves to terms with this society and with its values, that kids grow long hair and wear beards and dirty clothes as a sign of their revolt. But then, I think there are several boys now contending over which one will be the valedictorian at the Franconia College graduating exercises. One of them will win. And he will probably be the first boy on his block to buy a washer-dryer and a new refrigerator.

Let the long-haired unwashed giggle. That washer-dryer, that new refrigerator, is what every Congolese has been contending for by murdering missionaries, nuns, and fellow tribesmen.

Someone has always been smart enough to figure out that hard work pays off. Someone is clever enough to see that there is not all that much luck in the world and most of what there is is bad. No one will dispute me when I say that the only thing that overcomes hard luck is hard work. There's always someone clever enough to understand that the wise guy is the sucker every time. The wise  guy is the sucker because there ain't no free lunches anymore.

And the last of my knowledge consists of the admonition, never eat in a restaurant not bright enough to enable you to read your paper. The darkened lounge or salon will never pay off in food, service, or comfort.

## Harry Golden

Harry Golden is at once a newspaper publisher, a bestselling humorist, and an influential social critic. His major theme is the need for social and racial justice—although he never forgets that it is his theme, not Harry Golden himself, that deserves the reader's serious concern. Mr. Golden, the son of Jewish Austro-Hungarian immigrants, was born in 1902 on New York's Lower East Side. He left the City College of New York before getting his degree, worked as a teacher, hotel clerk, and newspaper reporter, and in 1941 finally settled in Charlotte, North Carolina. There he began publishing the now almost legendary Carolina Israelite, a witty, warm, irreverent journal of news and comment. His bestselling books include Only in America, For 2¢ Plain, Carl Sandburg, A Little Girl Is Dead, and Ess, Ess, Mein Kindt.

# ERIC HOFFER

## A Strategy for the War with Nature

---

$A$LL THROUGH adult life I have had a feeling of revulsion when told how nature aids and guides us, how likes a stern mother she nudges and pushes man to fulfill her wise designs. As a migratory worker from the age of eighteen I knew nature as ill-disposed and inhospitable. If I stretched on the ground to rest, nature pushed its hard knuckles into my sides, and sent bugs, burrs, and foxtails to make me get up and be gone. As a placer miner I had to run the gantlet of buckbrush, manzanita, and poison oak when I left the road to find my way to a creek. Direct contact with nature almost always meant scratches, bites, torn clothes, and grime that ate its way into every pore of the body. To make life bearable I had to interpose a protective layer between myself and nature. On the paved road, even when miles from anywhere, I felt at home. I had a sense of kinship with the winding, endless road that cares not where it goes or what its load.

Almost all the books I read spoke worshipfully of nature. Nature was pure, innocent, serene, health-giving, bountiful, the fountainhead of elevated thoughts and noble feelings. It seemed that every writer was a "nature boy." I assumed that these people had no share in the world's work and did not know nature at close quarters. It also seemed to me that they had a grievance. For coupled with

162

their admiration of nature was a distaste for man and man's work. Man was a violator, a defiler and deformer.

The truth about nature I found in the newspapers, in the almost daily reports of floods, fires, tornados, blizzards, hurricanes, typhoons, hailstorms, sandstorms, earthquakes, avalanches, eruptions, inundations, pests, plagues, and famines. Sometimes when reading about nature's terrible visitations and her massacre of the innocents it seemed to me that we were surrounded by devouring, pitiless forces, that the earth was full of anger, the sky dark with wrath, and that man had built the city as a refuge from a hostile, nonhuman cosmos. I realized that the contest between man and nature has been the central drama of the universe.

Man became what he is, not with the aid of but in spite of nature. Humanization meant breaking away from nature, getting out from underneath the iron necessities that dominate nature. By the same token, dehumanization means the reclamation of man by nature. It means the return of nature. It is significant that humanization had its start in the fact that man was an unfinished, defective animal. Nature dealt niggardly with him from the beginning. It brought him forth naked and helpless, without inborn skills and without specialized organs to serve him as weapons and tools. Unlike other animals, man was not a born technician with a built-in tool kit. Small wonder that for millennia man worshiped animals, nature's more favored children. Yet this misbegotten creature has made himself lord of the globe. He has evolved fabulous substitutes for the instincts and the specialized organs which he lacked, and rather than adjust himself to the world he has changed the world to fit him. This, surely, is the supreme miracle. If history is to have meaning it must be the history of humanization, of man's tortuous ascent through the ages, of his ceaseless effort to break away from the rest of creation and become an order apart.

Man became human by finishing himself. Yet his humanness is never finished and final. Man is not only an unfinished animal, he is an unfinished man. His human uniqueness is something he has to achieve and preserve. Nature is always around and within us, ready to reclaim us and sweep away all that man has wrought and achieved. Man's chief goal in life is still to become and stay human, and defend his achievements against the encroachment of nature. Nature is in almost complete possession of us when we are born. The child has to be brought up and made human. And no sooner is this accomplished than comes a crisis, the transition from childhood to manhood, in which nature reasserts itself. The humanness of the adolescent is a precarious thing. He has to be reborn to manhood, and be rehumanized. Indeed, every drastic change from one way of life to another constitutes a strain that may crack the uppermost layers of the mind and lay bare the less human layers. Hence a time of drastic change, even when the change is a leap forward, is a time of barbarization. Each generation has to humanize itself.

The contest with nature has the refined trickery we have come to associate with totalitarian wars. There are fifth columns, subversion, and a constant probing for soft spots. Just as man uses the forces of nature to subdue nature, so does nature use men to dehumanize their fellow men; and it is in the city that nature's fifth column finds its most fertile ground. The birth of the city was a crucial step in man's separation from nature. The city cut man off not only from the nonhuman cosmos but also from clans, tribes, and other primitive modes of organization. A self-governing city populated by more or less autonomous individuals has been the cradle of freedom, art, literature, science, and technology. But the city that has been a citadel against the nature around us cannot defend us against the nature within us—in our lusts and fears, and in the subconscious cellars of our minds. It is in the city that man's lusts and fears have free play, and that dehumanization spreads like the plague. The lust for power in particular has shown itself to be antihuman. We savor power not when we move mountains and tell rivers whither to flow but when we can turn men into objects, robots, puppets, automata, or veritable animals. Power is power to dehumanize, and it is in the city that this lust finds the human material to work on. It is easier to dehumanize man in the mass than any individual man. Thus the city has been the breeding ground of all movements and developments that tend to press man back into the matrix of nature from which he has risen.

A fateful feature of the war with nature is its circularity. Victory and defeat run into each other. Just when man seems to be within reach of his ultimate goal he is likely to find himself caught in a trap. Everywhere there are booby traps and pitfalls, and nature strikes back from unexpected quarters. A most recent example is the splitting of the atom. Man cracked nature's strongbox only to discover that he had cracked Pandora's box of ills and woes and evil spirits, and let loose the poisonous mushroom cloud of total annihilation.

One thinks of the fantastic spectacle of the nineteenth century when the Industrial Revolution seemed to make man's dream of total victory over nature come true, and the prospect of a man-made world blanketing the whole of the globe seemed within reach. The fateful fact that man was not inventive enough to automate his second creation, that his machines were half-machines lacking the gears and filaments of thought and will, set in motion a process of mass dehumanization that turned the machine age into a nightmare. Human beings had to be used as a stopgap for inventiveness. Men, women, and children were coupled with iron and steam, millions of peasants were scooped off the land and shoveled into the bellies of smoke-belching factories; the machines were consuming human beings as fast as coal. It was as if nature had infiltrated the metal of the machines and subverted the man-made world. Factories, mass armies, and mass movements combined to strip people of their human uniqueness and transmute them into a homogeneous, malleable mass. Lenin, the leader of a mass movement, recognized that the "hard school" of the factory was readying people for a totalitarian dictatorship. The mass armies trained people to obedience and mass action. At the same time, Lenin's revolution saw as its main task the conversion of peasants into factory workers and soldiers. Thus industrialists, generals, and revolutionaries worked hand in hand. And not they alone. Carlyle's glorification of brute force, Gobineau's race theories, Marx's economic determinism and his theory of the class struggle, Darwin's and Pavlov's zoological sociology, the dark forces of Wagner's music, Nietzsche's cult of the superman, and Freud's emphasis on the less human components of man's soul were all part of a blind striving to reintegrate man with nature. The deliberate dehumanization practiced by Stalin and Hitler was an intensification and acceleration of something that had been going for decades. There is hardly an enormity committed in the twentieth century that has not been foreshadowed and even advocated by some noble "man of words" in the nineteenth. Even such clear-cut opposites as the fascination with science and the romantic back-to-nature movements were actually pulling in the same direction—helping to equate man with nature, and cooperating in the dehumanization of man. They who leaped ahead and they who plunged backward arrived simultaneously at the gates of the twentieth-century annihilation camps.

One of the strangest features of man's war with nature is its undeclaredness. The men who are in the forefront of the battle are as a rule unaware that they are fighting a war. They are usually animated by a hunger for profit or for spectacular action. I have not come across a clarion call to mankind to abandon war between brothers and mobilize all its energies in a titanic struggle with the nonhuman universe. You can count on the fingers of one hand unequivocal expressions of the eternal enmity between man and nature. I can think only of Hardy's "Man begins where nature ends; nature and man can never be friends." Thoreau, who sided with nature, recognized that "you cannot have a deep sympathy with both man and nature" and admitted, "I love nature because she is not man but a retreat from him." Toward the end of his life Thomas Huxley realized that man's ascent was something different from his descent. In his Romanes lecture, in 1893, he warned, "Let us understand once for all that the ethical progress of societies depends not on imitating the cosmic process, still less in running away from it, but in combating it."

There is an echo of man's first blows against nature in some myths. The Babylonian god Marduk slew the dragon Tiamath and created arable land of her carcass. Prometheus stole fire from the gods and gave it to man to compensate him for the meagerness of his physical endowments. Yet, on the whole, the impression conveyed by mythologies is of a close relationship between man and nature in which nature always has the upper hand and must be supplicated and propitiated. There is a Darwinian motif in the totemic assumption of a kinship between man and other forms of life. The whole structure of magic is founded on an identity between human nature and nature. Both the scientist and the savage postulate the oneness of man and nature. The difference between them is that the savage tries to influence nature by means that have proved their efficacy in influencing human nature, while the scientist wants to deal with human nature the way he deals with matter and other forms of life. The scientist reads the equation "human nature equals nature" from left to right, while the savage reads it from right to left. Yet it is worth noting that Darwin, too, read the equation from right to left when he read cutthroat capitalist competition into the economy of nature.

In this as in other fields the uniqueness of the ancient Hebrews is startlingly striking. They were the first to enunciate a clear-cut separation between man and nature. Though monotheism was born of tribal pride—the desire to be the one and only people of a one and only God—it brought with it a downgrading of nature. The one and only God created both nature and man yet made man in his own image and appointed him His viceroy on earth. Jehovah's injunction to man (Genesis, Chapter 1) is unequivocal: Be fruitful and multiply, and subdue the earth. Nature lost its divine attributes. Sun, stars, sky, earth, mountains, rivers, plants, and animals were no longer the seat of mysterious powers and the arbiters of man's fate. Though man had to wrestle with the earth for his bread, he was the masterful male Adam, and the earth, Adama, a female to be beaten into submission. The writers of the Old Testament picked as the father of the race not Esau, a man of nature, whose garments, like those of Thoreau's ideal man, smelled of grassy fields and flowery meadows, but his twin Jacob, who was all too human in his anxieties and cunning scheming, and who preferred the inside of a tent to the great outdoors, and the smell of lentil soup to the smell of trees and fields.

It is true that the downgrading of nature had not prompted the ancient Hebrews to become mighty tamers of nature. Still, their endurance as a weak minority through centuries of persecution constitutes a grand defiance of nature, a putting to naught of the law of survival of the strong that rules the rest of life. Moreover, the mighty Jehovah did play a role in the rise of the scientific and technological civilization of the modern Occident. It is hard for us to realize how god-conscious were the scientists and technologists active at the birth of the modern Occident. Jehovah was to them the supreme mathematician and technician who had created the world and set it going. To unravel the mysteries of nature was to decipher God's text and rethink his thoughts. When Kepler formulated the laws of planetary motion he boasted that God had to wait six thousand years for his first reader. These early scientists and technicians felt close to God; they stood in awe of him yet felt as if they were of this school, and whether they knew it or not aspired to be like him. Perhaps one of the reasons that other civilizations, with all their ingenuity and skill, did not develop a machine age is that they had no god who was an all-powerful engineer whom they could imitate and vie with.

The first great assault upon nature took place in the Neolithic Age when there was as yet no writing; thus it remained unrecorded and unsung. Yet it is legitimate to wonder whether the presence of scribes would have mattered one way or another—whether the "men of words" would have been aware of the import of that which was happening before their eyes, let alone moved enough to declaim and sing. For when the second great assault came in the nineteenth century the "men of words" were not in the fight and, indeed, a great many of them sided with nature against man. It was precisely at the moment when the Industrial Revolution forged the weapons for a total victory over nature that scientists, poets, philosophers, and historians, seized with a mysterious impulse, began to proclaim with one voice the littleness of man and his powerlessness to shape his fate. Man, declared Huxley in 1860, "strives in vain to break through the ties which hold him to matter and the lower forms of life." Instead of being in the vanguard of the Promethean struggle we find the most gifted members of the species on the sidelines jeering at the clamorous multitude that set out to tame and straddle God's creation.

The intellectuals entered the nineteenth century flushed with the conviction that they were the new makers of history. Had not their words set in motion the earth-shaking events of the French Revolution? Coleridge boasted that the most important changes in the world had their origin not in the cabinets of statesmen or the insights of businessmen but "in the closets and lonely walks of theorists." Heine was more blatant: "Mark this, ye proud men of action; ye are nothing but unconscious instruments of men of thought who, often in the humblest seclusion, have appointed you to your inevitable tasks." Few of the educated knew in the first decades of the nineteenth century that they had an Industrial Revolution on their hands. Everywhere the intellectuals were strutting, posturing, and declaiming, each fancying himself a man of destiny. Then one morning they woke up to discover that power had fallen into the hands of their middle-class relatives—their lowbrow brothers, uncles, in-laws, who had not only taken possession of everything they could lay their hands on, and thus gathered the economy of the country into their pockets, but aspired also to impose their values and tastes upon the whole society. The revulsion from a middle-class society that came to dominate the nineteenth century alienated the intellectuals from the machine age. Writers, poets, artists, philosophers, and scholars poured their scorn on the money-grubbing, mean-spirited, sweating, pushing, hard-working philistines who dared vie with God. "The steam engine," cried Baudelaire, "is a negation of God." Flaubert described his joy at the sight of weeds overrunning abandoned buildings—"this embrace of nature coming swiftly to bury the work of man the moment that his hand is no longer there to defend it." One also wonders how much the refusal to countenance history made by a despised middle class contributed to the tendency of the learned during the nineteenth century to downgrade man as a maker of history.

The cold war between the intellectuals and the middle class that started more than a century ago has been gathering force in the twentieth century, and the intellectual seems to be coming out on top. In many parts of the world the intellectual is at present at the center of the stage as ruler, legislator, military leader, and large-scale industrialist. One of the greatest surprises of the twentieth century was sprung by the educated when they came to power. Gandhi once said that what worried him most was "the hardness of heart of the educated," and it staggers the mind that education rather than education of the heart often makes the heart savage. We have discovered that nature prefers to lodge its fifth column in the minds and hearts of the educated. We have yet to assimilate the fact that it took "a nation of philosophers" to produce Hitler and Nazism, and that in Stalin's Russia professors, writers, artists, and scientists were a pampered and petted aristocracy. These privileged intellectuals did not let out a peep against one of the most brutal tyrannies the world has seen. The Stalin cult was the work of intellectuals.

It is remarkable how worshipful of the machine intellectuals become when the economy of a country is in their keeping, and how naturally they take to treating human beings as a cheap, all-purpose raw material. They have processed human flesh and bone into steel mills, dams, powerhouses, etc., and it was all done in the name of a noble ideal. It needs an effort to realize that the twentieth century is the century of the idealists. No other century had seen so vast an expulsion of practical people from the seats of power and their replacement by idealists. In no other century has there been so powerful an attempt to realize ideals, dreams, and visions. The unprecedented dehumanization our century has seen was conceived and engineered by idealists.

Societies ruled by intellectuals tend to approach menageries; the fences and walls which usually enclose them are there not to keep anything out but to keep the animals from running away. The return of nature in these societies manifests itself not only in the attitude of the rulers toward the people, but in the attitude of the ruled toward the government. In a Communist country, for instance, people tend to view the government as a force of nature, and the misfortunes that overtake them as natural calamities. You do not protest or conspire against a natural catastrophe, nor do you feel humiliated when struck down by a natural force. You do not feel humiliated when the ocean spits on you, or the wind forces you to your knees. To outsiders, too, there is something terrifyingly unhuman about these societies. We tend to overestimate their power, and view them as implacable forces of nature. Every child is aware of Russia's and China's unhuman strength, while it needs an exceptional acuteness, a sixth sense almost, to have anything like a realistic grasp of America's capabilities.

Why should power corrupt the intellectual more than it does other types of humanity? One of the reasons is to be found in the assumption that education readies a person for the task of reforming and reshaping humanity—that it equips him to act as an engineer of souls and a manufacturer of desirable human attributes.

Hence when power gives him the freedom to act, the intellectual will be inclined to deal with humanity as with material that can be molded and processed. He will strive to arrange things so that he will not be thwarted by the unpredictability and intractability of human nature. The antihumanity of the intellectual in power is not a function of his inhumanity. An elite of intellectuals is more vowed to the service of mankind or of a nation than any other elite. But a savior who wants to turn men into angels will be as much a hater of human nature as a monster who wants to turn them into slaves and animals. Man must be dehumanized, must be turned into an object, before he can be processed into something wholly different from what he is. It is a paradox that the idealistic reformer has a mechanical, lifeless conception of man's being. He sees man as something that can be taken apart and put together, and the renovation of the individual and of society as a process of manufacturing. Robert Owen used a manufacturer's vocabulary to describe his intended reforms not mainly because he was a manufacturer but because he was a reformer. He spoke of his new social order as "the new machinery" that "will facilitate the larger production of happiness."

Another source of the intellectual's corruption by power is that no matter how powerful he becomes he continues to utilize the devices of the weak. It is curious how even at the height of their power Hitler, Stalin, Mao, and others tend to speak and act as if they were the leaders of "a company of poor men," of an oppressed tribe or a persecuted minority. Absolute faith and monolithic unity that enable the weak to survive are unequaled instruments of coercion in the hands of the powerful.

Finally, intellectuals in power are chronically afraid, and herein lies one more cause of their corruption by power. For the intellectual cannot admit to himself what it is that he is afraid of. When we are aware of the cause of our fear we can be afraid of only one thing, but when we cannot face the truth the fear becomes general. An elite of intellectuals is afraid chiefly of its own people and cannot admit it, hence its fear of the whole world; and when power is mated with a great fear it becomes virulent.

As we have seen, the war with nature proceeds both around and within us, yet we have no precise knowledge how the happenings on one front affect the other. Up to now, an increased command over nature around us did not automatically reinforce our humanness. On the contrary, in many parts of the world the taming of nature by rapid industrialization gave rise to a greater or lesser degree of social barbarization. Some thoughtful persons have questioned the wisdom of seeking further command over nature until means have been devised to prevent the misuse of the enormous powers we already have in our hands. Nevertheless, the overcoming of nature, so crucial in the ascent of man, can be a most effective agency of humanization in the decades ahead—if for no other reason than that it may divert aggressive impulses and wild energies from social strife. We are told that a decade from now sixty per cent of the people in this country will be eighteen and under. The Negro population is already more than half juvenile, and the same is true of the populations of Latin America, Asia, and Africa. The presence of a global population of juveniles spells trouble for everybody. No country is a good country for its juveniles, and even in normal times every society is in the grip of a crisis when a new generation passes from childhood to manhood. The enemy is within the gates. The trouble with the juvenile is not that he is not as yet a man but that he is no longer a child. He has lost the child's capacity for wonder and for total absorption in whatever it does, and its hunger to master skills. The juvenile's self-consciousness robs him of genuineness, while his penchant for self-dramatization prompts him to extremist poses and gestures. In his restless groping for an identity he will join any mass movement and plunge into any form of spectacular action. His humanness is a precarious thing, easily sloughed off. Both the Bolsheviks and the Fascists made use of juveniles to do the dirty work of killing.

My feeling is that the humanization of billions of adolescents would be greatly facilitated by a concerted undertaking to master and domesticate the whole of the globe. One would like to see mankind spend the balance of the century in a total effort to clean up and groom the surface of the globe—wipe out the jungles, turn deserts and swamps into arable land, terrace barren mountains, regulate rivers, eradicate all pests, control the weather, and make the whole land mass a fit habitation for man. A hundred years ago Alfred Russel Wallace envisioned the time "when the earth will produce only civilized plants and domestic animals; when man's selection shall have supplanted natural selection; and when the ocean would be the only domain in which that power can be exerted which for countless cycles of ages ruled supreme over all the earth." So, too, did the prophet Isaiah envision total domestication at the end of time when the wolf and the lamb, the leopard and the kid, the lion and the calf, the bear and the cow shall lie down together, and a little child shall lead them.

There is a phase of the war with nature which is little noticed but always impresses me. To me there is an aura of grandeur about the dull routine of maintenance; I see it as a defiance of the teeth of time. It is easier to build than to maintain. Even a lethargic or debilitated society can be galvanized for a while to achieve something impressive, but the energy required to maintain things is of a different order.

From talking with foreign-born longshoremen and ships' crews I gained the impression that the capacity for maintenance is a peculiarity of western Europe and the Scandinavian countries, of the Anglo-Saxon world and of Japan. The reports of travelers confirm this impression. Lord Kinross, while traveling in Turkey, was struck that though the Turks made excellent mechanics they had no talent for maintenance—"indeed, until lately, no word for maintenance existed in the Turkish language." Mr. André Siegfried sees the process of maintenance as "something which belongs essentially to the Westerner" and thinks "it is here that we must look for his distinct characteristic." Though the West has unprecedented powers to wreck and destroy, it cannot stand ruins. Still, it is strange that in Asia, where civilization had its birth, the separation from nature and the ability to hold it at bay should be much less pronounced than in the younger civilization of the Occident. In Asia, Africa, and Latin America the man-made world seems precariously stretched over the writhing body of nature. At the edge of every cultivated field, and around every human habitation, nature lies in wait ready to move in and repossess what man has wrested from its grasp. You see trees cracking walls, heaving blocks of stone from their sockets, and reclaiming once-mighty cities. In Australia nature reclaimed the dog from its human domesticator, and almost reclaimed man himself.

There is the story about Georges Clemenceau that when he traveled around the world in 1921 he came to New Delhi and was taken to see the huge Baker-Lutyen office buildings which were just then completed. He stood gazing at the buildings for a long time without uttering a word. Finally the British officer who was with him asked what he thought of them. "I was thinking," said Clemenceau, "what ruins these will make!" As so often with Clemenceau, his chance remarks threw a searching light on the human situation. Standing at the heart of Asia, Clemenceau felt himself primarily an Occidental and saw the British Empire as Occidental rather than British. He also knew that the days of the Occident in Asia were numbered, and that once the Occident withdrew its hand, the dragon of Asia would move in and sink its yellowed teeth of time in all that the Occident had built and wrought, and gnaw away till naught was left but a skeleton of ruins.

## Eric Hoffer

Eric Hoffer sprang to prominence in 1951 with the publication of his study, The True Believer, a brief, brilliant history of fanaticism and loyalty-to-leader in its myriad forms. In the years since, he has become known internationally as the longshoreman-philosopher who is read by the thinking community and consulted by Presidents. Mr. Hoffer, who was born in 1902, was all but blind till the age of fifteen, when his sight was suddenly restored. He then began to read voraciously, supporting himself meanwhile by working as a migratory fruit-picker, a miner, and a longshoreman. His books The True Believer, The Passionate State of Mind, and The Ordeal of Change are considered classics of contemporary social thought.

# ROBERT MAYNARD HUTCHINS

## First Glimpses of a New World

I HAVE BEEN PLAGUED all my life by two obsessions, the search for standards and the search for community. The reason is that ever since a few weeks before my twenty-fourth birthday I have been an officer of corporations not for profit.

Let me explain. An administrator in any corporation has to be concerned about what is to be done. This means that he has to decide, and he has to do so in the light of some notion of what his corporation is for. This supplies his standard. The definition of a corporation for profit states its purpose. The definition of a corporation not for profit states only what its purpose is not. Hence an administrator of such a corporation who wants to achieve its purpose has to begin to think about what its purpose is.

For reasons that will appear, I came early in life to the conclusion that an educational corporation ought to be a community of some kind. This seemed to be necessary to achieve its purpose. Hence the search for standards led me to the search for community.

Profit is a matter of numbers of dollars. Everybody knows what a dollar is, and everybody agrees that it is a Good Thing. Its great charm is that it can be counted. It is definite. It is simple. Everybody understands and appreciates it. There is no argument about it.

177

The American does not love the dollar because he is "material-istic." He will spend or give away money with a light heart. The Marshall Plan is unexampled in the history of mankind.

The American loves the dollar because he is philosophically timid, more so, I think, than any human being who ever lived. He is not at home with anything he cannot count, because he is not sure of any other measure. He cannot estimate or appraise quality. This leaves him with quantity.

About education we are totally ignorant, because all we can refer to are things that obviously do not matter. We talk of num-bers of students, teachers, buildings, acres, Nobel Prize–winners, books, dropouts, or graduates. A college degree means four years and one hundred twenty semester-hours, plus physical education. Yet we know it can't be so. We know that educations and educa-tional institutions differ in ways that can't be counted. But what are those ways? The most embarrassing question that can be raised in a university is, what are we trying to do?

The administrator of an educational institution is to be for-given if he evades this question and announces that education is what goes on in educational institutions. He can then regard his own institution as given and try to make it prosper in ways compre-hensible to his constituency. These ways are quantitative. Univer-sity presidents raise money, even when their universities are not much in need of it, because they know they will be judged by their success in this dispiriting task, and by this alone.

When I became secretary of Yale in 1923 the thoughts of the administration were almost entirely absorbed in building vast quan-tities of pseudo- or semi-Gothic architecture with Sterling and Harkness money. Yale seemed bent on making itself an example of academic splendor of the most superficial kind.

When I moved over into the law school as dean, architecture was in hot pursuit. Mr. Sterling was a lawyer, and the Sterling trus-tees insisted on giving the law school a building. Three times in my administration the faculty besought the trustees not to do it. When this appeal was denied, we suggested that, if we had to have a building, we would like a very cheap one, built in the slums. This was, perhaps, the first urban redevelopment plan. My friend Milton C. Winternitz, dean of the medical school, and I proposed to build a center of professional education over in the horrible neighborhood in which the medical school had been erected. We wanted to get away from the Gothic and the "college life" that characterized Yale in that distant day. If theology, medicine, and law could make a university in the Middle Ages, perhaps they could do so again.

Our scheme foundered when we met with the faculty of the divinity school, and George Dahl, the professor of Hebrew, said he did not want his students to associate with our students because his students would lose their faith. We replied that if they were going to lose their faith, the sooner they did it the better. After all, they could not always escape lawyers and doctors. This argument was rejected, and the divinity school went in the opposite direction, out next to the astronomical observatory. The law school got a magnificent $5,000,000 Gothic building that set it back ten years.

Yale at that time was full of good men, but they were scattered and ineffective. Dean Winternitz and I wanted a professional center because we wanted some kind of intellectual community in which every member would be better because of the presence of the others. Yale had no university faculty. Each school operated on its own, subject to the approval of the president and the corporation. The law school had reached a stage at which it was imperative that it break out of the isolation in which all Yale professional schools then languished.

The law school was not yet a professional school; it was still more or less a trade school. The object was not to educate students to understand the law, but to train them to practice it. The success of the school was measured by the success of its graduates at the bar. Success was defined in terms of numbers of dollars and headlines.

We wanted to be academically respectable. We knew what

everybody was beginning to learn in those days, that the only way to be academically respectable was to be "scientific." Since we knew almost nothing about science, we assumed that being scientific meant collecting the "facts" that would enable us to predict what the courts would do. We were, or wanted to be, among the first "value-free" social scientists. We had all been brought up on the big words, like freedom, truth, and justice. But since they could not be given scientific content or acquire content by scientific means, we knew they were just words. We thought philosophy, to say nothing of theology, was a thing of the past. I need not add that we knew little of either one.

It was true that Alfred North Whitehead had said that the object of education for a career was the mastery of the general principles underlying that career. But principles had no standing with us. We were going to be "realistic" as well as "scientific."

If we had been content to remain a trade school, we might have been content with our accomplishment. But we were haunted by the notion that a university law school had some responsibility to improve the law, not merely to teach what it was or was likely to become. We had to decide whether the courts were doing "right." Here we ran into the problem of standards.

At this juncture a simpleminded pragmatism came temporarily to our aid. It taught us that we could test the rules of law by asking whether or not they worked.

But we could not discover what worked. We could not explain in any defensible terms what it meant to work. If something worked out the way we thought it should, we were in favor of it. If it worked out the other way, we were against it. Since most of us were "liberal," we were in favor of those rules that seemed to tend in a "liberal" direction. We even said the others were "wrong."

But we would have been hard put to it to say why we were liberals. The best you could say for freedom and justice was that they were ideas; we were committed to facts.

So Max Radin, a great law teacher of the time, wrote, "Every one of us can remember the laughter of the class when the innocent freshman, after the discussion of a case, asks, 'But, Professor, is it just?'"

I dimly realized that though a trade school might be a community it was unlikely to be an intellectual community—what was there to think about?—and it could not be part of a larger community. Without a common language, a common education, and common goals, how could there be an intellectual community?

Yale at that date did not conform to the pattern of the modern American university. The prestige still clung to the college; research, graduate work, and professional education, which may all be summed up in the single word "specialization," had not yet taken over. It was clear, however, that the day of the dominance of specialization was dawning, even at Yale. The vulgar conception of science that we all entertained committed us to the pursuit and mastery of knowledge; we knew that this could be accomplished only by intensive investigation in narrower and narrower fields. This was clearly the way to the conquest of nature. We all knew that knowledge was power. It did not occur to many of us to ask how knowledge might be translated into wisdom, or even into understanding.

I went to Chicago in 1929, to a university of the modern type, where research and specialization had long held sway, and where in some quarters education was already looked upon as a nuisance. But the same questions of standards and community were raised, though in a different form. What was the purpose of the conglomeration called the University of Chicago, and how could unity within such diversity be achieved?

The reason even the most reluctant administrator finds it difficult to avoid such questions is that he has to try to make sense of his institution if only for the purpose of explaining it to others. To state the matter in its lowest terms, he cannot hope that in a pinch it will be supported merely because it exists. The administrator may want to think of himself as the man with the oil can and the monkey wrench, keeping the machinery going. It is a pleasing picture; he does not have to think, still less to have ideas. He finds the wheels in motion; he does not consider their direction, but only how the motion may be continued. The picture is pleasing, but it must dissolve in a crisis. Then somebody is sure to ask why these wheels should be moving this way, or at all.

But at first I devoted myself to tidying up the place in obvious ways, like abolishing the credit system and the requirement of attendance at classes and getting rid of one of the two university medical schools on the self-evident ground that one medical school was more than enough for any single university.

Then came the crisis.

The Great Depression conferred marked benefits upon the university, for it forced a reconsideration of the whole enterprise. The first thing I had to contend with was the demand that I cut everything twenty-five per cent. This made no sense to me. I thought what was important should be supported and what was trivial should be dropped.

In this way I trapped myself into thinking, what was important, and what was trivial? I could hope to find out only by thinking about the purpose of the university.

My prejudices could get me nowhere. The president of the University of Chicago in those days had no power. By statute the faculty controlled the curriculum, and the trustees controlled everything else. The president, if he wanted to do anything, had to persuade one or the other or both.

What did I want to persuade them to do? I gradually came to believe that I should try to persuade them to make the University of Chicago an intellectual community.

This would require the elimination of people who could not or would not think, of courses that did not require thought, of activities that interfered with the common intellectual life or that made no contribution to it. After this work of demolition, it was necessary to construct the community, and this was begun by involving faculty, students, and trustees in a continuing discussion of the purposes of education, the aims of the university, and the nature of the good life and the good society. This discussion went on for twenty years, and the curriculum and organization of the university were formed and re-formed under its influence. The university became an intellectual community, or more like one, by this process. It made little difference what the forms were that were decided upon at any given time. What counted was that the university gained its unity and its vitality from a perpetual argument that touched the lives of every one of its members.

Meanwhile, Mortimer Adler had taken my education in hand. We had been associated for several years when he was at Columbia and I was at Yale in trying to make sense of a subject in which I had come to specialize, the law of evidence. This is a fascinating maze of quips and cranks and wanton wiles developed by very clever lawyers over the years for getting at the truth in jury trials. Its central issue is, what does a jury believe, and why? The answer, of course, is, nobody knows, and there is no way to find out.

Nevertheless, in the interest of a "fair trial," whatever that is, some persons must be prevented from testifying, some persons may decline to testify, and some testimony must be excluded. For example, the hearsay rule proceeds on the assumption that the jury should not hear the words of a person not under oath and not subject to cross-examination. The thirteen exceptions to the rule indicate circumstances in which, as in the dying declaration of the victim in a murder case, the occasion is thought to be as solemn a guarantee of veracity as the oath and cross-examination.

The law of evidence makes an admirable trade-school subject. You teach the boys the rules and how to manipulate them. My examination questions showed what I was about; in a certain kind of case, how would you get certain testimony in, and how would you keep it out? No issue of principle, of right or wrong, of justice or injustice was raised. You can hardly get more trade school than that. I can only hope that my students rapidly forgot what they learned from me. The legislatures have repealed and the courts overruled most of what I knew. Even in the law, "the facts" have a high rate of obsolescence.

When some sense of responsibility dawned on me, when it occurred to me that the students ought to understand the law of evidence and not simply memorize and manipulate it, I had no resources with which to effect the change. The law of evidence seemed to be based on assumptions about human behavior and on a rough-and-ready logic. I had never studied either psychology or logic.

Mortimer Adler was a philosopher who had taken his degree in psychology. He was interested in what interested me, the problem of proof. It occurred to us that we might together find some way of making sense of the law of evidence.

During this effort Mr. Adler disclosed to me that he had been principally educated by studying and teaching in John Erskine's course in great books at Columbia. Since I had read only a few of these books, I wondered whether they might offer clues to the standards I was seeking. I was an easy mark for Mr. Adler when he represented to me that I was uneducated, that I was reading nothing but the telephone book, and that I had better join him in teaching John Erskine's course at Chicago.

These classroom discussions went on for twenty years. We conducted them at every level and in almost every part of the university. We argued about great books with students in the university high school, the college, the graduate school, the law school, and the adult education division.

From these two parallel experiences I began to get some idea of what I came to call the Civilization of the Dialogue, a phrase I am sure I stole someplace. I read in a book by a British scholar that has just come out, *The Experience of Higher Education,* that "The study of higher education is perplexed by two unanswerable questions—what is it for? and how do we know when it has succeeded?" I do not concede that the questions are unanswerable. I would say that the object of all education is to prepare all students to participate in the Civilization of the Dialogue and that the particular object of the university is to exemplify the dialogue and carry it further. A university that succeeds in doing this is a success, no matter what else it fails to do; a university that fails in this is a failure, no matter what else it succeeds in doing.

I have to admit that a successful university in my terms may now be impossible. It may be that the tasks of vocational certification, scientific research, technological development, and child care that we have imposed upon our universities prevent them from being universities in my sense at all, prevent them from being, that is, independent centers of thought and criticism. If this is so, we shall have to devise substitutes for them; for we cannot hope to maintain a democratic society and to advance toward a world community without something of this sort. Perhaps the Center for the Study of Democratic Institutions should be multiplied many times and relieve the universities of responsibilities they are no longer able to discharge.

Matthew Arnold described himself as

> Wandering between two worlds, one dead,
> The other powerless to be born.

This seems to me the human situation today. We are coming to the end of the old world; the new one may be powerless to be born.

The accumulation of knowledge, the mastery of nature, the acquisition of power over men and nations, these were the objects of the old world. The pursuit of these objects leads to paranoia rather than community. This is a disease that runs from the lowliest to the mightiest in our society, a disease necessarily and inherently

contagious, which afflicts whole populations and races. A community of paranoiacs is impossible.

So there are almost no intellectual or political communities
left in the United States. There is no serious discussion in which
even a minority of the people takes part, and what discussion there
is does not significantly affect public policy. Hence public policy is
largely a matter of pressure and deals. Demonstrations take the
place of reason.

The pseudoscientific attitude that dominated the old world
held that we must seek knowledge, for knowledge is power. There
is no use seeking wisdom; there is no way of transforming knowledge into wisdom. "Values" are unknowable and indefensible.
Standards are matters of prejudice and inheritance.

We are therefore all strangers except as we happen to be
united in our interests. There can be no community. There can be
only pressure groups. What we call community is merely a precarious equilibrium of pressure groups or, on a world scale, of nations.
Politics is power.

So de Tocqueville saw the American as essentially forlorn—
the individual living for himself alone, afraid of his neighbors,
afraid of government, afraid of foreigners, afraid of change, repeating to himself the phrase that epitomizes the American mood, "I
don't want to get involved."

Tolerance, the great virtue of the old world, merely meant, "I
won't persecute you if you won't persecute me—ideas are not worth
fighting about anyway."

I gradually came to see that there were no "scientific" solutions to human problems. We may have every confidence that
sooner or later we shall learn what everything is made of and how
everything works—everything, that is, except men and their societies. But, though we can say, for example, that democracy is the
most just form of government, we cannot determine with the precision of a mathematical formula whether a certain kind of democ-

racy is appropriate to a given people at a given time. Spinoza's effort to make a geometry of ethics was bound to fail. Since experiments with human societies are inconclusive and experiments with human beings are intolerable, attempts to develop the scientific laws of human nature are likely to have limited success and application.

But if human problems cannot be solved, they can be clarified. We can try to find out where we are, how we got there, what we know and do not know, and we can try to discern tendencies and probable results. Given tendencies that are discernible, what is the outcome we want? Or what is the outcome we ought to want?

Though there may be no precise, final answers to these questions, the questions and possible answers can be defined, discussed, and understood.

The Civilization of the Dialogue assumes that man is a social and political as well as a rational being. The world is to be united by a sense of common humanity, common destiny, common enterprise, and the warmth of human feeling.

Admitting that we cannot solve human problems, we can work together toward their solution. We can think and think together about how to transform knowledge into wisdom. The body politic then becomes an organic unity of sympathy and solidarity engaged in a common search.

The crucial problem of mankind today is posed by the difference between the appeal to reason and the resort to violence. Violence necessarily lies at the heart of the old world.

Is the new world powerless to be born? I think, in spite of all appearances, it is being born. The recognition of our common humanity is being forced in upon us by political and technological events. The futility and dangers of the old world become clearer every day. The world community exists, whether we know it or not. The task is to supply the intellectual foundations and the political institutions necessary to the Civilization of the Dialogue.

## Robert Maynard Hutchins

Robert M. Hutchins, educator and citizen-at-large, is an energetic practitioner and defender of the life of the mind. Throughout his notable career, he has been regarded as a prodigy, a polymath, and a farsighted intellectual innovator. He was born in Brooklyn in 1899, studied at Oberlin and Yale, became dean of Yale Law School at the age of twenty-nine, and was for twenty-two years president, then chancellor, of the University of Chicago. While at Chicago, he introduced a new working philosophy of education, one of whose outgrowths was the celebrated Great Books program. Mr. Hutchins has been associate director of the Ford Foundation and president of its Fund for the Republic. He is currently president of the Center for the Study of Democratic Institutions, in Santa Barbara, California. The Center brings leading thinkers together to examine various aspects of American life. Mr. Hutchins is also a member of the editorial board of Encyclopaedia Britannica. His books include Education for Freedom, The Great Conversation, and Some Observations on American Education.

# HORACE MEYER KALLEN

## How I Bet My Life

---

W HEN I ASK myself what, over my too many years, I have learned, I find that I'm not asking what it is that I have come to know beyond any doubt, but what it is that I have come to believe in enough to be willing to bet my life on it, aware that no bet can be a bet on a sure thing. I find that I owe the articles of my faith far more to the give and take of direct experience with places and persons, with their thoughts and their things, than to the discourses of the schools or the writings of the scholars, whether ancient or modern; and I find that I have a certain pleasure in examining the latter's writings for confirmation of my own credo—particularly if the confirmation defeats its author's intentions.

This may impress today's many—who cultivate "analysis," "semantics," or "philosophy of science" in order to grow the certainties which their Beat Generation no longer harvests from their elders' "perennial philosophy"—as another fall into the meaninglessness which they allot to meanings they do not accept. My meaning may figure for them as but another absurdity vainly interposed to delay their infallible deflation of the philosophies of the great tradition. Perhaps they imagine rightly, for I am, I believe, by disposition and habit, a philosopher, and I have been by training and lifelong occupation a professor of philosophy. The latter does not

189

necessarily follow, not to say follow from, the former. I have been lucky.

I am not sure when I recognized that one learns as one lives, and that the consummation of learning is more like undergoing a conversion than reaching a conclusion; the challenge, the anxiety, the travail are in unlearning the old far more than in learning the new. I became convinced of this early in my personal history, and it has stayed a gradient for my thinking about learning and teaching ever since. That which I found myself unlearning was a configuration of professions and practices embodying beliefs about Man, his world, his role, and his destiny in it, which I had become committed to, unknowing. I had grown up somehow living by them, yet feeling ever more troubled and afraid. What I learned and became converted to is the philosophic faith I have been confessing, reasoning about, and trying to give effect to in words and works these fifty years. It identifies me as a libertarian who had been a determinist, a temporalist who had been an eternalist, an individualist and nominalist who had been a universalist, a pluralist who had been a monist, without being alienated from what he had been. The sum of it—a Spinozist who became a pragmatist.

What I now believe about Man and how he got to be what he is in his becoming, about the ends and means which give form to his struggle to keep on struggling—that some call "existence" and others "survival"—is confluent with this philosophy; it orchestrates, I trust, the articles of this faith. With them, I am able to acknowledge the singularity of each event of experience as it passes, yet to find it as meaningful as the Christian drama of salvation that renders the banal flatness of the communion wafer for the true believer. Yes, any philosophy lived as well as spoken can effect a like transvaluation. Only the perennial ones must needs reduce events to unrealities, and then, in order to render them meaningful, each must needs practice its own mode of transubstantiation on them, while the analytic and semantic ones go on debunking every such transubstantiation into nonsense and futility.

As I see our life now, it is of the singularity of Man's manhood to practice transubstantiation. Everybody's doing it, everywhere. Everybody's creating his peculiar fetish, which shall secure him against his peculiar insecurity. Among the most highly relied on is "reason." The transubstantiation of the facts of reason into the diverse fetishes of rationalism and supernaturalism and scientism are among the most approved and emulated of human ways. The practice endows the passing experience, whatever it starts and ends as, however in itself banal, with saving power on which the true believer bets to win for himself the future he wants. Although to me it discloses the illusions that men's hopes generate, I may not grudge them those illusions, precious and real in that they are felt to guarantee the hopes. Willy-nilly, men live on by betting their lives and thereby investing what they bet on with the role of a magic engine of victory in their struggles to keep on struggling. This I have learned by unlearning.

Learning it has been an ongoing initiation, a rite of passage, from the dogma that the real is the One—One God, One Universe, One Humanity, One World, One Law of Nature, One Rule of Life for All Mankind—that the foreordained consummation of the last would be, "under God," universal brotherhood and universal peace. These onenesses comprised, in essence, the articles of faith of the orthodox Jewish household of my childhood and youth, which cleaved unto them regardless of their daily repudiations by events.

Repudiations were diverse. A pervasive one was anti-Semitism: My father, a Russian subject, serving as under rabbi in the small Silesian town where I was born, was *ausgewiesen* by Bismarck's Prussian government as an alien Jew. He found his way to Boston, where he brought me up in the faith of the fathers from my fifth year. In Boston, on the streets and in the schoolyards, the Christian kids taught me what they had learned the Jew should receive in payment for the salvation from eternal death which the death of their crucified Savior brought them. I could endure, and on occasion even overcome, because I knew that I belonged to God's

Chosen People and that my pangs and pains were linked in some salubrious way to the divine election.

But the Christians ganged up not only on the Christ-killers; they ganged up on one another, however Christian—as Protestants, as Catholics, as Yankees, as Micks, as Wops, as Polacks, as Dutchies (there didn't happen to be any niggers; these appeared later)—all, even as I, innocent carriers of the ways and views of their elders into the streets and the schools. At school, ever and anon, there came ceremonial occasions when the entire miscellany of pupils had to stand up and intone, "I pledge allegiance to the flag of the United States and to the Republic for which it stands; one nation indivisible, with liberty and justice for all." I don't recall whether the pledge was pledged "under God"—that phrase was added after my time as a student. I do recall how more and more puzzled I became each year I grew older.

The natural sciences which were a part of my schooling— physics, chemistry, biology of a sort—only deepened my puzzlement. For they seemed to subordinate unlike and incommensurable happenings to identical law; they seemed to digest the changes and chances we experience into a sequence of necessary connection which dissipated freedom in fantasy and novelty in illusion. The sciences, assimilating all differentiation into a system of eternal and universal Identity, always and everywhere One and the Same, yet refusing to identify this One as God in any form, I imagine, both confirmed and confuted the ancestral faith.

However, one day I chanced upon a German rendering of Spinoza's *Theologico-Political Tractate*. It set me free. I began to read English versions of his works and English commentaries on them. It was in the year of my graduation from high school that I became enamored of the man and convinced of his philosophy. His image, his thought, and his story became the point of no return in the ongoing alienation from my father and the ancestral religion. I identified with Spinoza. The reader may, if he wishes, write "unlearning" for "alienation from" and "have been converted to" for "identified with."

At college I was made aware of monisms other than Spinoza's, each purporting to be the only true one and to expose any alternatives as mistaken in fact and false in reason. They made up a diversity of competitors to be recognized as the unique revelation of the One which is, beyond every doubt, always and everywhere alone the Same. What I was reading and learning about religion and science disclosed a like rivalry. Both told of ongoing struggles for the establishment and continuation of beliefs—each at one time taken for true by some minds and false by others—all sooner or later displaced by different ones which had been rendered more acceptable to the same minds or others of their kind. The "body of knowledge" I saw was an ever-changing body in which truths of the past become errors of the present, and truths of the present are struggling not to be reduced to errors of the future. How, then, could anything "real" be always and everywhere the same—even Spinoza's substance, his *deus sive natura*?

What I had painfully learned is that the condition of fallible people was the condition of their infallible truths, no less! It made no sense. And how could one keep up the struggle to keep on struggling unless one could make sense of it? William James, who "gave up logic" and developed reasonableness, showed me how sense might be made of it. All I have learned since the time I first came under his influence has its vital root in the man and his teaching.

The empiricism I learned from James is "radical." It takes not only the events of experience as they come, each with its own singular presence, it also acknowledges the reality of the multiple ways the singulars join together and move apart, no less identifiable than the presences they relate. To perceive any is at the same time to perceive its helping or hindering the struggle to keep on struggling which from birth to death compounds into the person that one goes on becoming. An event's role in the struggle makes it value for the struggler as he strains to assimilate it into all else that he has already appraised as true, false, good, bad, right, wrong, beautiful, ugly, rational, absurd, reality, appearance, meaningful, meaningless. He labors at an ongoing identification of the diverse; and everywhere in the world, every variety of mankind's endeavor is a striving to transvalue the diversities they encounter into some One they choose to take for the one Real, and for the harmonizing ground and goal of the embattled manynesses—the One which somehow guarantees their everlasting safety and well-being.

That no inquiry has yet disclosed such a One, that each quest adds one more figure to those already demonstrated and advocates one more way of reaching it, seems not to abate the ardor of the quest. Let the seekers be Albert Einstein hot for his Unified Field; let them be his epigones striving to overcome the ongoing multiplication and diversification of their briefly ultimate particles by means of an overruling "symmetry"; let them be Julian Huxley projecting an Evolutionary Humanism, or Teilhard de Chardin spanning creation between the Alpha and Omega of his transcendentalist evolutionism; let them be Norbert Wiener and his epigones, with their cybernetic grounding of the computerization of human relations and of the scientific, religious, political, and cultural economies they shape up. Each envisions some singular unity responsive to his particular business and desires. The unity continues to be a hidden unity, ever a *deus absconditus*, ever believed in, never encountered—an article of faith, not a fact of life.

Men know from birth how much of life is a war of the faiths, each becoming different as it struggles to master or destroy the different ones that beset it and to attain incarnation as fact by itself alone. Each unity is at once the end and the means of the warfare. The earliest fact, and the latest, is differences increasing and multiplying, with *Homo sap* struggling to lasso and harness their circumambience for the varying uses of his struggle to keep on struggling. And when a harness is believed so to serve, the user changes its status, giving value precedence over existence; he translates his tool into an idol and worships it exclusively for the goods and services he hopes it will provide. *So Homo sap's* inveterate fetishism has until this day transvalued his pecking orders and his gods; so the priesthoods of the present age transvalue the arts and sciences. The fetishism sprouts from what William James has called "a certain blindness in human beings."

He started me toward a cure of this blindness, and it began where I lived. My unseeing had come with a dumb anxiety over my Jewish identity. Non-Jews were troubling my days and nights because, through no fault of my own, I happened to be different from them. My difference diminished me, shackled me, deprived me of my liberty and subjected me to injustice. I must needs rid myself of it and make myself the same as my apparent betters. I must needs change from Jew to—what?

None of the people I was encountering were, in each other's esteem, themselves undiminished by some differences; and all, even the weakest and most humble, seemed to be penalizing others as they could for not being the same as themselves. Following Spinoza, I had come to believe that difference, seen clearly and distinctly, made no real difference, that in substance all the families of mankind are one. What I had learned about the faith that shaped the Republic at first reenforced this belief. Did not the Declaration of Independence tell the world that "all men are created equal, that they are endowed by their Creator with certain unalienable rights," among them "life, liberty, and the pursuit of happiness"? That men institute governments in order to insure the unalienable against alienation? That the just powers of government rest upon the consent of the governed who institute it? So what could "equal" mean, save what it used always to mean—"the same"?

Yet in the business of living, "equal" signified not sameness perceived or achieved but scorning and fleeing some particular difference—by an individual, scorning and fleeing whatever keeps him, with all the self-diversification that growth is a word for, *this* one and no other; by a group, a style of living, thinking, working, and fighting together—a culture, a self-altering tradition of faith and works which joins the group's members to one another. As it obtains, the group's association is a process of union, not a state of unity. Some unions are shotgun marriages, enforced by preponderant power, as among racist and other totalitarian formations; others get their shape from the free teaming up of their members, and grow more cohesive and powerful as their uncoerced participation prolongs—which is the case among the freer societies. I have learned to qualify the varieties of the latter as orchestrations, and to signalize education as the vital center of their survival and growth, which indeed it continues to be in every society.

During my youth "Americanization" became, here at home, the word for manifold ways of dissipating differences, all directed to self-alienation by the different. One favored way was unquestioning conformity to requirements of those who claimed to be the nation's elite and used their power to enforce their claims. Another, not a little resisted by the claimants, was to emulate them, more widely signalized as "keeping up with the Joneses" or "bringing up Father." Still another was willy-nilly melting the Joneses together with oneself into an undefinable new super-identity in Israel Zangwill's "melting-pot." The true American of the future was to be this unique homogenized new *Homo sap.*

As I pondered such often violent divergences, it came home to me that the different signers of the Declaration could never have meant their "laws of nature and of nature's God" to intend "the same" and write "equal." For thus, the divine intention eliminates no differences; it only sanctions one kind of difference, taking privileges and laying penalties on other kinds. So, what is not the same cannot be "equal"; what is different is required, as *different*, to stay unequal. No person, no faith, no occupation, no way of life, no culture might sustain its identity and be equal in those human rights declared to be self-evidently unalienable, and against whose alienation Americans declared their revolution. Was not this Declaration discounted as "glittering generalities," "self-evident lies," or held to be valid only for "superior races"? Does it not continue to be so appraised, everywhere in the world?

The revolutionary meaning of "equal," however, repudiates such appraisals. This means by "equal" equal as different; it affirms the parity of the different; it recognizes that their equality does not abolish their diverse natures but preserves and liberates them, jointly and severally to live on and to grow, to succeed or to fail, by their own power, on their own merits, at their own risk. "Equal," I came to believe, intends the right to be different as the unalienable right—so long, so cruelly, and so diversely subjected to alienation—of which all other rights declared to be unalienable develop as diversifications. I learned that, at least for Homo sap, "to be" and "to be different" are synonyms for the reality of his struggle to keep struggling; that my Jewish difference could be no less real, worthy, and honorable than any other I might be fleeing to; that unlearning it might more greatly diminish me than living and orchestrating it.

And if this were true of my Jewish difference, how not of my friend Alain Locke's Negro difference, which had presented this poet, scholar, man of letters, and philosopher with a challenge of identity far more poignant and critical than mine? We talked much about answers to it the year we both were at Oxford. And if my Jewish and his Negro difference are ours of right and not by sufferance, then, in the nature of things, so are all such differences. It was, I recall, during my talks with Locke that I first used the phrases that have become clichés—"right to be different," "cultural pluralism," and "pluralistic society."

My experience elsewhere than in my field nourished the perceptions which the clichés named, and the reasonings they crystallized. I found that my pragmatist pluralism shaped my reflections about persons and peoples, nations, religions, arts, sciences—their economics, and their rivalry and cooperation with one another. Their de facto diversities, not their de jure onenesses, stayed in the foreground of my sentiment and the reasonings it prompted. I came to judge the onenesses as either imaginative aspirations compensating for lived actuality, or projects to reshape actuality closer to the heart's desire. E pluribus unum became for me the directive agreed upon by a configuration of individuals and companies whose communions joined them into communities of culture as diverse, and as diversely associated, as themselves. The generations of them somehow pledge themselves, as they come, to maintain their union of differences in such wise that all together undertake to assure to each separately equal liberty and equal safety.

Such undertakings would, if successful, be the actuality of peace. As things are, peace is a multitude of struggles short of war. Like war, it suggests a search for a moral equivalent. I have come to believe that the Republic must, among other things, be also such an undertaking, which its citizens covenant to advance and protect from ongoing aggressions within and without, old and new—aggressions which keep on testing, as Abraham Lincoln observed at Gettysburg, whether a nation so conceived and so dedicated can long endure.

To date, the nation has endured. So far, from the Civil War on, the American people have, against no little resistance, tugged and pushed, bullied and bawled their country into less imperfect actualizations of the declared rights of the different to equal liberty and equal safety. Someone's always doing it with regard to the economy at home and the circumambience abroad.

Since the turn of the century, disputes among Americans have mostly concerned the doubted means, not the declared ends, of the world wars, hot and cold, and of the local wars between and after. Few, if any, have challenged Woodrow Wilson's great design "to make the world safe for democracy"; or Franklin Roosevelt's projection during World War II for "survival" of his "Four Freedoms"; or John Kennedy's reformulation of both as struggling "to make the world safe for diversity"; or no-less-utopian Lyndon Johnson's recent "We have learned to despise the witch hunt, the unprincipled harassment of a man's integrity and his right to be different." Few, if any, have challenged the manifold specifications of the right to be different that compose the Universal Declaration of Human Rights, whose professors purport to represent almost all the peoples of the world. Not a little in consequence of the American experience, even the Roman hierarchy, through Pope John XXIII's Ecumenical Council, has given reluctant recognition to men's right to be different and to their joining together to assure to one another equal liberty and equal safety in differing.

That Mankind's professed goals may be, and largely are, pretensions with which they mask practices is so all-pervading a commonplace that it need only be mentioned. The record, however, discloses that professions can and do project new goals with new ways and means to them; it has persuaded me that to date, at least, the ever-revolutionary American credo and the American people's experience and reformulations of it have prompted societies everywhere on the globe to turn to new goals and to seek new ways of which the beginning without end is the right of the different to equal liberty and equal safety.

Does the record as I read it bring me confidence that *Homo sap's* struggling will achieve its goal? What odds do the statesman, churchman, scientist, or bookmaker give on peoples' diverse struggles thus to live on? How do I bet, in view of the once unimaginable odds these struggles have created since the turn of the century? In view of the new knowledge and the new know-how incarnate in the engines that harness atomic power with atom smashers, atom bombs, automation, computers, rockets, and new chemicals? In view of the anxieties, the tears, the fears, the preoccupation with death, including the death of their gods, which the rationalizing Cassandras of the gospel of absurdity celebrate and demonstrate?

Having learned that reason serves best as neither a power nor an energy but as a prophecy before, or an accessory after, the event, that the event is the decision after decision which compounds into the individuality of each one's struggle to keep on struggling on decisions which reason serves as a viable aid or a formal hindrance —I bet on the struggler over event. I do not see that, first and last, any human life requires a sanction from any other existence, human or nonhuman, natural, supernatural, or unnatural. Nor do I find this a cause for tears and not for laughter; existentialist tearfulness seems to me as comic as perennial philosophy's cheerfulness. The circumambience, however its components be imagined, discovered, or constructed, comprises the conditions of each one's struggling on; if any become an authority that a struggler relies on, or a master he believes, obeys, and fights for, it is by the struggler's consent, because he has so taken it.

I do not see that extinction by dying can in any way render meaningless the living of life as it is lived. The living makes its own meaning, *is* the meaning, is all the meaning there can be. For each person it consists of this and no other singularity of faith and works struggling on, maintaining its integrity. Long or short, lives end with death; they become the nothing that they were before birth; their meaning perishes with them.

Epigones who afterward study, evaluate, reprobate, or worship the image they make up from a dead person's less perishable residue endow it with meanings or meaninglessnesses which but utter their own business and desires. To itself, no life lacks meaning, even if, like some professors and poets, it cultivates its own meaning by charging everybody else's life with lacking any. For all lives, their going on is goal enough.

Ever so often I recall Job, challenging omnipotence, declaring, "I have no hope, I know that he will slay me; nevertheless will I maintain my ways before him. Mine integrity hold I fast and will not let go; my heart shall not reproach me so long as I live." On

occasion, I recall how Pericles told his Athenians, in that unforget-
table funeral oration, that the secret of happiness is freedom and
the secret of freedom a brave heart. On other occasions I remember
de Tocqueville—"The man who asks of freedom anything other
than freedom, is born to be a slave."

I do not believe that in the nature of things there are many
such askers. I believe that those whom others judge to be such are
individuals who, still struggling against alienation of their unalienable right to be who they are and to become what they want to be,
get so absorbed in securing the means to their freedom that they
lose awareness that it is also the unalienable, all-deciding beginning
and end which chooses and changes the means. Like Arthur Miller's
salesman who died, they become aware again, if only to die.

Having learned and unlearned as I have, I find myself dis-
posed, when I encounter such an awareness, absurdly to seek conso-
lation from the feelings it arouses in the ever-resurrected cliché of a
laughing Roman: *Homo sum; nihil humanum a me alienum puto.*
Its absurd peer, in my own vernacular, would be: *There, but for the
grace of Lady Luck, go I.* If I have become a secularist and a hu-
manist, it is on these terms.

### Horace Meyer Kallen

*Dr. Horace Meyer Kallen has for six decades been one of America's
most stimulating philosophers. As a teacher of philosophy he is perhaps
best known for his long, distinguished tenure at the New School for
Social Research, where he is now professor emeritus of philosophy, and
research professor in social philosophy. He was born in Germany in
1882, and came to the U.S. when he was five. After graduating from
Harvard magna cum laude, he attended Princeton and Oxford, then returned to Harvard and received his Ph.D. in 1908. He has been a notable
figure at the New School since its founding in the 1930s. His works include* Art and Freedom, Cultural Pluralism and the American Idea, *and*
Liberty, Laughter, and Tears: Studies of the Role of Tragedy and
Comedy in the Freedom of Man.

SALVADOR DE MADARIAGA

# The Dangerous Lure
# of Parrotland

---

THE DARK NIGHT hangs like a black curtain before my idle, useless eyes. There is nothing there. Presently, the forerunners of the dawn announce that the light of the day is coming; dull, dumb lines emerge from nothingness, foreshadowing shapes; and no sooner has the ball of light burst over the edge of the hill than the world stands before my eyes in all its glory—the green treetops and the brown trunks and the green grass and the rivulet that runs leisurely through its velvet, carrying in its wavelets tail ends of blue sky, and the cottage, a cool white in the shade this side of the corner edge and a dazzling white beyond where the horizontal lines start downward, and the red tiles above—every detail so clear, so well defined, outlined, differentiated, and the whole now so full of sense!

Such is the joy of the human being who casts on the world of things the light of his intellect. In so doing, he creates the world— so far as he is concerned. He endows the world with a sense, and everything in it with an outline of its own. I have never grown weary of that joy, and can still remember the days when I felt man's reason capable of grasping and disentangling everything. I can still remember the pleasure of reading it all compressed in Pascal's wonderful formula, *L'homme n'est qu'un roseau, le plus faible de la nature, mais il est un roseau pensant*—"Man is but a reed, the weakest in nature, but he is a thinking reed."

I have learned that the relation between man's thought and life is more complex than that. Thought is but part of life and a part cannot grasp the whole. "Ah, but if I stand aside and look at life and see it all, am I not grasping it?" The argument is tempting but not convincing. Thought can grasp the thought of life. Life itself evades its grasp. And this revelation sobers—or ought to sober—wise philosophers.

If knowledge means the reduction of "that there outside me" to a set of ideas acceptable to the intellect, life is unknowable. That I came to learn. I am not sure, though, that I had not already guessed it by intuition—not by a flash of it, as the saying goes, but by a mist of it, so to speak. Thus I never could apply myself seriously to philosophic thought, and seldom read philosophers. If their books are well written (which is seldom the case) I enjoy them. I read Bergson with more zest than Balzac. But I still have to read a book of philosophy which convinces me of the truth of what it says or stands for. Though here and there fruitful and enjoyable, it all seems to me as a general lore an idle if most sophisticated exercise or game.

Science is—was—another matter. Truly, here was the light of day creating the world and giving it a sense. What joys could equal those of analytic geometry? To discover that every point in space could be described by three numbers and every curve by an equation—was there a more beautiful fairy tale? And, that the easiest way to calculate a dynamo was through the use of the square root of $-1$, which does not "exist," and yet the dynamo works?

But calculus is only a vehicle that conveys what is trusted to it from one point to another. It adds nothing to the knowledge of what is being conveyed. And I was led to think that science is but the accurate picture of that aspect of the world which we could grasp. Later I became even more modest. The world revealed to us by science is but a projection of our own minds on reality, mirrored back by reality on our own minds.

I have come to think—or at least suspect—not only that reality *an sich* is unknowable, but that it is unthinkable. Any variation in the scope of our senses would fundamentally change our perception of it—new colors and new sounds would suddenly become part of our experience. And who knows what Titians or Beethovens we are missing who would express themselves not merely through our senses enlarged but through other senses than those we do possess? The world we see and hear, smell and touch, is but a tiny part of a world we don't know. Nay, we only know this world as it is because the senses we have outline it so for us—because, therefore, of the limitations of our senses and because of our lack of other senses. What the world would be like for us, were we endowed with other or better senses, we have no idea. What the real world is like, we can imagine still less. Has the concept *real world* any real sense? Or would *reality* be just the verbal symbol for an urge, a guess, an intuition of the permanent or eternal under the constant flow and ebb of appearances?

I should thus set down as my first lesson a conversion from faith in the power of the intellect to a modest view of the intellectual powers of man which would put actual, real knowledge beyond man's hope or faith. The most we can hope for in this field is to understand and describe certain aspects of the relations between man's mind and the Mystery. The Mystery itself remains impenetrable.

While, with the years, my faith in the powers of the intellect has gradually become fainter, my confidence in human sensibility has grown. In other words, while I believe less and less that we can grasp "nature," I believe more and more that, at least at fleeting moments, we may feel, experience, taste it. This privilege goes by the name of grace. It may come to the saint or to the artist. It may come to any human being who lives a moment of sanctity or of inspiration. These moments are rare, intimate, profound, and apt to be protected by a mist of shyness. The favored one is not likely to speak about them. They may be more frequent than meets the eye or the ear.

Were I therefore asked whether the philosopher or the scientist on the one hand or the saint or the poet on the other can get closer to the Mystery, I should not hesitate, for the philosopher and the scientist endeavor to penetrate the Mystery, while the saint and the poet let themselves be penetrated by it. So, in my dramatic poem in French, "*Le Mystère de la Mappemonde*," Rosemonde says to Mercure:

> *By action unceasing*
> *I will penetrate the meaning;*

But Mercure retorts:

> *Rather let it be the sense*
> *Which penetrates your being.*

And this is another lesson learned in life: Thou must know how to remain passive before the world. Let the soul hollow itself in the shape of a riverbed for life to flow undisturbed by the untutored movements of the self, and the vital flow will vivify the riverbed and make it feel and taste that which is.

This conviction, gradually grown by experience, has enlightened me about my instinctive ambivalent attitude toward information. Knowledge is the usual word, or perhaps scholarship. Now, though possessed by an insatiable curiosity about everything, from mathematics to theology, I also feel a definite repulsion toward acquiring concrete, precise facts. At first sight, this feature might seem a paradox or even a contradiction—"I am curious but I do not want to know about things"—and as such it has struck me when I began to observe this double trend in my nature. It is, though, less paradoxical than it sounds. Curious about the essence of things; averse to details and so-called facts. So, in the end, I was able to explain that odd feeling I had that, throughout my life, I had spent a good deal of ingenuity dodging knowledge.

Since this trend to dodge knowledge was there before I observed it, I can hardly say that I have learned it. What I did learn was how to account for it. This discovery confirmed and invigorated another of my spontaneous tendencies—that which led me from the first to seek in character and personality the root of all happenings between men. Born and bred at the time when the controversy over Marxism was at its height, I was never able to generate any interest in the primacy of either politics or economics. Both seem to me mere forms of psychology; and age and experience have but confirmed my first intuition. Character, both individual and national, is, I gradually learned, terribly constant. Variable, of course, but constant. Another paradox? By no means. A hyperbola and a parabola vary but are constant and faithful each to its shape and equation. In other words, you can train a wild pony into a good saddle or draft horse, but you will never train it into an elephant. This, then, I learned in life: that a man's actions and reactions are like the fruit of a tree, and you cannot expect apples from a pear tree. And the same goes for nations.

A sobering, indeed a melancholy, thought. It does not altogether abolish the value of education, moralizing, advice, guidance; but it considerably reduces its scope—the scope, I mean, optimistic pedagogues attribute to such things. I will own that I was slower in realizing this truth in what concerns nations than in the case of men. I believe I can adumbrate the reason for this. In the case of individual behavior, it soon dawned upon me that man acts on impulses determined by complex systems of rational and irrational forces and influences, the shape of which is peculiar to the individual concerned. In the case of collective action, it is tempting to think that, since individual action is always at least in part irrational, the group can only coordinate its collective will by shedding these irrational, individual elements. In other words, reason would (in this view) be the common ground on which to build collective action.

This way of thinking seems to me to have inspired the founders and advocates of the League of the Nations. We were, of course, mistaken. It is quite possible to reach a consensus of collective action in utter irrationality if and when the individuals concerned share the same irrational passion. A few years of service as an international official in Geneva, followed by another period of years as Spanish Representative, soon convinced me of this fact. Nations remained faithful to themselves, faithful above all to their own peculiar form of foolishness. No pears from the apple tree.

There is another lesson I owe to those years rich in experience. It is also sobering and melancholy. I should like to come to it by way of my symbolic French play. Mercure says to Rosemonde he is to lead her to the Land of Parrots, whereupon Rosemonde asks:

> Does such a country exist?

And Mercure answers:

> All that resists does exist
> and nothing resists the spirit,
> as a well-trained parrot.

Parrots. Parrots all or most of us. Terrible thought. Mercure formulates it ruthlessly:

> As your wisdom becomes severed
> from your being, it topples down.
> Your wisdom becomes your thought;
> your thought becomes your words;
> and your words turn into parrots.

This is the bitterest lesson of all. When our wisdom is severed from our being it rapidly degenerates. Wisdom sets into thought, thought into words, words go . . . parrot. It seems to be inevitable and fatal. I am feeling it at the moment I write these words. There goes my wisdom down the path to parrotry.

Project all this onto the plane of institutions. The movement will begin with a faith. The faith will push the faithful to collective action. They will start a church. The church will need a sacristy. And lo and behold, soon the church will have overgrown the faith and the sacristy will have overgrown the church; and the poor faith will have to be content with burning modestly in some obscure chapel, the darker for that little flame burning in its night. Here again, it all seems inevitable and fatal.

A warning to spiritual leaders. Holiness proclaims peace among men. Politics pleads for peace in Vietnam. Holiness may think the time has come to plead for peace in Vietnam. It must, however, be clear that in so doing Holiness runs a risk, a terrible risk—that of toppling down the cascade into thought, words—parrotry.

Politics nearly always does. When Rosemonde and Mercure arrive in the Land of Parrots, treading on the narrow path that separates the White from the Red Parrots, four White Parrots (or Red, it doesn't matter) in succession say:

> Something that stirs.
> This is very disquieting.
> It is not a red parrot.
> Therefore it is a white parrot.

The deeply felt wisdom, grown from the seeds planted in us by Socrates and Christ, severed from our lifeblood, has become thought—Locke, Rousseau, Marx—and inevitably gone parrot. The tumult of it! As for knowing, finding out, concluding. . . . Many years ago, an Englishman arriving in Montevideo asked a

Uruguayan companion on board ship, "What is your political setup here?" And this was the answer. "We have two parties; one composed of all the good men, patriotic, competent, decent; the other made up of all the rabble and thieves of the country. *But we don't know which is which.*"

The trend of our day is dispersive—it leads to analysis, specialization, details. That way lies Parrotland. We shall not rescue our communities from that misery unless, at least now and then, we dive to essentials. Unfortunately, the era lives under the sway of empiricism, and one of the direct consequences of this trend is a real obsession with economic problems. However, both the political and economic approaches are bound but to skim the surface of things, since both politics and economics are forms of an essence which is the soul of man. The true approach therefore is through psychology and ecology.

I was fourteen when I first read on the frontispiece of French official buildings the famous trinitarian slogan: LIBERTY. EQUALITY. FRATERNITY. I was attracted by its conciseness as well as by a triangular quality that fitted the neoclassical architecture of most of the buildings which it hallowed for the French freethinker. Throughout the years, I have learned to probe the meaning and value of its second term, the most controversial and perhaps—not for the philosopher but for the psychologist—the most important.

Liberty evokes a need. Fraternity, a hankering or an ideal. But Equality stakes a claim, utters a protest, forecasts a rebellion. It is at the root of the class war and of the struggle for a classless society.

I believe it was in some writings of Leonardo that I came across the definition of classes. There are three. They are natural. They are permanent and unchangeable. *Those who see. Those who see when they are shown. Those who do not see.* It is a marvelous classification. It bears some mulling over.

To begin with, the human beings who compose these three classes may vary according to the aspect of lore or life that is being considered. Einstein would be in Class 1 on mathematics; but I have heard him on politics and he was, well, he was not in Class 1. This brings in some comfort. But by and large, we may accept Leonardo's classification as providing the framework for the ideal form for a human society.

I had been led to think, on similar though not identical lines, that one might consider three classes: the aristocrats (in the original sense of the word), the bourgeoisie, and the people; the first, being led by intuition and working for the future; the second, being ruled by reason and concerned with the present; the third, impersonating the instincts and rooted in the past.

These two classifications are models—paradigms. They are to our societies what a sphere is to a potato. Our political tensions correspond to the distance in shape between our society and its classes, such as they are, and the models they tend or long to be. These tensions express the dissatisfaction caused by a double injustice; and it is this double character of the injustice which I deem to be here the important lesson I learned. First, a divine, natural, or prenatal injustice. One is born first, second, or third class in the natural—i.e., Leonardo's—scale. We can do nothing about it. Then, a social injustice: One is born first class by nature, but into a second or third by rank—or any other combination that can be imagined—all of which, except that which combines nature, vocation, and social first class, give rise to a tension.

It is the sum total of these tensions which gives substance and impulse to the claim for equality. I have come to think that it is an unreasonable claim, because it does not conform to the facts of nature. (No one disputes equality before the law. That is another point and an obvious one.) In fact, I have come to think that a society without differences of level would not work; and I suspect that the many difficulties most prosperous societies are encountering are due to the rubbing out of level-differences by a number of causes, but in particular by the machinery of the Welfare State. (Nothing wrong with Welfare—everything wrong with State.)

.     .

I have been enumerating lessons learned through meditation and experience—none of them, it must be owned, of an exhilarating nature. Is there a ray of light somewhere, though? For otherwise, why live? The balance must be positive, somehow, since we do carry on, and the number of suicides is not striking. Our problems do seem to be insoluble, so why try to solve them? Here is the chink through which the ray of light may penetrate. *Our problems are not there for us to solve them but for them to solve us.* Hence, our zest for life. Whether we know it or not, our aim in life is— happiness? No. Not happiness. Shrewd though he was, Jefferson did doze here. We are not in this world in order to flutter about from flower to flower in pursuit of the pollen of happiness, but to find out all about ourselves through thought, passivity, and activity. And for that aim our problems, our insoluble problems, are our best tools.

It is on this thought that I learned to found my liberalism. Liberty is the bread of man's spirit, for the aim of man is to realize himself in experience, and experience without freedom is like that landscape in the night with which I began. It is simply not there. Traveling on this road, I soon came to think that the argument for liberty should not be founded only on the dignity of man but on his indignity as well, or at any rate, his unworthiness. On his dignity, because since Christ died on the cross every man has been shown to possess that spark of divinity which every other man must respect; on his indignity because, since Socrates has shown that the world is so subtle and complex that no man can by himself comprehend more than a tiny corner of it, no man's opinion can be held to be the truth; and that therefore no man can claim to be wise enough to coerce his brother's thoughts.

Thus I learned to see freedom of thought as a necessity, not merely for the citizen as a man but for the community as a collective human being, since without the free discussion of as many individual views as possible, the community could not know itself.

The form of government is a problem that has long fascinated me. Why should a mere *form* arouse such passions in men? And why, in our old Europe, the politically most successful nations should all be monarchies with the exception of Switzerland? I believe I came to solve this conundrum, in the framework of a psychological picture of Europe. From what I later will say on my *Portrait of a Man Standing*, let me borrow the system of coordinates which I there sketched: a cow and a tree—the cow symbolizing the horizontal, herdlike, collective; the tree, the vertical, individual tendencies in man. Let me also guard against any reproach of exaggeration. I simplify so as to be clear; but, of course, all tendencies live in all men.

The flash, I believe, was a phrase of Bayle which I found in a book on *The Praise of Drunkenness*. It put forward the view that the Europeans could be divided into lovers of Venus and lovers of Bacchus; and when Luther and Calvin split the faith of the Continent, the lovers of Venus remained Catholic, while the lovers of Bacchus became Protestant. This revelation led to many more. I then saw why the Protestants locked up their bottles and the Catholics their girls—with equal success or lack thereof. But how could I remain blind to the fact that the political success went also with Protestantism and with the monarchial system (always excepting Switzerland)?

The next step came from my international experience. I shall picture it thus: Put Europeans round a table; throw a problem on it; and the Europeans will roughly fall into two groups: Those who ask, *What* is to be done? Those who ask, *Who* is going to do this? Let us describe these two groups as "the peoples-what" and "the peoples-who." The former are interested in the thing. The latter, in the person. Thing, in Latin, *res*. Therefore, by nature, no matter their regimes, the peoples-what are republican; and the peoples-who are monarchist. Hence the solution of my conundrum.

The peoples-what, being interested in the thing, deal with it effectively. Public affairs run a normal and, on the whole, a smooth course. There is, therefore, no need to alter the system. The form of government inherited from the past is allowed to carry on. In most cases it was a monarchy; a monarchy it remains. In one case—that of Switzerland—it was a republic. And it remains a republic.

The peoples-who are interested in the person. They neglect the thing. Public affairs don't work; ill humor, irritation become general, and make matters worse. Public opinion turns against the regime. It used to be a monarchy. It was thrown overboard. A republic replaced it. It was thrown overboard. And so on.

Conclusion: Only republican peoples can run a monarchy—or a republic.

This success in the handling of their collective affairs may be the cause of the arrogance observable in the Nordics. The corresponding feature in the south is pride. Arrogance is collective, herdlike, "cow." Pride is individual, lone-beast-like, "tree." These then would appear to be the two poles of the European psyche, best incarnated respectively by Britain and by Spain. France oscillates between her Protestant-arrogant "cow" north and her Catholic, proud "tree" south. You will say all Frenchmen are atheists. Well, not all. But many. Yet one can be an atheist in a Protestant and in a Catholic way; the first argues God out of court, the second fights against Him for dear life. So atheists and believers may differ in the substance but not in the form and attitude of their faith or lack of it. At present, France is living on the Catholic side of the pendulum —all pride.

Few men realize nowadays that a number of European ideals, dreams, were day-to-day realities which some of us have known in our lifetime. Until 1914, a European could travel from Lisbon to Stockholm, from Dublin to Athens, with no papers whatever, let alone visas and such things; and in France, Belgium, Switzerland, Italy, and Greece, the silver and gold coins of the five countries circulated with equal freedom. The period 1871–1914 was in Europe remarkably quiet. Scandals, such as the *affaire Dreyfus* or the shooting of Ferrer, later the Sacco-Vanzetti case, shook the world with indignation. I was present as a schoolboy at the impressive gathering of the Paris Cour de Cassation which finally exonerated Dreyfus. I helped a Paris barrister who led the campaign of European protest against the shooting of Ferrer. I more than once discussed the Sacco-Vanzetti case with Frankfurter (later of the Supreme Court) both before and after I had a window of my car broken, as it stood one night at the parking court of the League of Nations building, by a body of irate pro–Sacco-Vanzetti enthusiasts who, for reasons unknown perhaps even to themselves, made the League of Nations responsible for the execution of the two anarchists.

Let this relative placidity of those days be my excuse for having fallen into the naïveté of feeling that Hitler's invasion of Austria was a monstrous, unimaginable crime. I still remember my astonishment and indignation when the news came through the tape as I stood in Scott Mowrer's room in the Chicago *Daily News* building. We all had to confess that we had forgotten that man carries within all the savagery of animal creation. Hitler and Stalin made us learn bitter lessons. We should never forget them again. The wild beast is there under the civilized citizen of the world community.

This lesson was the most humiliating of all. It raised a host of question marks in the mind. First of all, political. Plebiscites, direct votes—are these crude methods legitimate in a civilized community in order to ascertain the will of, what? The people? The mass? The nation? An avenue which would take too long to explore here. Let me say this only: I came to think that a number of time-honored ways adopted by liberal democracy needed revising, and their underlying ideas needed to be rethought.

A mass is not worth consulting, for it is a rough, collective female human being which longs for a male. It does not become a people until it is organized into institutions. A nation is a people conscious of itself. Therefore, a nation is not the mere sum total of its individuals, but the integration of its institutions. It follows that direct universal suffrage does not conform to social nature, for it rests on the idea of mass, not of people or of nation. I am fully aware of the unpopular character of these conclusions, but I believe they happen to be right. A powerful draft of the fresh air of liberty must come to strengthen the true basis of democracy, which is the municipal community. The power descending from the top must be checked and balanced by the power rising from below; for otherwise, the absolutist trend of democracy will wipe out liberty from our midst. This lesson I learned from the British before they forgot it themselves.

Then the appalling cruelty of Bolshevism and Nazism drove me to think again over the problem of violence in public affairs. One still reads in books written by honest people that what is wanted in this or that country or in the world is a revolution, preferably with a capital "R" and preferably violent. I believe that this faith in revolution is utter trash. I do not say that faith in the aims or even in the results of revolution is trash. That would depend on which revolution is being discussed. What I am saying is that faith in revolution as a political method is trash. For instance, the French Revolution brought nothing but blood, tears, and delay to an evolution which, without it, would have achieved the same good results much better and much more quickly. Likewise, if the American people had listened to Jefferson's advice on slavery, they would have spared themselves the Civil War.

I am not saying that revolutions and civil wars should not happen. I am not arguing against political earthquakes. Revolutions just turn up. Men prove unable to get on with the work of collective life without enough of them sitting tight on their prejudices and privileges until another set of them loses patience. What I am saying is that we must not glorify revolutions. For a nation to say, "In 1789 (1688, 1784, etc.) I went through a glorious revolution," is just as foolish as for a man to say, "In 1946 I had a glorious appendicitis."

Finally, this dreadful outburst of animal cruelty our generation has witnessed raised again the problem which tortured so many minds, and which Dostoevski dramatized in his novels. If God, why evil? I have tried to tackle it in *Portrait of a Man Standing.* This book is mostly a discussion on what happened with the quadruped when he became a biped, and why he chose to do so. While on this trek, I try to "spy on the Creator" in the hope of catching glimpses of His mind at work. I think I have learned a number of things in the process, but I could hardly state them clearly enough at the end of this essay. Needless to say, the problem of evil remains unsolved.

The evening begins to fall. Gray mists begin to soften the outlines of the landscape. Soon the black curtain of the night will fall on the scene and on the play. But one thing will remain as a certitude, the chief lesson of all: The Artist that created the world —nay, the Artist that creates the world—ever at work, directs evolution not merely cowlike, horizontally, from bones to bones, but vertically, like a line of trees, from inspiration to inspiration in His ever active Spirit.

### Salvador de Madariaga

*Salvador de Madariaga is an internationally active and renowned writer, philosopher, and diplomat. When he writes of world affairs and of human dilemmas he brings to bear on his subjects not only a brilliant sensibility, but a wide range of practical experience. He was born in 1886 in Corunna, Spain, obtained his higher education in Madrid and at technical institutes in Paris, and began his working life as an engineer and technical adviser for a Spanish railway. Later he became a journalist and literary critic in London, gravitated to the League of Nations, became*

Spain's chief delegate to the League, and eventually was made Spanish ambassador to the United States and to France. He has taught at Princeton, Oxford, and the University of Mexico, is an honorary fellow of Oxford and lives in Oxford, England. His books include Portrait of Europe and Portrait of a Man Standing.

# ROBERT MOSES

## Confessions
## of a Reformed Reformer

---

I AM a Boethian among the philosophers. In such company any profession of faith or ultimate aim, by one who is often characterized as a bulldozer, is bound to seem sophomoric. If any apologia is called for, I am a middle-of-the-road pilgrim, content, like the great convert Cardinal, to take one step at a time toward the distant goal. I have no lively expectation of more than a glimpse of the Promised Land, and perhaps a forlorn hope that at the Pearly Gates some accredited friend among the faithful may vouch for me, but expect to hear no trumpets on the other side.

I have learned nothing that has changed my mind about limited objectives or which leads me to believe that, in state and local government especially, contemptuous disregard of the past, clowning, daily inspirations, rosy promises, importation of more and more experts who do not know the points of the compass in a strange environment, application of analogies which do not apply, reorganizations on paper along functional lines, are substitutes for painfully slow, persistent, indefatigable, step-by-step progress. These are the stuff of politics, not effective administration. No doubt we must ordinarily tolerate politics, and in easy times this is not too unpleasant a diet, but there must be an embargo on it where genuine crises and malice domestic must be met and really drastic improvements are required. It is a kind of war, and in war we are supposed to be united.

I fear that my excursion into philosophy will appear trite and crudely practical. I know that it does not follow that because a man has been through a lot he must have come out of it a deep thinker. The builder rarely has time or patience to stop and try on another man's shoes. Maybe it's all just a matter of pace. Perhaps the hare is simply hurrying faster into the hassenpfeffer and the tortoise more slowly and just as inevitably into Terrapin Maryland.

The other day I picked up a typical promotion advertisement from *American Home* picturing the scientific millennium which is just ahead of us. Here are a few quotations:

More radical changes in the American Way of life will occur during the second half of the twentieth century than in all the preceding sixty-six years. . . .

Microwaves will cook food. Laser light beams will disintegrate the household garbage. And, ultrasonic waves will replace water for dishwashing. The housewife will shop via closed-circuit television and after registering her selections on a punch card, a computer will automatically total the cost and deduct the amount from her bank account. Disposable towels, sheets, and pillow cases, self-cleaning curtains, and mahogany styled, never wear aluminum floors will further shorten domestic labors. . . .

The pure and healthy atmosphere of the home will have been automatically set through light, temperature, and humidity controls. Domestic water and heat will be economically reused, making the house independent of outside supply. Fresh oxygen will be created by converting carbon dioxide, while solar storage batteries will be turning the sun's rays to heating water and powering appliances. . . .

Allowing for Madison Avenue burble, this pronouncement fills me with longing for the shack on the barrier beach and the lodge in some vast wilderness. The goal looks more like a mechanical labor-saving museum than a triumph of civilization. I entertain the hope, alive in the heart of every park and outdoor man, that somehow we shall be able to provide a month's vacation away from the charged American home in the city or suburb, approached by Whitman's long brown path and the corduroy road, boardwalk, and sandy trail which will lead from the best parkways and expressways money can buy and we can build to the borders of the shore and the wilderness.

What else have I learned in my peregrinations?

First, as to democracy, with the generic small "d." I have learned to be chary of political slogans, patriotic claims and assertions, clichés, and Fourth of July oratory. Whatever they may accomplish in battle, slogans are no good in controversial public works. The progression is always the same. First the slogan, then the demagogue, then extravagant promises, then delay, disappointment, disillusion, resentment, cynicism, contempt for public authority and order, and finally any handy weapon to get even with society. At best a slogan is little more than the hoarse défi of a football song in the late fall. It needs youth or nostalgia and probably a flask to put it over.

I believe in democracy as a matter of faith, hope, and charity, not as an unchallengeable dogma beyond debate. I do not agree with the sour criticism of Henry Adams that this dogma is being eroded and degraded to a level at which its survival is doubtful. This Adams was one of the last of a great breed, a bored New England intellectual, an aristocrat happiest abroad, who had lost the common touch and the grip of his ancestors on the American dream. I go with Lincoln, who indulged in no frantic boast or foolish word, but prayed that this nation, so nobly conceived, might not perish from the earth.

My skepticism, or shall I say caution, about threats to the further implementation and early realization of the democratic dream has been reinforced by recent experiences with new republics, notably African, at the New York World's Fair. I read astonishing books on the East and West African slave trade and thought off and on about the millions in other lands who could live handsomely off our garbage. We met leaders and learned something of their problems. One state head, a big, attractive, and impressive personality, was assassinated shortly after his visit to Flushing Meadow, and no one seems to have been able to find out how it came about. Another, a distinguished pediatrician who was temporarily detached from his hospital in a republic of over three million people carved out of the French Sahara, when questioned about the number of college-educated men in his nation, said there were thirteen. In another case all the highest-court British judges were kept on pending the graduation and training of natives from a law school just opened.

The internal feuds in African states were a byword and beyond comprehension by strangers. Some of these countries do not have a viable economy. Some have all their resources in an area at odds with neighboring provinces. All this is trite. It adds up to a question of how long at best it will take to establish stable governments and economies and whether, regardless of their unpopularity, dropping the pilots so fast makes for anything but shipwreck. The World's Fair also taught us that national independence, rising from dated colonialism, and annihilation of distance do not necessarily produce friendship, but that healthy rivalry in the competitive Olympic tradition and spirit is the best way to promote mutual respect and peace.

Another question raises an ugly head—do we in fact ourselves have ideal solutions to offer? Have we done so well recently that we are anointed of the Lord to recommend our formula or prescription to others of very different antecedents and ideologies? After the Spanish-American War, General Leonard Wood, who narrowly escaped the Presidency, handed Cuba a government exactly like ours on the curious assumption that what is good for us must be equally good for the Cubans. Behind the façade of the Cuban Constitution, the traditional Caribbean apparatus continued as before.

This brings me to our new concept of representative government. What is representative government? Surely it is government by trusted elected officials at various levels, chosen to use their brains, experience, and courage to meet current issues on the basis of pledged principles, planks, and platforms. These representatives are supposed to exercise judgment. If they fail or the public changes its mind, they may be replaced by others. In the interval they will, of course, study the shifts and vagaries of public opinion, and would not be either human or effective if they were not influenced by the trends. But what can be said for government by public opinion polls and pressures and the unwillingness of our representatives to act until every conceivable interest, class, group, federation, minority, and club affiliation has been canvassed and the net results weighed and balanced in terms of votes?

It is beginning to be realized that recent excursions of the Supreme Court into the thicket of political organization may be more dangerous to democracy than subversion. Take, for example, the one man–one vote dictum which gives no representation to acres as against people and concentrates all power in crowded municipalities. Our entire Federal Government depends on the equality of representation of states in the Senate. Why does not the same logic apply *within* states? The one man–one vote dictum is now being applied by the inferior courts all the way down through state legislatures to county supervisors, city and village boards. Area representation is permitted, but only by fractional voting. We seem to have invented The Fractional Man.

All drastic reforms based on slogans —and one man–one vote on honest reflection *is* a slogan—are to be viewed with suspicion. I am a reformed reformer and have learned that gadgets and devices of government do not produce the millennium and would make the world a dull place if they did. In international affairs the United Nations, like its predecessor, has become a Tower of Babel echoing noble pronouncements. True, we know nothing better. In state and municipal affairs I have seen the short ballot, executive budget, consolidated departments, efficiency and economy systems adopted, proportional representation tried and found wanting, and the literacy test tossed in the ashcan on the assumption that it is not necessary to speak and read English to vote on complex political issues. The fate of most reports or white papers is oblivion. The public official concerned releases them to the press with assurances of action and then forgets them. The forum is strewn with the *disjecta membra* of investigations.

An honest observer must conclude that men, not measures, and leadership, not absolute equality, in the final tests determine the results. All people are not the same size, and denial of superior talent and leadership is fatal in a highly competitive society. Demagoguery is not leadership. It ends with tyranny. Ostracism may keep it within bounds, but only his mortality makes man bearable. It is true that the greatest of leaders unfortunately sometimes become tyrannical with time. France, having been saved, has bequeathed to the world the Cross of Lorraine.

I have learned that enterprises of great pith and moment with currents running against them are not to be achieved by diplomacy, magic, and charm. At a meeting at Niagara on the power program, with all its ramifications reaching into homes, plants, streets, rails, and scenery, before an audience which could hardly have been called enthusiastic, I remarked that on a similar occasion a public official, returning home, was asked what kind of a reception he had received. "Mixed," said he. "Good and rotten." I told the Niagara folks that as chairman of the State Power Authority I would be respected, didn't care a damn about immediate popularity, but hoped some affection might develop. It worked out that way.

The same thing happened on the St. Lawrence. Here I cut the working time from seven to five years. We saved on the American side some $11,000,000 by this simple device, and we built an international project without a written contract between New York and

Ontario. "You can't build by law," said Governor Smith—meaning that only informal methods and personal trust between heads of big enterprises get results. The late Beardsley Ruml once said to me more or less facetiously, "If the end doesn't justify the means, what does?" I suppose he meant that the ends are paramount and the means secondary and that most bureaucrats are concerned only about safe, orthodox means. Beardsley was much more than a wise-cracker. I suppose he also implied that we must at times accept compromises however distasteful, expensive, face-saving, and fool-ish, provided the principle remains in sight.

Along the Niagara and St. Lawrence they put my name on some landmarks. These, however, may not be durable memorials. I recall a ferry boat on the East River named after a borough presi-dent who was caught off base, tagged out, and sent to the hoose-gow. What to my astonished eyes should appear but a new name on the bow and stern. The *Maurice Connolly* had become the *Gold Star Mother*. Such is fame.

Leaders without supporters are of no avail, but there must be teamwork, that is, loyal aides, not merely *muchachos* who like the leader, but a self-respecting staff devoted to principles. One of our prominent elective officials, following a meeting to which I brought my top men, asked me to stay and then said, "How do you get such people?" I replied, "You have to *earn* that." I have learned that earning colleagues has become more difficult. The number of younger men with an instinct for the jugular and a thirst for mar-tyrdom seems to become smaller.

I have learned to revaluate the old-line political bosses. They had their virtues. The ancient loyalties which the old roughneck bosses exemplified included not only generosity, no doubt usually involving some direct or indirect public expense, but gratitude, which is increasingly rare and never purchasable. The old paternal-ists, it must be admitted in retrospect and by comparison, had few embarrassing standards. They had bluff, kind hearts, a merry twin-kle in the eye, and no illusions of divine guidance or moral superiority. Their handouts, inevitably taken over by government and institutionalized and bureaucratized, had a pleasant human quality not found in what John Boyle O'Reilly called "a cautious, statistical Christ."

Shrewd observers of government will recall the old chestnut about the political leader who met a treacherous former pal at a bar and asked him to explain why he had deserted him. The Benedict Arnold replied, "You ain't done nothing for me lately." This familiar attitude was perhaps more elegantly described by the witty Talleyrand in a cozy talk with Alexander of Russia. "Sire," he said, "loyalty is a question of dates."

The New York Times, usually enthusiastic about all municipal reform, said recently:

Deputy Mayor [of New York] Timothy W. Costello, a former professor of psychology at New York University, is recruiting an unpaid Council of Psychologists to concentrate on such major city problems as crime, addiction, and alcoholism. Dr. Costello also wants some of them to observe meetings of city officials, including Mayor Lindsay's cabinet, in order to "contribute to increased rationalization of decision-making in municipal government."

Dr. Jacob Chwast, immediate past president of the New York Society of Clinical Psychologists and head of the screening committee for Dr. Costello's proposed council, demurred somewhat. "Let us say," Dr. Chwast put it, "that we will help to maximize decision-making efficiency by eliminating noncontributory factors."

Take your choice of stated objectives, assuming you will find them comprehensible. Either way, putting politicians under psychological observation in their habitats will provide few surprises for the psychologist. They will find that the political "decision-making" processes are complicated by such elements as sibling rivalry, inordinate desire to please, rational and irrational fears, sublimated and unsublimated aggression, obsessive impulses, uncontrollable anxieties, delusions of grandeur, and recurrent ambivalence. . . .

In the process of learning, next to catchy slogans and mechanical gadgets, planning clichés are to be viewed with suspicion, accepted with reservations, and never regarded as cure-alls. Clichés are the *ipse dixits*, assurances and pontifications of articulate professional planners who have acquired status and utter commandments. In the humbler ranks and levels of municipal, metropolitan, and regional works the new reformers denounce almost everything that happened before they appeared on the unspoiled scene, deplore selfish, unregulated, unimaginative, unpatriotic growth and development which are ruining the land and its people, and either sink in nostalgia and longing for the good old days or demand an entirely new approach regardless of practicality and common sense.

Ruskin never tolerated the Industrial Revolution and George Eliot only reluctantly accepted the universe. The world has passed them by. But we have our doleful prophets who limn the decay of cities and demand magisterially that we wipe them out and start over. They go way beyond philosophy into actual building, for which they have no talent or tolerance. Constructive planners in the end must produce something more than words, something visible, palpable, tactile, livable, and workable. The others offer at most stimulating alternatives but nothing to serve as a guide to the less messianic laborers in the vineyard.

I have nothing against the philosophizing of the super-planners and their absorption in the higher strategy and the eternal verities. It is only when they itch to get their hands on practical problems that they become dangerous. Why must a thinker fool with steel, stone, and landscaping? In the ascending scale of benefactors of mankind, the philosopher undoubtedly ranks far above the ditchdigger, but the two classes should not be confused. I doubt whether the practitioners disagree about the lessons of their experience or claim any originality or novelty. We simply confirm and reinforce what has been said and done before. I have found from experience that solving a relatively small public works problem in a big city like New York takes all the talent of a first-class man. The roster of Baron Haussmanns who can achieve major comprehensive transformations is short indeed.

This brings me to Frank Lloyd Wright. Frank was an original and we shall probably not look upon his like again. He was a distant roundabout relative of my wife, who introduced me to the Cornish and Welsh fraternity in Wisconsin. Frank's uncle, Jenkin Lloyd Jones, was a Unitarian minister, civic leader, and reformer, immensely respected in Chicago. He boasted a benign countenance framed in a Santa Claus beard and was one of the great evangelists of our time. He christened my daughter Barbara. I called for him when the Ford World War I Peace Ship, which was captained by him and Dr. Aked, a New York Presbyterian minister, docked. The slogan of the ship was "Out of the trenches by Christmas." The irreverent and irrepressible Franklin P. Adams said it sounded more like a pedigree than a slogan. At any rate, some notion of Uncle Jenk's cheerful other-worldliness may be gained from a remark he made to me as we drove uptown from the pier. I asked him what the voyage had accomplished. He replied, "Well, Bob, we made a deep impression in the neutral countries."

Frank Lloyd Wright had at least a touch of genius, maybe more. Time will tell. There were also elements of the fearless pioneer, the Welsh bard, and the ham actor. Frank and I had a debate at the Princeton Bicentennial on planning, the arts, and architecture. Frank put it all over on me and was the center of adoring GIs and their brides, but his talk, as it appeared in print later, was pretty sorry stuff.

Our New York Commissioner of Buildings, Bernard Gillroy, who had risen from the inspectional ranks, insisted that Frank follow the Code in building the Guggenheim Museum. Frank modestly referred to himself as a genius and said all codes must yield to genius. From then on, as might have been expected, Gillroy threw the book at him. There was hardly an innovation which was not challenged.

At a luncheon in Florence, at which he received a gold medal, Frank told the Florentine Academy, a moribund institution revived for the occasion, that all his life Michelangelo had tried to get this medal, but that it remained for a simple lad from the dairy country of Wisconsin to earn it. The audience was flabbergasted, convulsed, and completely won over.

Anyway, from Frank I learned that if you think a builder is pedestrian and unimaginative you call him a mole and modestly insinuate that you yourself are a skylark. Frank was really humorous, forgiving, and completely without side. He did not try to impress his friends. That was reserved for public appearances. His larger planning excursions into roadside towns, thousand-story skyscrapers, and fantastic ramp garages were stimulating but never got beyond Frank's fantastic draftsmanship. One of his great disappointments was not having been invited to join the UN headquarters Board of Design. He told me they simply couldn't build it without him, but they did.

The list of clichés we learn to combat is too long for an exhaustive review supported by enough evidence to confound or infuriate the critics. In road building it includes dogmatic assertions that all elevated structures are bad and unnecessary, that traffic peak loads can be fully accommodated by forethought and recourse to imaginary funds, that rubber must pay for rails, that metropolitan transportation is all one thing and that an administrative umbrella should cover all its phases, that fatal as distinguished from minor accidents are due to faulty design of cars and incompetence of drivers rather than speed, that air pollution can be completely eliminated by drastic ukases, crackdowns, and official pronouncements rather than painful, long-range, step-by-step realism.

The same logic must rule earnest, honest attacks on pollution of streams and shores, noise, school integration, slum clearance, and the substitution of high modern residential buildings on small coverage of land. Hardly any other field of reform has been as grossly misrepresented as comprehensive slum clearance and few other officials as recklessly maligned as those in charge of it. The extension of the supreme power of eminent domain and huge write-downs in the cost of land acquisition were declared constitutional because of the paramount public interest in the entire elimination of housing ghettos. Slum clearance as such was the objective to be followed by whatever best suited the neighborhood. There was no requirement that all or part of the cleared area was to be devoted to the lowest income housing. In fact this would have been wholly unacceptable in the case of an area like Lincoln Square, keeping in mind the loss of taxes due to tax-exempt cultural lessees. It should be noted in passing that the fight for the new Fordham University campus for colleges of social sciences and law, largely replacing a Puerto Rican slum—as nasty and bigoted a performance as I can remember—was carried all the way to the United States Supreme Court on the issue of using public funds for a private religious institution.

It would take too long and invite too much misunderstanding to attempt to characterize the attitude of the modern press, and the communications, advertising, public relations, and image-projecting professions. The lesson I have learned, especially at the World's Fair, is to expect little steady, reliable press and air support, but much concern with "angles," sensational disclosures, fomenting controversies, and accentuating the negative. In journalism, in Gogarty's words, "Oh, boys, the things we have seen, the things we have seen." We have seen one big metropolitan newspaper after another fold, readers forming new habits, viewers not too happy with telescoped air news, and the old gossipy weeklies still flourishing.

A Wisconsin weekly I see now and then, going into its second century, has always carried the banner headline IT'S THE GLAD TYDINGS WE AIM TO BRING TO YOUR HOME. Where shall the conscientious official who is not a headliner find his news media and his support? More and more he must depend on readable, illustrated reports. The price of first-rate reports is lost in the cost of the tremendous sums we spend on design, administration, and building. No public official has a right to immunity from criticism. A certain amount probably does him good and reduces swellings. But snide, captious criticism terrorizes the weak, reduces the attractions of public work, and drives the strong into the comparative quiet of private business.

I have learned that critics build nothing. They did not deserve a World's Fair. The fault-finders denigrated the city, aggravated the malaise which affects the world, intensified differences, and fomented disorder. They made the tasks of management tougher, but we succeeded in spite of them. Over fifty-two million visitors testify to it. The critics arm their blowpipes with lethal arrows dipped in curare and shoot in all directions. Regardless of the victims, they are happy as long as there are fatalities.

I have learned to be ready to admit that higher education for every youngster is a dream of the future. Our colleges become too large, the teachers too far away, and the talent to profit by cultural as contrasted with practical courses beyond high school or junior college instruction is too limited. A college degree should not be the open sesame to earning a good living any more than a Ph.D. should be indispensable to a teacher. Almost every president of a small college wants, as the social workers say, to "eventuate on a larger scale," that is, to spread, create a university, add graduate schools, recruit football and basketball stars, a large hockey goalie, and a good baseball battery, and to have a huge silver mace carried in front of him in the academic processions.

I would settle in the immediate future for any educational system through high school and junior college which teaches pupils how to read, write, and speak simple English. We need not inculcate style or knowledge of the tyranny of words and the trickiness of metaphors—just a respect for simple unlatinized English. I would also require students to read music, not write or play it. I can't read a note myself but have learned to mark time.

As government proliferates and Parkinson's Law becomes more and more provable and less and less an amusing, farfetched academic witticism, public officials turn to Washington for contri-

butions to the arts, performing and static, and the amenities, inci-
dental and prevailing. Manifestly philanthropy cannot foot the bill
for all the fringe benefits of public works and all the rising demands
of a public clamoring for the good things of life, for self-expression,
for new manifestations of the eternal verities, and for cultivation of
increasing leisure. No wide-awake official can afford to be against
such things if he expects to keep abreast of the times, not to speak
of remaining in public favor; but must it all come from the Santa
Claus at the White House? The conservative local official wants to
go easy, remembers that there are unresolved wars with frightful
threats of annihilation, and that you can't have a truly great society
in a torn atomic world.

Those of us who function at the lower government levels,
viewing Washington from afar, learn that we are only pawns in a
cosmic chess game. In international affairs we live in a continuing
crisis. We don't know whether to step up containment in distant
disturbed danger spots regardless of future repercussions or to go on
with almost superhuman patience to cultivate and aid those who
march to a different drum. And with this puzzle goes another—
whether to continue to assume that huge, generous investments in
a Great Society and picking up the tabs for every municipal need
and adventure are consistent with prudent, audited foreign aid and
foreign military containment.

I have had some responsibility for several major self-supporting
public works, each costing a billion dollars, and have some notion
of the difficulty in spending so much legitimately, effectively, and
economically. Our professional almoners, the Commissioners of
Bread and Circuses, compete today for Federal gifts in no sense self-
liquidating, beyond the fondest imaginings of the prisoner in the
Chateau d'If, who later became the Count of Monte Cristo. This
abandoning of home rule and municipal and state responsibility
and begging the Federal Government for every variety of handout to
meet every local problem, has become known as creative federal-
ism, surely one of the trickiest, most dangerous slogans of our time.

We humble ditchdiggers suspect that the diagnostician or gynecologist with the glad hand, cheerful smile, and professional bedside manner may not be a better doctor than the old-fashioned general practitioner who frankly reports that the illness is serious and the outcome doubtful.

Here endeth the lesson. The local builder who has the nerve to say these things will probably be ridiculed, if not stoned, and suffer considerable hardship before time, native common sense, and decency come to his rescue. I verily believe that in the end the truth is mighty and will prevail, but the end sometimes seems a long, long way off.

### Robert Moses

*In more than a half-century of public service, Robert Moses probably has done more than any other individual to change the face of New York City and much of New York State. Departments, authorities, and commissions he has headed have directed construction of bridges, tunnels, power projects, parks, parkways, and other public works. Among them are New York City's Grand Central, Henry Hudson, Whitestone, Marine, Belt, and Hutchinson River Parkways, the Verrazano-Narrows and Triborough Bridges, Jones Beach State Park, and the New York–Canadian St. Lawrence River hydroelectric development. He has been New York State director of public works, secretary of state, parks commissioner, and chairman of the State Power Authority; New York City parks commissioner and a member of the City Planning Commission; and president of the New York World's Fair, 1964–1965. He is now chairman of the Triborough Bridge and Tunnel Authority and a member of the board of Lincoln Center.*

*He was born in Connecticut in 1888; holds degrees from Yale, Oxford, and Columbia; and is the author of many magazine articles. His books include* Theory and Practice in Politics *and* Working for the People.

# REINHOLD NIEBUHR

## Some Things I Have Learned

M Y SEARCHINGS of memory, mind, and heart have made me aware of the contrast between the critical nature of my opinions and the conventional nature of my vocations. I hasten to add that the critical nature of my opinions was due to historical circumstances and not to peculiar or private insights.

My conventional vocations included a Protestant pastorate in Detroit in the beginning of my career, followed by more than four decades of teaching on the faculty of Union Theological Seminary in New York, an interdenominational Protestant school for the training of ministers, where I served from 1928 until my retirement in 1960.

The critical nature of my opinions was occasioned by the general revolt against the culture of the eighteenth, nineteenth, and early twentieth centuries, in short, against the culture of a bourgeois period in Western history. The Industrial Revolution, two world wars, and a world depression had served to challenge the individualism and optimism of this culture in its estimate of the moral capacities of men.

Protestant liberalism shared the optimism and individualism expressed in this bourgeois culture. These views were drawn from the eighteenth- and nineteenth-century dogmas of the perfectabil-

233

ity of men. The secular element in the culture hoped that increasing rationality and the beneficent fruits of democratic institutions would change self-seeking behavior into a sense of responsibility for the welfare of one's neighbor. The religious element in the culture believed that religious norms and disciplines would transmute self-love into love of one's neighbor.

The whole of human history, however, refuted these illusory hopes. Men, according to the evidence of history, were driven both by self-regarding and by social impulses. But of the two, the first motive was undoubtedly dominant. Moreover, collective self-regard was revealed to be more powerful and persistent than individual egotism.

The new industrial civilization made these old facts about human nature more vivid, partly because its greater dynamism intensified class rivalries, which had been less obtrusive in agrarian feudalism. But this advance also meant that the industrial workers understood better than the peasants the nature of economic interests and the ideological elements in the moral explanations of the conflicts of these interests. The Marxist belief that the whole of history could be comprehended in the pattern of the class struggle was a dogmatic simplification of complex historical facts.

Obviously, collective self-regard was bound to defy the norms of pure love and disinterested reason. Men, acting in classes, races, and nations, might achieve a tolerable harmony with their fellows only by arbitrating their competitions by standards of discriminate justice, or by stratagems that would discover the point of concurrence between the more parochial and the more universal interests.

My critical views of the old optimism and individualism were first induced by a radical variant of Protestant liberalism known as the social gospel. This movement may be described as a belated response of the Protestant conscience to the injustices of modern industry and to the moral irrelevancies of liberal norms to modern collective problems. I came under the influence of this movement in my graduate studies at Yale University. When I assumed my academic career thirteen years later, I found that this same movement was responsible for the redundant definition of the subject matter of my courses as "Christian Social Ethics." Could anyone doubt that moral theory must include social relations?

The social gospel supplied what had been lacking, the emphasis on social justice. Walter Rauschenbush and others had rediscovered the principles of social justice as preached by the prophets and revered by both Jew and Christian.

Armed with this variant of Protestant liberalism, I completed my graduate studies at Yale and assumed the ministry of a small church in Detroit. The lessons I learned about religion among the saints and sinners in this my first and only pastorate must be postponed while I recount the lessons I learned in my first direct encounter with industry.

In 1915 Henry Ford had only recently performed the miracle of putting the nation on wheels, and the city of Detroit was burgeoning with a growing auto industry that used the methods of mass production. These methods required only semiskilled labor for most of the assembly line. Only a fraction of the labor force consisted of skilled toolmakers and diemakers. This new industrialism aggravated most of the problems of industrial justice it claimed to have cured. The pretended cure was quite simply a more benevolent distribution of the new wealth of mass production.

Henry Ford was the most plausible symbol of such benevolence. He combined mechanical genius with social and historical ignorance, and humanitarian and power impulses were compounded marvelously in his complex personality. His five-dollar-a-day wage created a worldwide reputation for humanitarianism. This wage, however, did not obscure the fact that his labor costs were shockingly low, or that his annual wage, with no compensation for enforced monthly layoffs, did not match the annual wage of his hard-boiled competitors with their piecework wages. Ford achieved such disproportionate symbolic significance in the education of a young parson because his moral pretensions were such shining examples of the ideological taint in all moral pretensions. Needless to say, when the Wagner Act finally gave industrial workers the right to organize and bargain collectively, they still had to fight for that right in bloody battles with the private police force of the benevolent autocrat.

The reaction to this industrial situation was more mixed in Detroit than in the rest of the nation. My particular concern was with the reactions of the churches. Fortunately, many religious leaders, in and out of Detroit, knew very well that social justice was a relevant norm for institutional relations.

The conventional Protestant churches, both liberal and orthodox, were completely irrelevant to the struggle for justice in the new industry. Their business was to help people lead respectable lives but not to interfere with the production of automobiles.

The liberal Protestants preached sacrificial love, which is a moral norm relevant to interpersonal (particularly family) relations, and significant for parents (particularly mothers, heroes, and saints), but scarcely applicable to the power relations of modern industry. Traditional Protestantism in America emphasized the economic virtues of diligence, honesty, and thrift. The implication was that the possession of these virtues, or their lack, was responsible for the disparity between wealth and poverty in modern industry. Unfortunately a moribund Calvinism contracted a strange alliance with Spencer's Social Darwinism. Therefore the comfortable classes could find religious or scientific reasons, or both, for not alleviating social distress in a sea of social discontent.

It was one of the goals of radical Protestantism to rescue the honest souls in the Protestant community from this double-plated ideological shield of moral complacency. Since this is the story of American culture from a viewpoint of a critical clerical observer, it may be worth recording that the Detroit situation was typical of industrial America in the early twentieth century. The Protestants, as a class of industrial owners, were most in need of, but actually were most bereft of, moral norms relevant to their place in the scheme of things in industry. Their labor force in the growing industry was composed, on the whole, of Jewish and Catholic immigrants.

The Jews had a social ethic inherited from the prophets and the traditions of the rabbis. The Catholic social norms were consistently misunderstood by non-Catholics, secular or religious. These norms were in fact involved in a long and complex history. When the Church conquered, and was conquered by, the Roman Empire, it had incorporated the classical standards of natural law and consigned the perfectionist impulses of Messianism to the category of "counsels of perfection," to be observed by the ascetics. The metaphysical base of natural-law standards made them rather too inflexible. But this did not prevent the gradual displacement of early Stoic equalitarianism by Aristotle's justification of social inequality. The standards of natural law thus provided ideological instruments for later feudalism.

The inflexibility of the social standards and their justification of a feudal culture made them old wineskins incapable of containing the new wine of modern life. The new forces, which could not be accommodated in the old norms, consisted of the rising nations, a growing commerce, an enlarged bourgeois class, and its insistence on the franchise of open societies. When the Reformation and the Renaissance ruined the imposing temple of medieval culture, it seemed logical to dismiss all medieval social standards.

But the Church survived as a religious institution. It later showed that it could relate itself creatively to the problems of technical civilization. It was able to preserve its insight displayed in feudal ages into the social substance of human existence. Meanwhile it revealed that when industrial workers rather than feudal lords were its clients, standards of justice according to natural law had quite a different savor. Modern Catholicism of the West had, compared with its medieval past, illustrated the lesson I was gradually learning. It was that the intimate relation between ideals and interests makes for curious transformations of moral norms into ideologies—and vice versa.

My Detroit experience contained one more lesson about the collective behavior of men. Race riots broke out after the First World War as a result of the immigration of both Negroes and Southern whites to the auto industry. The mayor appointed a race commission, of which I became chairman. We conducted the usual survey of housing and employment opportunities for the Negro minority. Our recommendations undoubtedly would seem elementary in the light of the present racial crisis. But as chairman I learned that the pride of a racial majority can be a greater hazard of justice than the economic motives that had preoccupied me so long.

The next lesson about the collective problems of human communities I learned after I left Detroit in 1928. The whole period of the long armistice between the two world wars showed the brutal facts of international relations. These had to be digested, not with the help of religious and national traditions, but in defiance of them.

Any intelligent student of history might have known, for instance, that while force can be only a minimum component of political power and authority in the domestic life of democratic nations, even the most democratic nations are bound to resort to maximal force in their relations to other nations, and this for both good and bad reasons. The problem of proper moral norms for legally autonomous nations has been long unsolved, though secular and religious pacifists claimed a solution by ruling out force in international relations. This perfectionist solution seems highly irrelevant because it would attempt to persuade, through love or reason, the most unlikely candidates for moral redemption.

My lesson about the moral norms proper for sovereign nations contradicted two of my cherished traditions, religious and national. The religious tradition of the social gospel was, for all its realism in domestic politics, pacifist and perfectionist in its attitude toward the international problem. Our own nation was, of course, not consistently pacifist. But from Jefferson to Wilson the illusion persisted in our national life that only monarchies were prone to military ventures.

The First World War shattered the security of a nation with its ocean moats, but it accentuated our sense of innocence, partly because President Woodrow Wilson was under the illusion that we were "the most unselfish nation on earth." But our conscience was both aroused and eased because the German military policy was unusually ruthless by the standards of a pre-nuclear age. The British conscience was outraged by the violation of Belgium's neutrality. Our conscience was aroused by the inhumanities of Germany's unrestricted submarine attack upon our ships.

Thus we had moral reasons for entering the conflict which even a reluctant Wilson could not disregard. When we entered the war, Wilson immediately proclaimed an ideal, rather than the real, reason for our participation. It was a crusade, "a war to make the world safe for democracy." All idealists, including myself, of course, were satisfied—and engaged in war efforts with passion.

The sorry realities of the Draconic peace of Versailles naturally disappointed all idealists and revealed the moral ambiguities in the designs of even the most democratic nations. Wilson had one more arrow in the quiver of his idealism—the League of Nations. This was expected both to correct the obvious injustices of the Versailles peace, and to beguile a hitherto irresponsible nation into accepting responsibility for keeping peace.

The nationalists, suspecting Wilson's idealism, charged that the League did not properly guard our own national interest. It proved impossible to submit their indictment to the test of history, because the charge was sufficient to prompt the nation to reject the League. The rejection broke the heart of a dying President. It also tore off the only fig leaf, and exposed the naked political realities of the Versailles peace.

Since the reaction of the whole nation was more important than that of the minority, though intimately related to it, we must pause only long enough in recounting the well-known history of our nation in the long armistice between the two world wars to confess that I postponed the learning of a much-needed lesson about the structure of nations, and about the moral norms appropriate to the field of international relations, by joining the pacifist Fellowship of Reconciliation and swearing that we would never, never have recourse to military force again.

The reaction of the whole nation was important because it represented the anxiety of a whole community to postpone learning the lessons suggested by a strange experience. It was dumped out of its cradle of continental security by the storms and tumults of a budding "community of nations." Its response was an almost neurotic neutralism.

We were, of course, rudely awakened from this sleep of adolescent daydreaming by the rise of the Nazi peril in Europe.

Our initial reaction to this peril was an "America First" movement, with two incompatible partners. The nationalist partners wanted to preserve our neutrality because our security was not directly imperiled. The perfectionist partners wanted to guard our neutrality because they were under the curious illusion that abstention from overt conflict would guard our previous innocence. This conviction implied, of course, that an irresponsible complacency about evils, remote from our lives, was not a violation of a law that enjoined responsibility for the neighbor's welfare.

I found this perfectionist reaction so revealing and its complacent partnership with national egotism so dishonest that my reaction induced a crisis in my life. It was a crisis because I had come belatedly to realize that the "idealism" of both my religious and national traditions had failed me in the process of learning. They prevented me from seeing an obvious fact about man's collective behavior, particularly as it expressed itself in the behavior of sovereign nations. In short, both traditions had deluded themselves about the power and persistence of collective self-regard.

The attack on Pearl Harbor ended our shivering indecision about a war in which our destiny as an hegemonous nation in a nuclear age was proved to be involved. My own reaction is unimportant, except as part of the record of what I have learned from life. I resigned both from the pacifist organization and from the Socialist Party. I helped to found a Protestant journal to challenge the pervasive pacifism of liberal Protestants. I also cooperated in founding an interventionist organization, Americans for Democratic Action, whose purpose was to challenge the neutralism of the various social forces, agrarian and labor, that first brought Roosevelt to power.

I can only add that the peace after the Second World War may have been even more disappointing than the Versailles peace. But the nation did not revert to irresponsibility. Its hegemonous power had taught it that power means responsibility. Our new sense of responsibility was immediately tested when the Communist and democratic allies, responsible for the defeat of Nazism, revealed the brevity of wartime alliances.

Events have moved swiftly in the quarter-century of the cold war. The destructive power of the new weapons has obviously made nuclear warfare suicidal and therefore unreasonable. But the new situation did not eliminate other contests of power. We were in fact engaged in a tremendous contest between two blocs of nations. The one, the so-called free world, had its core in the culture of western European bourgeois democracy. We were the hegemonous nation in that bloc. The other comprised what was in fact a new culture, rooted in a utopian religio-political dogma. The

U.S.S.R. was both the hegemonous and the holy nation of that bloc.

The present period, beginning with the limited test ban agreement between the U.S.S.R. and the U.S.A., may represent a new achievement and challenge in the age-old problem of enlarging political authority to a universal community. It may initiate a partnership of mutual responsibility for the avoidance of a nuclear catastrophe. In that case it may herald the slow growth of a center of political authority, equipped with the necessary instruments of prestige, power, and force, that abstract world constitutions lack.

But this budding hope represents more of a challenge than an achievement for the moral imagination of mankind. The bridge is built across a deep ideological chasm. We must determine whether the chasm can be bridged, even if one element in it is the non-negotiable value of an open society. It survived in the West precisely because it vindicated itself by conquering the social injustices of early nineteenth-century industrialism. It thus refuted the Marxist indictment that political institutions were merely the stooges of economic power. The Communist rebellion therefore proposed the socialization of all property as a solution for all social ills. The dogma, despite its absurdity, unleashed social forces that enabled a feudal-monarchial and agrarian culture to achieve both technical competence and industrial equipment in a brief period.

The polemics of the cold war could easily be modified if the new partnership were important enough. The Russian polemics against Western democracy relied on nineteenth-century evils long since eliminated. Our polemics against the Communist system as a "despotism" relied on the more recent, but also eliminated, evils of Stalin's period.

Even the gradual elimination of these polemical falsities cannot hide the difference between an oligarchic system, sworn to uphold a dogma upon which its whole culture is founded, and an open and pluralistic culture, presumably hospitable to all dogmas and viewpoints. Russia is not a budding democracy, but the seeds of freedom may well be sown in the rivalries of its competitive oligarchies, political, managerial, and military.

Meanwhile the necessities of technical civilization have modified both the "free enterprise" and the collectivist dogmas. The Russians are forced to obviate the capricious bureaucratic decisions by allowing their industries to seek profit by their own enterprise. We, on the other hand, are forced to establish more and more control by the state.

Should we be tempted by a too optimistic hope for this prospective center of world order, it is well to remember that history gives us no warrant for assuming that the resolution of ideological differences will eliminate conflicts of power.

The emergence of China as a great, and potentially nuclear, power is an even more vivid challenge to our moral and political imagination, reminding us that history constantly presents moral problems to nations, despite their limited moral capacities. In this case the challenge obviously reminds us that a world authority, based on the partnership of two technically competent and white, affluent nations, will be hard put to yield justice to a group of nations that have the common characteristics of color, technical backwardness, and poverty. China seems determined to lead this bloc of nations. The revolutionary creed it shares with Russia is an aid rather than a handicap in its contest with Russia. For China simply presents a more radical version of the common creed, and accuses the Russians of possessing a complacent and bourgeois version of Communism. Since Russia is bound to be more interested in preserving its great gains than in exporting revolutions, the Chinese are quite ready to supply the need for revolutionary zeal. They are exporting revolution everywhere in Asia, Africa, and Latin America.

Their zeal may be fraught with the peril of revolutionary chaos. But this peril will merely remind us of a perennial problem of the political order. Communities, both parochial and international, are bound to place order first in their hierarchy of values. But justice comes as a quick second in the political hierarchy, because unsatisfied desires are bound to challenge every order, whatever may be its prestige, power, or force. The growing tension between the colored and poor nations and the white and affluent nations may serve to remind us that historical development tends to present perennial social and moral problems in higher and higher dimensions. This may also disclose that seemingly permanent ideological differences are as ephemeral as the contests that inspired them. In short, we cannot escape the moral problems of the international order, provided we understand that the morals of sovereign nations have a distinct and unique anatomy.

The dimension of this new problem of order and justice may tax both our imagination and our institutions to such a degree that the avoidance of a nuclear conflict in the next half-century seems highly improbable. Such avoidance could be achieved only if the two giant nuclear powers possessed an imagination, not usual in the history of statecraft.

Ironically enough, the American illusion of omnipotence might shatter the nuclear peace even more than the illusions of a closed dogmatic society. It might tempt us to contain the age-old Chinese penetration of the Asian continent by pure military force, even though our policy would serve only to give one Communist adversary, Russia, an advantage over the other, China, in their inevitable contest over supremacy in Asia.

I must conclude my report on the lessons life has taught me by an account of what I learned about religion. I acknowledged earlier that my calling either as minister or as professor was conventional from the vocational standpoint, while my convictions were critical in confronting liberalism, secular or religious.

My vocations were determined by my inheritance. This included the tradition of home and family, as well as the liberal Protestantism both of my father and of those teachers who influenced me at Eden Seminary and at Yale Divinity School. This inheritance gave me an understanding of religious faith as trust in the meaning of human existence. At home, the emphasis expressed in family worship and in instruction was on gratitude for the blessings of life. This interpretation remained with me and was deepened through the give-and-take with colleagues and friends, particularly through endless dialogues with my late brother, H. Richard Niebuhr, and at home with my wife, herself a scholar and a teacher of the history of religions.

Religious faith interpreted as basic trust in the meaning of human existence would explain why religion has survived—despite obvious weaknesses—even in a secular age.

Trust in the meaning of human existence is, in short, uniquely a human extension of the natural impulse of survival. It is not rational in the sense that a scientific or philosophic explanation might be. Yet such explanations of natural and historical coherences would not satisfy the anxious individual, confronting the many incoherences and ills in his own life. Therefore it is impossible to construct religious faith "within the limits of pure reason" (Kant), for "religion is not transcendently true, but is transcendently important" (Whitehead).

The studies of Erik Erikson, from *Childhood and Society* on, have proved of inestimable value for those of us who interpreted faith as basic trust. His work has given clinical evidence for the importance of basic trust as rooted in the securities of the child's family and home. At the same time, significant clues are given for the reasons and occasions of the corruptions of religion.

The basic trust of the person of faith may be childlike in its singleheartedness, yet this basic trust can be changed into a childish belief that God is on the side of the believer, and that this faith, which is belief rather than trust, merits the reward of special favor.

I was shown the difference between faith as basic trust, and faith as possessing vested rights, in the very beginning of my Detroit ministry. Two old ladies, whose characters I had not known, but who were, by conventional standards, equally devout, faced certain death. The one old lady asked me to read her psalms of praise and gratitude. She was particularly grateful for the love of two splendid daughters, whom she had put through nursing school since her husband's illness made her both homemaker and breadwinner for the family. The other old lady was in a fever of anxiety and resentment. She recounted all her virtues with the implication that it was unjust for a righteous woman to suffer her pains. I learned from the one that gratitude is the natural response of a life lived in faith as trust in the goodness of life. I learned from the other that faith is frequently corrupted by childish peevishness about the lack of special favors for the righteous.

The tendency to claim God as an ally for our partisan values and ends is another childish, but also universal, corruption of religion. This is the source of all religious fanaticism. Abraham Lincoln, in his eloquent Second Inaugural, took pains to disavow this corruption as revealed in the American Civil War. He said, "Both [sides] read the same Bible, and pray to the same God; and each invokes His aid against the other. . . . The prayers of both could not be answered—that of neither has been answered fully."

This fallacy is part of a special problem that has to be faced by all religions that seek to comprehend history in the realm of meaning. Impatience with such faiths has prompted some to turn to mysticism, to neo-Platonism in its many forms, or to Buddhism. But the price of such alternatives is high. Mysticism projects an undifferentiated eternity that swallows up time and history. It therefore reduces all historic responsibilities to insignificance, and denies any meaning to this life.

The Biblical faiths, Hebrew and Christian, tried to express their faith in an ultimate triumph over all evils of history by their messianic hopes. According to the Hebrew prophets, "the wolf shall dwell with the lamb, and the leopard shall lie down with the kid." Thus there would be an ideal messianic age in which a transformed nature would guarantee the fulfillment of all historic hopes. But a naturalistic culture found this hope incredible and substituted instead a utopia, a heaven on earth, with nature untransformed. But this utopian hope proved as dangerous as the older hope was incredible, as the despotism of Stalin has shown.

There is in Judaism and Christianity, because of their historic particularity, this tendency to limit the universality of God in their own favor. Yet also there is criticism and correction ("Thou art our Father, though Abraham does not know us and Israel does not acknowledge us"), and in the New Testament parable the goats will sit down in the Kingdom of God, rather than the sheep, who are the flock of obvious elect ones.

The ironic twist given in this parable illustrates the peculiar genius of the Bible. The ultimate and transcendent character of God challenges man's own conception of piety and goodness—"My thoughts are not your thoughts," etc. The faith of Israel gave the world this vision of a God transcendent over historic process, who also is intimately related to history and to man, and is "as a father who pitieth his children." As transcendence and historic relatedness were bound together in the drama of God and Israel, and of God and man, so also were love and justice held together in the schema of the law. Jesus reiterated this faith of Israel, for it was "the first and great commandment" . . . to "love the Lord your God with all your heart, and with all your soul and with all your mind and with all your strength." The ultimate transcendence was beyond man's exact understanding, for "no man can see God and live," and the glory of God cannot be measured or its mystery plumbed, yet the character of God was made known in "his ways" which were the fulfillments of the law. Thus transcendent mystery and transcendent love were to be made plain in the historical measures of justice, in the proportionate interchanges of responsibility and concern between man and man; "the second [commandment] is this, you shall love your neighbor as yourself."

The New Testament reiterates this theme in story, parable, and saying with simplicity and immediacy. To his followers, the words and the ministry of Jesus so expressed the message of love (mercy) and justice (righteousness) that he became exemplar and example of "the ways of God."

For nearly forty years I preached almost every Sunday in various parts of this country. This experience taught me much. "Making sense" out of the symbols and professions of faith has always been the responsibility of preacher and of teacher. Since we must use symbols to define the reaches of the human spirit beyond definable knowledge, we must realize that these symbols are tangents toward the ultimate, and therefore fruits of the human imagination. These symbols create a penumbra of mystery around every realm of meaning within the bounds of verifiable knowledge.

The penumbra of mystery is able to enrich the realm of meaning, provided we are modest enough to distinguish the mystery of the unknowable from the tentative mystery of the unknown, which is constantly subject to diminution by advancing knowledge. Such modesty might well be prompted by the suspicion that no neat system of coherence is able to comprehend the beauty and terror of life.

## Reinhold Niebuhr

*Reinhold Niebuhr is a world-renowned theologian, an unflinching social activist, and—a label he probably shrinks from—the elder statesman of contemporary Protestant thought. The hallmark of his work and witness* has been his consistent attempt to relate man's spiritual dilemmas to man's total role in our vexed modern civilization. Dr. Niebuhr was born in Wright City, Missouri, in 1892, is a graduate of Yale Divinity School, and is currently professor emeritus at Union Theological Seminary, and co-editor of the magazine Christianity and Crisis. His books include Moral Man and Immoral Society, Pious and Secular America, Christian Realism and Political Problems, and The Self and the Dramas of History.

ALAN PATON

# The Challenge of Fear

---

ONE OF the big lessons that life has taught me is that my earlier understanding of man and his society was wretchedly inadequate. An extraordinary thing, is it not, that one should begin to acquire an understanding of them both when one is drawing near to the end of his acquaintance with them? The richer one grows in wisdom, the shorter becomes the time in which to use it.

Just how it happened that my understanding was so inadequate I don't quite know. My parents certainly never taught me that man was growing better and better and that the future was therefore in some way assured. They certainly taught me to seek after righteousness, but they never taught me that righteousness would in a temporal and political sense be successful. Nor did I ever learn this at school. Yet that is what I grew up believing. Why should this be so?

I can only think that it was taught to me after all, not by father or mother or teacher or priest, but because it was a basic assumption of the pre-1914 society into which I was born. I am surprised to find that this view of man and life was shared by many all over the world who were born at that time. I am surprised because my own particular world was a very particular one indeed. It was the town of Pietermaritzburg, Natal, founded by the Afrikaner trekkers, but intensely British at the time of my birth in 1903, most of the trekkers having gone to the Transvaal after the British annexation of Natal. My world was intensely pro-Empire, devoted to the royal family, moved to excitement and pride when the red-coated soldiers of the British garrison marched down the street past our home, with arms swinging and drums beating and fifes blowing, to the old Polo Ground to parade for the King's birthday.

There were thirty thousand people in Pietermaritzburg in my boyhood, more than half of them Africans and Indians, of whose existence we knew and of whose lives we did not. They were not persons. The Africans were servants or they dug up the roads. The Indians sold fruit and vegetables, in baskets fastened one to the front end and the other to the  back end of a flexible strip of bamboo carried on the shoulder, the baskets swaying up and down with a springy motion.

This faulty understanding of man and life has been called by some the romantic illusion, and can be entertained in different places and at different times in history, but in our illusion the might of the British Empire, the indomitable British Navy, and the *Pax Britannica* were particular elements. The world was good and it was going to stay good, perhaps even become better.

I had no conception at that age of the way in which man could create tremendous, noble-sounding slogans, and could shout them aloud while doing ignoble actions; and what is more, the louder the shout, the greater the ignobleness could be. I had no conception of the need of so much of mankind, while it was actually employed in self-seeking and self-securing, to cling simultaneously to unself-centered religion and altruistic ethics. Nor did I realize that man could so easily deceive himself that his highest religious and ethical values were identical with his own self-interest. And there must have been a great many people like me; otherwise why did George Orwell's *1984* create such a sensation among us?

The extraordinary thing about all this is that I ought to have known it. My parents gave me a religious upbringing, and the reading of the Gospel story should have prepared me better for the world with its scribes and pharisees and the crucifixion of Jesus through the instruments of church and state. I take that story seriously, for I believe that in some societies one cannot be true to one's highest beliefs without paying for it in suffering. This is more true in the totalitarian and the semitotalitarian societies (of which Nazi Germany is an example of the first and South Africa an example of the second) than in countries such as America and Britain. In South Africa, one may say with safety that apartheid is misguided, but it is dangerous to say that it is cruel or to oppose it too vigorously.

Not only the Gospel, but history also should have taught me to know better. There is, for one thing, the tale of man's innumerable wars, and of his inhumanity to other men. The early Christians were persecuted by the state, but when Christianity became a state religion, it was not long before the church began persecuting and burning heretics. For centuries, the Jews suffered unspeakably at the hands of Christians, who had no difficulty in believing that they were doing a good thing, and doing it in the name of Christ, who taught that one must love one's neighbor as oneself and had made it very clear who one's neighbor was.

Not even the World War of 1914 shattered my pre-1914 world, though today to read of the terrible and useless slaughter of the bright youth of Britain, France, and Germany leaves one appalled. It was Adolf Hitler who finally destroyed for me—and for many others—the romantic illusion. Dachau, Belsen, Auschwitz— these places gave me an education which was not available in Pietermaritzburg. So one suddenly learns in age the truth of a saying heard in youth—namely, that life is the greatest teacher of them all.

What Hitler taught me about man and nature was sobering enough, but life taught me two further lessons. The first was that, whatever Hitler had taught me about man, I must on no account forget that all over the world men and women, both young and old, would offer their lives in the fight against totalitarian rule and the doctrine of race superiority because they believed them to be evil. The second lesson was quite different, and that was that some of these same men and women twenty years later would begin to support the very things that they had fought against, and to approve of the punishment without trial of those who opposed the doctrine of apartheid, but had committed no known offense.

And why do they behave like this? Have they suddenly, or even gradually, become corrupted? And if so, why? Surely the answer is that the nature of their security—and that means the nature of their self-interest—has changed. In 1939 their security was the British Empire and the Navy. In 1967, amid the turbulence and uncertainties of modern Africa, their security appears to them to lie in white supremacy and apartheid. With the change of one's self-interest there comes also a change in one's ideology, one's values, one's principles.

This discovery of the complexity of human nature was accompanied by another—the discovery of the complexity and irrationality of human motive, the discovery that one could love and hate simultaneously, be honest and cheat, be arrogant and humble, be any pair of opposites that one had supposed to be mutually exclusive. This, I believe, is not common knowledge and would be incomprehensible to many. It has always been known, of course, by the dramatists and the novelists. It is, in fact, a knowledge far more disturbing to other people than to writers, for to writers it is the grist to their mills.

Nor was I aware when I was young (both as boy and as man) how powerful a motive is fear, even though I myself had many fears. As I write this I am searching for an explanation of the fact that under some circumstances men readily admit fear, and under other circumstances do not. I assume that readiness to admit fear is part of a general readiness to look at the world as it is, and therefore at oneself as one is, while unwillingness to admit fear may be a strong element in self-esteem. One does not readily admit to a fear of which one is ashamed.

Now, while fear has its important uses, such as causing an outflow of adrenalin which helps one run away faster, it is a wretched determinant of conduct. There is nothing more pitiable than a human being whose conduct is largely determined by fear. Furthermore, it is a destroyer of reason and the rational life. What can be done to control it, check it, or even eliminate it?

Here I must use language which will be out of fashion for some, and I must use reasoning which will seem quite unreal to others. Life has taught me that John uttered the plain and simple truth when he wrote that there is no fear in love, but that perfect love casts out fear. In one sense, the opposite of fear is courage, but in the dynamic sense the opposite of fear is love, whether this be love of man or love of justice.

It is clearly not enough to tell a fearful man that if he would only love more, he would fear less. In an age when leprosy was feared much more than it is today, that rich and spoiled young man, Francis of Assisi, impelled by some sudden and irresistible emotion, got down from his gaily caparisoned horse and embraced a leper in the road. From that day he feared nothing, and taught thousands of others to fear nothing. Yet few of us are visited by such irresistible emotion.

How does one help ordinary men and women, if not to eliminate fear, at least to keep it within bounds, so that reason may play a stronger role in the affairs of men and nations and so that men may cease to pursue policies which must lead to the very disasters they fear? To me, this is the most important question that confronts the human race.

I note that it is more and more widely held that poverty and inequality of opportunity are among the greatest causes of tension between man and man, between race and race, and between nation and nation. I believe that race tension in my own country would be amazingly abated if the disparity between average white income and average black income were not so overwhelming. I believe that tension between America and Russia has declined since Russia became one of the productive nations. Yet when men are ruled by fear, they strive to prevent the very changes that will abate it.

Fear of change is, no doubt, in all of us, but it most afflicts the man who fears that any change must lead to loss of his wealth and status. When this fear becomes inordinate, he will, if he has political power, abrogate such things as civil rights and the rule of law, using the argument that he abrogates them only to preserve them. In my own country the government, in order to preserve Christian civilization, uses methods incompatible with Christianity and abrogates values which are essential to any civilization which calls itself Christian. If only a man would say, "I do this because I'm afraid," one could bear it; but when he says, "I do this because I'm good," that is a bit too much.

I see no hope for the peace of society or the peace of the world so long as this fear of change is so powerful. And this fear will remain powerful so long as the one side has so much to gain and the other so much to lose.

I should like to make one point clear, and that is that I do not believe that a more equitable distribution of wealth will automatically bring the Great Society. The point I am trying to make is that if it is not done, there will never be any Great Society. Nor will there by any peace for the world.

Can a school prepare our children for the complexity and waywardness of man? Is it not more likely that these lessons can be taught only by living? There would be the danger that some children might learn to believe a contrary illusion, namely, that man is cruel, cunning, and deceitful. If I remember my childhood and boyhood correctly, and perhaps even my experience as a young teacher, one actually protected children against knowing too much of the worst sides of man's nature. My readers know, no doubt, the story of the businessman who put his young son on the roof of the house, and, standing below, said, "Jump, son, and Daddy will catch you." So the boy jumped, and Daddy didn't catch him, but instead said to him, "Son, that will teach you to trust nobody." One could hardly do that. But one could, while holding up the goals of honesty, kindness, loyalty, tolerance, integrity, tell children a bit of what the world is like. I would also assume that the children of 1967 know far more about man and his nature and society than did the children of the pre-1914 days; it must be almost impossible for children of today to cherish the old romantic illusion.

One must not suppose, however, that because children have lost the romantic illusion and look upon life and the world and their parents with a more calculating eye that they are now free of illusions. In South Africa many white children cherish the illusion that they are, in many important ways, superior to other children, and I regret to add that many nonwhite children entertain the illusion that they are, in many important ways, inferior to white children. Another powerful illusion handed down to many white children is that their country is perfect and their government wholly just and benign, so that they lose all faculty for self-criticism.

I have known people who, when their romantic illusion is finally destroyed, cease to believe anything except that man is bad and life intolerable; who feel that they have come, to use Thomas Wolfe's magnificent words, from the prison of their mothers' flesh "into the unspeakable and incommunicable prison of this earth." I presume they would say that this is what life has taught them. It is my fortune to be able to say that though life destroyed my romantic illusion, she did not teach me the contrary illusion. It would appear either that she does not teach the same lessons to everybody, or that other factors operate besides experience, such as temperament, character, religious faith, and sheer luck and good fortune.

I certainly had good fortune, in marriage and children and friends—especially those friends who, with me, have challenged the beliefs and practices of a color-bar society—and it is these personal relationships that have saved me from the melancholy that besets the wholly disillusioned. I call this my luck because it is very difficult, and perhaps impossible, to achieve such a state by act of will. You may say to a friend, "Don't worry; worry changes nothing," but that in itself will not stop him from worrying. Life has taught me—and this is my luck—that active loving saves one from a morbid preoccupation with the shortcomings of society and the waywardness of men.

I should again make it clear at this point that I am not saying that human society is unimprovable. What I am saying is that the problems of creating the Great Society are immensely greater than many of us were taught to believe and that we would have been better equipped to deal with them if we had understood their nature and difficulty better. To give up the task of reforming society is to give up one's responsibility as a free man. The task itself is endless, and large parts of it, sometimes the whole of it, must be performed anew by each succeeding generation.

Now, while life was teaching me these lessons, she was leading me in what would appear to be a quite contrary or at least contradictory direction. Here I must refer directly to my own local and particular situation as a white South African. While, on the one hand, I was discarding the romantic illusion about men and society, on the other I was beginning to rebel against the man-made barriers of race and color that divided man from man and to cherish a new ideal of society, which would be judged by some to be an illusion no less romantic than the one it was replacing.

When I first set out in this direction, the road was certainly unusual, whereas later it was to become dangerous, owing to the coming to power of a government which took to itself supralegal powers enabling it to banish, silence, confine to small areas, debar from certain occupations and from attending any social or political gathering, any person who in the opinion of the minister was "furthering the aims of Communism." Many non-Communists were dealt with in this way, without charge, trial, or sentence; some of these were my own fellow liberals, whose only offenses had been that they had ignored conventional race barriers or had been active in providing legal defense for political prisoners and aid for their dependents.

Whereas South Africa teaches many of its people to fear and to hate racial mixing (and I use the word "mixing" in its widest, not its narrowest sense), here it was teaching me the opposite, and teaching me to see our future as being that of one nonracial society and not a collection of strictly separated and individual race groups. The whole philosophy of apartheid is based on the fundamental assumption that there can be no such thing as a nonracial society, and that each individual realizes himself only through his membership in his own racial group, and that, therefore, it is the duty of the government to preserve these racial differences, in language, education, sex, marriage, sport, entertainment, and so on and so on. The apostle of apartheid would further declare that it is only another romantic illusion to imagine that an Afrikaner Calvinist, an English-speaking Anglican (Episcopalian), a colored (that is, of mixed blood) Roman Catholic, an African Methodist, an African ancestor-worshiper, an Indian Hindu, and an Indian Muslim—not to mention those who profess no particular faith—could operate a common nonracial society. The apostle of apartheid says he is a realist and that a person like myself is a sentimental idealist. But when this apostle is angry with me he would call me dangerous, and could, if he wished, restrict my freedom in the ways I have mentioned above.

He will, almost certainly in 1968, make it an offense to operate a nonracial (and multiracial) political party. One learns the lesson at first hand that the practice of the art of political persuasion can be made impossible by the state. One learns how the whole character of a people can be changed by a powerful state. Having Germany in mind, I do not say fundamentally changed; but even if the change is not fundamental, it is terrible enough.

Yet, in spite of all this one goes on believing in a nonracial unity that can transcend racial difference. This is something that one has come to believe through experience of personal relationships, and it may be that what is possible in personal relationships is not possible in society. There have been many examples in history where two individuals from mutually hostile groups have greatly loved one another.

Now, is it possible or is it not possible to realize in society what one has realized in personal relationships? I believe one cannot answer the question. All that one can say is that there is within one an impulse to try to realize it, that this impulse is an integral part of one's self, and that it must be obeyed, for to disobey it is to do damage to the integrity of one's self. And what is more, one has fortunately already learned the lesson that a failure, or a measure of failure, to realize some social or political aim can be compensated for to a tremendous degree by the depth and warmth of one's personal relationships.

What has life then taught me after all? She has taught me not to expect too much, though not in the sense of the cynical beatitude, "blessed is he who expecteth nothing, for he shall not be disappointed." Life has not taught me to expect nothing, but she has taught me not to expect success to be the inevitable result of my endeavors. She has taught me to seek sustenance from the endeavor itself, but to leave the result to God. And the strange thing is that my parents taught me all this more than half a century ago. It is a lesson that—for me—had to be learned at least twice. When I learned it in my youth, it meant Sir Galahad and the Holy Grail.

When I learned it in my age, it meant Christ and the road to Golgotha. And looking back upon it all, I would not wish it otherwise. Indeed, I cannot see how it could have been otherwise.

To try to be free of self-deception, to try to see with clear eyes one's self and others and the world, does not necessarily bring an undiluted kind of happiness. Yet it is something I would not exchange for any happiness built on any other foundation. There is only one way in which one can endure man's inhumanity to man and that is to try, in one's own life, to exemplify man's humanity to man. "Teach me, oh Lord, to seek not so much to be consoled as to console."

### Alan Paton

*"He pulled up the barbed wire fence and planted geraniums," someone once said of Alan Paton's courageous achievements in bringing prison reform to his native South Africa and in focusing world attention on South African racial problems. Throughout his remarkably productive career as a writer, teacher, penologist, and political leader, Alan Paton has applied humanitarian and innovative energies to the alleviation of the racial and social injustices plaguing his country and the African continent. He was born in Natal in 1903 and educated in South Africa at Pietermaritzburg and Natal University. Currently, he is president of the struggling South African Liberal Party. He is a recipient of the Freedom House Award in the United States. His first novel,* Cry the Beloved Country, *won world-wide acclaim in 1948; other works include* Too Late the Phalarope, South Africa in Transition, Tales from a Troubled Land, *and* South African Tragedy.

# CHAKRAVARTI RAJAGOPALACHARI

## What Man Cannot Know

I CAN PUT in a few words what I have learned from life: Life is God's *leela*. This Sanskrit word *leela* is not just "play," although it is generally so rendered in English. The Sanskrit word expresses what to us is the more important negative result of any attempt to unravel the mystery of life; namely, that we cannot make out the design though undoubtedly there is design, order, and law. The nearest approach to an explanation is that the great Master of the Universe amuses Himself, but we cannot unravel the mysteries of this highly organized divine play except that the inexorable law of Karma governs it—every action brings with it, inescapably and unfailingly, its results. I have also learned this—that the greatest happiness results from being good; that is, from following the moral law in spite of every seeming pain and privation associated with it.

I have also found that any attempt to define what is good is futile, because of the various results of every action. One man's good is almost invariably another man's pain or privation. Good can only be relatively determined. The teaching of the Gita of the Hindus contains the soundest advice, namely, do what is laid as duty on your shoulders in the context of each moment and do it unselfishly and surrendering yourself to God. One man's duty may differ from

261

another's and what is good at one time may not be the right thing at another time. Unselfishness and unbroken reliance on God and faithful use of one's reasoning powers must decide what at each juncture, public or private, one's duty is. This is not Hinduism alone or the Bhagavad-Gita alone. It is the teaching of every great religion. But the Gita expatiates on it as if intimately dealing with a tough skeptic.

These being the lessons I have learned from life as well as from good books and the company of good men and women, what is my present personal summing-up of the world situation? It is at present a rather sad one—of disappointment and retarded hope.

When the atomic bombs were exploded over Japan and World War II was brought to an end, I was among those who rejoiced but were also deeply alarmed. I rejoiced that the victory of the Allies and the defeat of Hitler, with his brutalities and terror, were steadily approaching; but when the actual end came in the way it did, it filled me with sadness and a terror unequaled by anything inflicted by Hitler and his satanic power.

I watched with dismay and grief the race in nuclear production that immediately followed. The world was in the grip of terror out of which it had to escape; but instead of doing what should end the terror, powerful nations went on adding to the danger and the terror.

A stage was reached when the new weapons of total annihilation no doubt served to prevent war, but they did this by adding to the danger in ever-increasing measure, for if ever the poised balance of terror failed, war would arrive.

This form of peace soon resulted in the withdrawal of all the support against injustice and aggression that the weaker nations had obtained from more powerful nation-friends. In the pre-atomic period, the more powerful nations gave help to their weaker friends; after the nuclear terror arrived, everyone was afraid of "escalation" of the defense of a weaker nation into a terrible world war.

This led to a period of greatly increased activity by way of debate, discussion, and negotiation in the world forum. The United
Nations organization assumed great importance and seemed rapidly
to approach the role of world government. The great book of Clark
and Sohn, *World Peace Through World Law*, is a demonstration
and a symbol of the hopes that the role of the UN raised during this
period. It was a complete, very carefully drawn-up draft bill for the
nations of the world to adopt, by which the UN would be transformed into an effective world authority acting under world law
and there would be an end to war and the fear of war.

The grant by the British Parliament of complete independence
to India and Pakistan in 1947, followed immediately by similar
withdrawal of all imperial power from Burma and Ceylon, was a
great landmark in world history. The British Empire was peacefully
liquidated by the British Parliament. This was a signal for the termination of colonialism throughout the world. America with its con-
genital bias against colonialism and Russia with its slogan of anti-
imperialism both hurried to grant independence to numerous big
and small nations spread over Africa, Asia, and elsewhere. The
United Nations organization admitted all these new nations as
units, all of them being equal to one another whether big or small,
powerful or insignificant. This was an advantage, but it carried with
it the great disadvantage of the organization's being overloaded
with "have-not" units carrying no power behind them. Soon the
United Nations organization was infected not only by the old cold-
war poison but also by a new poison distilled out of the old anti-
imperialist feelings. Blocs began to be organized in the UN that
blasted the hopes of its growing into an effective world authority
under world law. Nationalism grew again into a dynamic force replacing the internationalism that had marked the end of the Second World War and had raised vast hopes in the minds of world
statesmen. Today that internationalism and that great hope have
both nearly disappeared. The powerful French President is the big-
gest symptom of this new nationalism. The polarization of the na-

tions of the world into free and Communist tended to replace nationalism by a world outlook pulling either one way or the other. Each side hoped the other side's consolidation would break up as a result of nationalist forces. But what actually happened is that both sides underwent that change—and world consolidation has suffered badly as a result. The regenerated nationalism of the big nations of the world and the persistent anti-West feelings of the newly emancipated small nations have both become great roadblocks in the march to a world government. The goal appeared near enough some years ago but it has receded very far now.

And as a result of this setback, the old cold war which seemed to be disappearing has got a fresh start. China is in the front line of this new phase of the cold war and Russia can but join her comrade —willingly or otherwise. The prospect for the world has become indeed bleak.

Let us, for the some relief, go back to the divine *leela*. There could have been nothing conceivably more vicious than the slave trade, which planted a large number of Africans in the United States of America. The Negroes of America are no longer slaves but are a significant section of a free and great nation. Their present movement for full integration with the white majority is today a point of irritation—like the one within the oyster that makes the precious pearl. Similarly, this present irritation in the United States will lead to something great and precious—the breakdown of one of the most stupid of superstitions, that the color of the skin makes a real difference between man and man. The defects, intellectual or moral, in a Southern white person appear to many, if not most, white people in the U.S. as tolerable and remediable, but the same defects in a black man are felt by the same people to be intolerable and permanently associated with the skin pigment and therefore unchangeable. This is an attitude hard to cast out. Often one's intellect and reason would admit the attitude to be baseless, but sentiment persists against intellect. The prejudice disappears only when the pigment is outbalanced by talent, wealth, or enlightenment. Even where it is overcome, it is often only an external conquest, not a complete internal annulment.

This color superstition is not confined to white against Negro, but prevails throughout the world in some form or another. In India it takes the form of caste prejudice and in a higher value stupidly and openly set on a fair complexion. And this in a country where the races got hopelessly mixed up many thousands of years ago.

The criminal slave trade made for the ultimate coming into being of a great number of Africans who are as enlightened as the natives of Europe who lived and progressed in America. These enlightened Negroes have a great mission cut out for them after integration with their fellow citizens in the U.S. It will be the uplift of their cousins in Africa—uplift not in the superficial sense of political stir, but in the real sense of a rise of level in enlightened living. This would be a capital demonstration of good coming out of evil— in the not too distant future. And perhaps there will be exchange of good on both sides, for the black people of Africa have something valuable to give to their cousins in America, who have adopted American culture.

The evolution of human civilization takes its course through what is obviously good and gentle as well as through oppression— through ambition and conquests as well as through the voluntary consolidation of groups of humans, and through their joint activities. What has been recorded in history as activities of ambitious and wicked leaders of men has all helped toward the evolution of what we now recognize as progress and civilization. The British occupation of India is a patent example of how good comes out of evil. It is not an exception. It is only one patent illustration of what has been going on in God's leela from time immemorial. The regions and the human groups now divided into separate nations as

Ceylon, India, Pakistan, Burma, Tibet, Malaya, Nepal, Bhutan, Sikkim, Nagaland, and so on in Asia were all one vast region under Britain and could have entered the UN as one unit.

I remember when India was legally released from Britain and the question before us was whether to be completely isolated from the United Kingdom or to remain in the Commonwealth as one of its units recognizing the British sovereign's symbolic status as head of the Commonwealth. Jawaharlal Nehru, no doubt under the subtle influence of Earl Mountbatten, told me that he was inclined to remain in the Commonwealth, because, as he put it to me, it is good for world peace and progress that nations come together rather than be isolated, and the Commonwealth was a big consolidated reality, which we should keep and nurse rather than break up. His inclination was a pleasant surprise to the rest of us and it became a great decision that moved the incorrigible imperialist Winston Churchill to tears of joy. Projecting our thoughts from this point, we can imagine that it would have been better for the world if other imperial consolidations that had been brought into being through ambition, fraud, or force had not been hastily dissolved but, rather, exploited for the ultimate good of humanity. Again, we cannot dive into the inscrutable play of the Divine Master but must submit and do our relative duties honestly, and reverently strive to take humanity forward in spite of all the difficulties and contrary forces. Internationalism has in great part unfortunately yielded again to reinvigorated nationalism. The spirit of resistance, anger, and hatred generated in the struggles for liberty persist even after liberation when such feelings have no place or meaning. All this and other difficulties have to be overcome and will be overcome because the good is stronger than the evil, and truth must prevail over error, however seemingly more energetic evil and error may appear to be for a time.

America should not lose interest or faith in the UN or develop a feeling of antagonism to it. What now appear to be setbacks may indeed turn out to be just what was necessary to prevent some greater evil. Let us struggle and God will ultimately help us. His *leela* is no doubt complicated and inscrutable. There is much apparent evil that we cannot explain on the basis of a just and merciful all-powerful guardian of the human species. But what we have experienced is enough to prove Him to be good and omnipotent. Let us strive, therefore, with faith in the ultimate result. Let us cultivate serenity and patience and let us act our parts justly in His great and unending play, at each moment doing our duties to one another and to society and humanity as a whole; and even further, by doing our duty to all living beings. Endowed with the wonderful endowment of the human mind, we have duties toward all the living beings on earth, with whom we are really one and indivisible.

Brisk trade is developing between the Western nations and Soviet Russia and her allies, and is operating as a catalyst to dissolve the cold war attitudes. This is a development promising much good, especially when the selling is accompanied by long credit terms.

We can see the difficulties and complications in the administration of a small welfare state. We see the same difficulties multiplied tenfold in the large nation-states. We can do no good without inflicting pain on someone or other. Infinitely more complicated must be the divine administration of the whole planet on any welfare plan! If we extend our thoughts beyond human pain and pleasure and admit that the all-merciful Supreme Master's charge includes also living beings other than man, the complications increase more than a millionfold.

The pain and destruction we inflict on sentient beings to find out and practice methods to relieve human pain and human hunger and wants is immeasurable. Indeed, we are even led to conclude that there is no way of creating pleasure without creating an equal quantum of pain. These thoughts take us back to the inscrutability of the ways of the Master who governs this vast universe of which our planet and the human population on it is an infinitesimal part. Closing our eyes to the dizzy heights of the universe and concentrating our imagination on the problems of man only on this planet, do we not see, as plainly as anything can be made plain, that all our difficulties arise out of disobedience of the moral law? This moral law is not absolute but relative and flexible to suit every context. There can be no solution for unhappiness except by firm reestablishment of this moral law. And this is what we should aim at with determined minds.

Notwithstanding every advance made through observation and experiment to unravel the mysteries of the universe in which we live using the superb instrument for investigation with which we are endowed—the human brain—there is an irreducible residue of an unknowable, inscrutable nature. We may spell the Inscrutable with a capital letter or we may follow our forefathers' way of spelling it with three simple letters of the alphabet—it comes to the same thing. Darwin summarizes his investigations with the revolutionary laws that, according to him, brought about the infinite number of species of life on earth, with the deeply pious as well as scientific observation that it is no derogation of divinity to discover an evolutionary process at work through millions and millions of years in place of a single act of creation, and that, indeed, it is an enhancement of God's almighty character to understand and appreciate the automatic power with which he invested the lowest forms of life to develop ultimately into man, that the law he ordained worked unceasingly and brought about the wonder that we call the universe, and that in this planet it brought into being the marvel that is man and his mind. The discoveries of science, be it in physics or in zoology, cannot do away with the primeval cause—aadi moolam, as the Hindus call it—to which they offer adoration. That inscrutable gap is an irreducible one. The discoveries of science only enhance the wonder and the inscrutability of the Supreme Being. This humble confession leads to hope and saves us from despair in the midst of the most depressing circumstances. Optimism is not a creed but an inescapable attitude of mind that has an evolutionary function.

## Chakravarti Rajagopalachari

Chakravarti Rajagopalachari is one of the most beloved and respected political and philosophical figures in India. He was educated at the Presidency and Law Colleges in Madras. A long-time leader in India's turbulent political history, he is currently a key member of the Swatantra Party, an important opposition group in the Rajya Sabha, or upper house of the legislature. From 1948 to 1950, the stormy formative years of the newly independent country, Mr. Rajagopalachari was India's Governor-General—the culmination of more than two decades of work with the Indian National Congress led by Mahatma Gandhi, whom he met and joined during Gandhi's Satyagraha campaign and noncooperation movement in 1919–1920. Mr. Rajagopalachari's devotion to Gandhi was total. He was jailed five times for his Congress activities. While Gandhi himself was in prison, Rajagopalachari edited his Gandhi, Young India. Mr. Rajagopalachari's own pervasive interest in philosophy and literature is brought out in his several reflective works, including Hinduism: Doctrine and Way of Life and Voice of the Uninvolved. He was born in the Salem district of India in 1878.

# SIR HERBERT READ

# What Ever Happened
# to the Great Simplicities?

IN THE heart of London, just to the north of Trafalgar Square, there is a statue of an almost forgotten heroine of the First World War, Nurse Edith Cavell, and on the pediment are inscribed the words: PATRIOTISM IS NOT ENOUGH. I have been told that the saying is apocryphal; in any case, like most sayings of the kind, it is ambiguous. Nurse Cavell was executed by the Germans in 1915 for treason, and what presumably is meant by the saying is that it is not sufficient to profess a sentiment such as patriotism—there is above it a love of humanity that does not distinguish between the members of one race or another.

What is patriotism? Love of one's country and of one's fellow countrymen, but that love has been sadly confused in our time with nationalism, which usually implies hatred of all foreigners and a determination to assert, by force if necessary, the selfish claims of one's own country. Dr. Johnson thought that patriotism is the last refuge of a scoundrel, and in our time it is generally considered more altruistic to proclaim oneself a citizen of the world, to profess the brotherhood of mankind; and that perhaps is the real significance of the words on Nurse Cavell's monument.

I have learned to distrust all such words, and the lesson began about the same time that Nurse Cavell was sacrificing her life. I very nearly sacrificed my own life in that same war, and all those four long years I was asking myself, for what purpose? Not—decidedly not—because I was inspired by any patriotic feelings, or any feelings of hatred for the enemy. I was caught by the war, like a young animal that had sprung some trap, and I went into it without the least trace of patriotic sentiment, without enthusiasm of any kind except a vague desire for adventure and for an ordeal that would test my courage. Those vague desires were quickly dispelled by the crude horrors of the actual experience. I endured these to the end, but long before the end I had lost the adolescent enthusiasm that lent some glamour to the early days of training and embarkation.

As the war proceeded and hundreds of thousands of my fellow-infantrymen were slaughtered—many of them I knew and loved—I acquired a deep hatred of those slogans with which the war was being justified by our politicians and journalists. I did not yet have the necessary experience to guard against the substitution of other, equally deceptive slogans—or "rogue words," as Ruskin called them—and though I hesitated between socialism, communism, and anarchism to describe the political ideals I was formulating (the last was the one I eventually adopted), there was one word I did not hesitate to use—pacifism. I continued to fight, for the very good reason that I could not desert my companions, and for the less good reason that I did not wish to be thought a coward, but I did not hesitate to write and publish poems condemning war and expressing a longing for peace. I have remained a pacifist all my life, and if I am told that pacifism is merely another rogue word, devoid of realism and apt to deceive innocent people, I answer that it presents the essential creed of all the profoundest teachers the world has ever known—Lao-tzu, Confucius, Christ, St. Francis, Comenius, Kant, Tolstoy, Gandhi, and many others.

Pacifism must, of course, be defined; and aggression, which it opposes, must also be recognized and defined. Pacifism is not a negative doctrine; it is the science of diverting aggressive instincts into creative channels. Such a science is now well understood, and scientists such as William James, Freud, Jung, and Konrad Lorenz have removed the roguery from the word. Peace is now a realistic alternative to war.

But it has not yet replaced patriotism and other rogue words in the politics of our time. The most thriving of our present slogans, in the Western world, is the one which H. G. Wells first formulated as "making the world safe for democracy." It was immediately countered by a similar slogan—making the world safe for communism, and half a century of political chaos has by now surely taught us that both slogans are meaningless. Democracy, as just a political concept, is meaningless for any society larger than a small city or a rural commune. Our so-called democracies in the Western world are oligarchies subject more or less to periodical revision (which never changes their oligarchical structure), and in this they do not differ essentially from the oligarchies that rule the Communist world. The people, in any human corporate sense, do not determine any policies outside their backyards. The world is governed by the representatives of industry, finance, technology, and by bureaucracies in the paid service of these powerful groups—governed, not in the interests of the people as a whole, not even of all the people in any one country, and not even nowadays for personal profit, but primarily for the self-satisfying exercise of power.

So much for the ideals I lost through the experience of war. But there were some that I gained from the same experience, apart from a belief in pacifism. I gained—or rather, I was confirmed in—a belief in the essential goodness of man. This may seem to contradict what I have just written about democratic politics, but it is not man—common man—who is engaged in such politics; the common man is exploited by politicians in every country. My belief in the common man arises directly out of my wartime experience.

Who were the men I fought with? For the most part, miners and agricultural workers from the north of England, with a sprinkling of clerks, teachers, and professional men drawn willynilly into the vortex of war. To men accustomed to mines and ditches, the trenches were perhaps not physically daunting. There were, of course, a few exceptions, men with some built-in neurosis; but the great majority accepted constant danger and the frequency of death with a willingness for which, for some reason, the French word *insouciance* seems appropriate. It was not that they wished to die, but they knew that death was in any case their human lot— that every bullet, as they used to sing, has its billet. Words such as bravery or courage they would have rejected—they groaned when some visiting general called them "my brave men." They were, simply, fatalists, and that is perhaps the philosophy of all men who are engaged in a dangerous calling—miners, sailors, soldiers, airmen, mountaineers. This was the basic characteristic of the men I became familiar with—useful in warfare, but not induced by it. The quality that then emerged among these fatalists I have been inclined in the past to call "solidarity" (it has nothing to do with the conventional *esprit de corps*), but recently my attention was drawn to some words of Conrad's (himself a man who had lived dangerously) in the book he called *A Personal Record:*

. . . Those who read me know my conviction that the world, the temporal world, rests on a few very simple ideas; so simple that they must be as old as the hills. It rests notably, among others, on the idea of Fidelity.

Fidelity is the word I need to describe the simple idea that was revealed to me in the First World War—the fidelity of one man to another, in circumstances of common danger, the fidelity of all men in a group to one another and to the group as a whole. I read, either

274 WHAT I HAVE LEARNED

during the war or shortly afterward, Kropotkin's great book, *Mutual Aid*, and there I found this simple idea enshrined in a philosophy of society; and to this simple idea I have now been faithful for more than fifty years.

It is a striking paradox that this idea of fidelity, highly valuable as a social bond, is not a moral idea. It came to me in the midst of war, and it characterized groups of men who were, after all, engaged in the beastly business of killing other men. We had sufficient contact with the enemy to know that they, too, were inspired by the same fidelity to one another; and, of course, the idea is not confined to men at war. It can characterize any group engaged in a dangerous occupation, even groups of criminals—gangsters, as we significantly call them. The lesson here is that social virtues are not necessarily moral virtues—courage, fidelity, self-respect, and even love are social virtues, and as such are inculcated, not by precept, but by example and habit.

This lesson that I learned so early in life has, I think, been the profoundest of all, and in some sense it determined the rest of my life. But it is by no means the only lesson that I have learned, and it was not, in the usual sense of the phrase, a disillusioning lesson. What was disillusioning was the discovery that an ideal that had proved to be so necessary in war was not viable in peacetime—that fidelity and mutual aid were powerless against the political establishment at home. I have spoken elsewhere (in my autobiography, *The Contrary Experience*), of the intense disillusionment that followed the First World War, a disillusionment shared by ex-combatants in every country, not excluding Russia. This disillusionment has been prolonged for more than half a century, has been intensified by another world war, and is now aggravated by what we call the cold war. It has found expression in all kinds of movements and revolts, and has provoked noble utterances from such outraged men as Gandhi, Russell, and Camus. But what has been achieved?

Even the delusive emancipation of India has led only to the martyr-dom of Gandhi, to religious and racial strife, to political chaos and famine. The simple idea of fidelity has not prevailed, least of all in India.

I must now speak of the more intimate lessons I have learned —not in my personal life, for that, apart from the inevitable trage-dies of death and separation, has been happy. The severest lessons have been those which have taught me to moderate my personal ambitions. My greatest ambition was to be recognized as a poet, but I soon learned that the modern world has little use for poets in general, and less for me in particular. Against such a statement might be brought in evidence the careers of Yeats, Valéry, Rilke, Frost, or Eliot—poets who have been acclaimed and honored by the whole world. But what do these poets themselves say about their so-called success? They are full of personal bitterness, con-tempt for society, spiritual disillusionment. They knew that their fame was a hollow and insubstantial show, that their public was largely sycophantic or hypocritical, and that their influence on their fellow men (compared with the influence of a Dante, a Milton, or a Wordsworth) was nil.

It is true that their verse was not so "uplifting" as the verse of the great poets I have mentioned; it would have been false if it had been, for the poet today is called upon not to uplift but to reveal— to reveal the tragic situation of modern man. Such a tragic vision is not welcomed by the citizens of an affluent society, and all these poets (not notably "democratic" in their sentiments) have been ignored by that society. Their reputations are academic, or at best "aristocratic"; they mean nothing to the technocrats who are mak-ing the modern world, nor to those who are content to live in such a world.

In my own case I have to confess rather ruefully that I was not born with a tragic view of life—my ideal was to celebrate in poetry not so much nature as man's triumph over nature, in the manner described by Eric Hoffer in a previous contribution to this series. I remember many discussions with Eliot and other contemporaries of mine on this question of the necessity of a tragic sense of life, and though, under the influence of Nietzsche, Unamuno, Freud, and T. E. Hulme, I had come to accept such a necessity *intellectually*, I could not bend my muse in this direction. I attempted one tragic poem of adequate scope—"The End of a War"—but even this had to end with an affirmation of hope.

The lesson I learned from this experience was that as a poet I was not in tune with the age—in spite of the fact that I was a modernist in technique and had never relaxed the intolerable struggle, as Eliot called it, to match words to feelings. It will be said that in my case the feelings were not profound enough; I prefer to believe that they were not fashionable enough. But I do not say this in any spirit of arrogance; merely I affirm once more Conrad's conviction that the world rests on a few simple ideas, and I do not find that the ideas prevailing today are simple enough.

I come now to an experience that may be said to have redirected the course of my life. My interest in the fine arts had been aroused at the same time as my discovery of poetry, and in the intellectual vacuum of the years immediately following the First World War (in England almost a physical vacuum caused by the slaughter of so many young men of my generation) I was drawn into the struggle to establish the new ideals in painting and sculpture—my first art criticism was written already in 1919. The interval between the two wars was a period of intense activity—a new kind of war, the modernists assailing the entrenchments of tradition and authority. Eventually, that war was also won, and one learned much from a struggle distinguished by bitterness on one side and arrogance on the other. But such experiences were shared by many others, and do not call for special comment in the present context.

The particular and personal experience I have in mind occurred during the Second World War. An organization called The British Council was created in 1940 with the purpose—to quote from its Royal Charter of Incorporation—"of promoting a wider knowledge of Our United Kingdom of Great Britain and Northern Ireland and the English language abroad and developing closer cultural relations between Our United Kingdom . . . and other countries." A Fine Arts Committee was formed to "project" British art abroad, and in the years that followed it was to prove very effective. But while the war lasted it was impossible to send valuable works of art across the seas, and as an interim measure it was decided to substitute collections of drawings by British children which could be packed in light parcels and framed when they reached their destination. I was given the task of selecting such drawings, and for this purpose visited a number of schools throughout the country. Several exhibitions were sent abroad, and one such exhibition was shown in Paris. Picasso came one day and spent a long time looking at the pictures. When he had finished he turned to me and said, in French, "When I was the age of these children I could paint like Raphael. It took me many years to learn how to paint like these children." The story has often been repeated, generally in a distorted form, but this is the authentic version.

In the course of collecting such drawings I came to a small village in Cambridgeshire and was there shown a drawing by a five-year-old girl which she called *Snake Round the World and a Boat*. It had been drawn by the child at home (she was the child of working-class parents) and was entirely spontaneous in origin. I was deeply moved because what this child had drawn was one of the oldest symbols in the world—a magic circle divided into segments and known as the mandala, the symbol of the self as a psychic unity, a very ancient symbol found in Egypt and the Far East and throughout Europe in the Middle Ages. In Tantric Yoga such a symbol represents the dwelling place of the gods. But the symbolism of the child's drawing does not end there, for the snake round the world may be identified with the Uroboros, again an ancient symbol found in Babylon, in India, Egypt, and elsewhere (among the Navajo Indians, for example).

There are many interpretations of this symbol, many of them having to do with time and eternity, but symbols are never meaningful in the rational sense, and of course this child could not attach a meaning to the symbol she had drawn, and was not even aware that it was a symbol. (The boat, she explained, was for crossing the seas.) I, with my more sophisticated knowledge, could recognize the drawing as a symbol that was archetypal and universal. Such knowledge on my part had been acquired largely from my reading of Jung's works, but what had been an interesting hypothesis had suddenly become an observed phenomenon, proof. This child of five had given me something in the nature of an apocalyptic experience.

This was not the only experience of the kind. Symbols are present in children's drawings everywhere, and at all ages. But on the basis of the material I collected for the British Council during the war I made a close study of the subject which was published in 1943 as *Education Through Art*. The more I considered my material the more convinced I became of the basic significance of the child's creative activities for the development of consciousness and for the necessary fusion of sensibility and intellect. In the course of writing my book I came to regard the theme as more and more polemical. I do not claim to have discovered any truth that was not known to teachers such as Franz Cizek in Austria and Marion Richardson in England, but I added my observations to theirs and put forward a hypothesis that was nothing less than a new system of pedagogy.

My point of view was accepted by many teachers, at first in England and then throughout the world. A society for Education Through Art was established in the United Kingdom, and in 1952 an International Society for Education Through Art was founded, sponsored by UNESCO, and held its first General Assembly in

Paris in 1954. INSEA, as it is called, now has branches throughout the world, but this does not mean that its claim—that art should be made the basis of education—has been widely recognized. It conflicts too directly with the technologically motivated education of advanced industrial societies. But the progress of this simple idea in twenty years has been amazing, and I believe that it may yet conquer the world.

It may—I do not express any confidence, for mankind seems to drift toward self-destruction in blind disregard of all that its wise men have said or can say. What, indeed, is there left to say? We need not go back to the wisdom of the East, to the sermons of Buddha and Christ, the simple Way of Lao-tzu, or the *Analects* of Confucius; to the wisdom of the fathers of the Church or of the philosophers of the Enlightenment. We have our own prophets who have spoken in clear voices—Tolstoy, Gandhi, Schweitzer, Freud, Jung, Buber. We know what we should do but we do not do it. We prefer to remain not so much in an outer darkness—for lights of wisdom blaze round us—but in a bemused euphoria of material "progress" which offers mankind a high standard of living in exchange for his spiritual freedom.

The greatest single deception in my life, as in the life of many idealists, has been the failure of socialism, in which term I include communism. This failure springs from one error and one only, "the most fatal error," as Shelley called it, "that ever happened in the world—the separation of political and ethical science." Tolstoy placed Shelley's statement as an epigraph to one of his later writings, *An Appeal to Social Reformers* (first published in 1900). Tolstoy recognized that the pursuit of power, whether by the individual or the state, is the root of all the evil we endure, and against power only a spiritual weapon can prevail.

This spiritual weapon is simply the one known long ago to men, which has always destroyed power and always given to those who used it complete and inalienable freedom. This weapon is but this, a devout understanding of life, according to which man regards his earthly existence as only a fragmentary manifestation of the complete life, and connecting his life with infinite life, and recognizing his highest welfare in the ful-fillment of the laws of this infinite life, regards the fulfillment of these laws as more binding upon himself than the following of any human laws whatsoever.

Only such a *religious* conception, Tolstoy concluded, can truly de-stroy power.

But is this a religious conception? Nicholas Berdyaev, a sympa-thetic but severe critic of Tolstoy, thought not—"The Good for him was God. This shows his greatness, but also his limitations." For Berdyaev something more is necessary—an awareness of "the significance of irrational processes of life that permeate us, get hold of us, imperil us, and thereby transcend our rational and moral aims and ends. . . . True, no one perhaps had experienced the horror of evil, particularly when it parades in the guise of the Good, with such intensity as Tolstoy, but he remained blind to the dark, irra-tional, metaphysical source of evil." That, too, was Jung's opinion, not of Tolstoy particularly, but of all social reformers who think that the world can be changed by rational means.

And so we come to the spiritual void that opens in my own path. I have read Berdyaev and many other Christian apologists, and have been moved especially by two of them, Kierkegaard and Simone Weil. Above all by Simone Weil, the greatest spiritual writer of our time, far profounder in my opinion than Teilhard de Chardin or even Martin Buber. The difficulty I experience with all such Christian apologists is that they rely, for their final argument, on the necessity of grace. They admit that this state of mind is an arbitrary phenomenon—"Grace fills empty spaces but it can only enter where there is a void to receive it, and it is grace itself that makes this void" (Simone Weil). It is not even a simple chance— the odds against the unbeliever are doubled.

In desperation, we have recourse to the science of the self, to individual psychology, which teaches us surely enough that reason alone no longer suffices. In particular, reason cannot deal with the problem of evil (consider the miserable failure of our present educational and reformatory measures against crime), nor can it deal with force (which is not necessarily always an ally of evil). In despair of reason, we now substitute fear—fear of organized crime, fear of nuclear war—if only we are fearful enough, we assume, we can control such evil forces. But fear is not even a positive instinct; it is the inhibition of all instincts, good as well as bad.

What we need is the peace of mind that comes with self-knowledge, and self-knowledge implies the knowledge of the unconscious processes that cause fear and aggression, envy and crime. This self-knowledge may in rare cases come from inner illumination, and happy are those who are vouchsafed it. For mankind at large it must come from what we must call education, ambiguous as the word is, an education that above all takes into account the symbolic needs of the unconscious—therefore, an education through art. The ideal to be achieved might be called serenity—the condition of mind, Buber once said to me, that he found only in England. I fear he was confusing serenity with our famous sang-froid!

Education is perhaps a poor and misunderstood process on which to rely for the salvation of mankind, but I know of no other. If we remember its literal meaning, then it does imply bringing to consciousness what is undeveloped, unrecognized, misunderstood, or despised. We must become whole men, and we cannot become whole so long as we leave the foundations of the psyche on tremulous ground. I agree with Jung that the process of education (which he called the process of individuation) may lead the individual back to God—or, as he would have said, bring God back to the individual. But these are questions for the future, and largely questions of nomenclature. The present and urgent necessity is to admit the sickness of man's soul and take practical measures to cure it. I would emphasize the word practical, and even substitute for it the

word pragmatic, for it is no longer a question of moral exhortation
or of religious revivalism; it is a question of having faith in a few
simple ideas, for only such simple ideas have the power to transform the world.


## Sir Herbert Read

Sir Herbert Read, prominent British poet and a leading interpreter of
modern art and literature, was born in 1893 in Yorkshire, England, the
eldest son of a farmer. He studied at Crossley's School, Halifax, and at
the University of Leeds. Although a pacifist by political conviction, he
served in World War I in France and Belgium, attaining the rank of
captain. He has been a professor or lecturer at the University of Edin-
burgh, the University of Liverpool, Harvard, and other institutions. His
extensive writings include: Education Through Art, Art and Society, A
Concise History of Modern Painting, A Concise History of Modern
Sculpture, Reason and Romanticism, Anarchy and Order, and several
volumes of poetry.

# JOSEF HANS THIRRING

## Can a Scientist Be an Optimist?

---

THERE ARE many people who doubt that real progress in the human society is possible. I have often heard the saying of pessimistic historians, "The only lesson which history taught us is that man has not yet learned anything from history." Being rather optimistic on that score, even willing to grant that there may be some truth in this saying, I feel that the emphasis in this sentence should be laid on the words *not yet*.

What I am writing in this article is a kind of first guide on how to learn from history. It is quite instructive to compare the past of mankind with its possible future. The age of *Homo sapiens* in his recent physical constitution is about a million years. About five millennia of a historical epoch lie behind us. The steam age began less than two centuries ago, that of electricity about a hundred years ago, radio and air travel only a few decades ago. All these periods are infinitesimally small compared to the possible future of mankind.

Certainly we are now passing through a critical phase of history which began with the accumulation of sufficient annihilating power to extinguish civilized life. This crisis will end only if we reach an agreement on general and complete disarmament. But should we succeed in surviving the next few decades and become mature enough for total disarmament on a global scale, the chances for a better and long future are excellent. Our scientists and technicians will be given more time and money for improving human life instead of finding means for its destruction. Medical doctors and educators will be efficient enough to save us from degeneration by an overdose of civilization and from the population explosion.

The natural end of life on earth will be caused by radical changes of solar activity which are, however, well over a billion years in the offing. Thus, comparing the almost endless time usable for futher human development with the ridiculously short period of world history, we find that our civilization is in the stage of a new-born baby that opens its eyes for the first time.

This thought is apt to alleviate somewhat our feelings of anxiety over the unsatisfactory state of affairs both in private life and world politics; all these shortcomings of our civilization—the cultural lag, the barbarism of warfare, the petty quarrels between individuals and between groups, the money, goods, and labor squandered on military purposes regardless of a miserably undernourished majority of the world population—all these are nothing but the children's diseases of our still quite infantile humanity.

There is also some hope that those teachings from history that are needed most urgently will be understood before a nuclear holocaust wipes out our civilization. We are living in a period of quick changes, many of them quite radical. Just compare the new look of our young girls of today with that of all their ancestors as far as we can look back. Almost as quick as the change of fashion is that of technology. I remember well the days before the first flights of Orville and Wilbur Wright (1903) when a wise uncle of mine tried to dampen my enthusiasm for an around-the-world flight. His argument was, "Man is neither a bird nor an insect. Since the beginning of the world his way of moving went along the earth's surface, and this will remain so forever."

He grew old enough thereafter to confess his mistake. But, on the other hand, it was only a few years ago that I heard a professor of history declare, "There have always been wars between the nations. Hence, wars will occur as long as men exist." I am afraid that it will be only the grandson of this historian who will acknowledge that the old gentleman guessed wrong. The two prejudices, "war in all eternity" and "man cannot learn from history," are somehow interconnected. Hence, a less irrational understanding of past mistakes would be of great help in avoiding future wars.

Of course, it will take some time to adapt formal education to the spirit of "constructing the defense of peace in the minds of men," as proclaimed in the charter of UNESCO. But whatever we learn in school can be greatly enriched by intelligent use of our thinking abilities in order to draw conclusions from significant events of history and of our time. Also from personal experience. Here is how I learned some important knowledge which I was not taught in school.

One of the earliest observations that impressed me, at the age of about fifteen, is something which seems to happen to all strata of society—perhaps particularly to the upper class. It struck me that pain and suffering among men are caused more often by basically avoidable evils than by unavoidable ones such as the loss of a loved one, serious illness, extreme poverty, or catastrophes occurring in nature. Most cases of unhappiness seem to result from petty feuding with one's fellow man or from inner conflicts. This unhappiness derives to a large extent from frustrated desires and vain abmitions, or, speaking generally, from a false sense of values. Many people feel miserable without being either poor or physically ill; others feel badly injured though nothing but their vanity has been hurt.

As far as I know, nobody has yet made any comparative study of troubles arising from avoidable and unavoidable evils. But I would guess that the former occur perhaps ten times more frequently than the latter. This is a striking symptom of the backwardness of our age. A radical reorientation in this respect seems to me of supreme importance.

The first rule I gathered from my personal experience was:

*Beware of being misled by a distorted hierarchy of values.* In observing that rule I grew more self-confident and soon was able to feel sorry for people handicapped by vain ambitions, prejudices, and touchiness. At that stage of my gradual development into a mature human being, my attention to a proper hierarchy of values was limited to personal matters, where it proved to be extremely useful. A decade later, however, I realized its importance in a far wider field.

Till 1918, the name day of the saints Peter and Paul on June 29 was a holiday in Austria. On that day in 1914, I spent the afternoon with friends at the house of a colleague of mine when extra editions of the papers brought the news of the assassination of Archduke Franz Ferdinand, heir to the throne of the Austro-Hungarian Empire, who was shot in Sarajevo near the Austro-Serbian border. Understandably, our small group centered its discussion upon this event and its foreseeable consequences. Although we all felt that most likely war would break out against Serbia, our opinions differed concerning the wisdom of taking such a drastic step. All the officers and most of the male civilians in our group declared that it was a point of national honor for every loyal Austrian to teach those Serbians a lesson for having bred the assassin and possibly supported his action.

I was among the few who opposed this opinion. For I began to visualize the consequences of a modern war and tried to make my friends realize the risk which our country and the dynasty would run by using the deed of a fanatic youth as a pretext for waging war in one of the most explosive areas of Europe. My arguments were rejected, however, by most of my friends, who saw the major issue of the whole affair in the injured honor of Austria which "had to be defended at whatever cost."

I am reporting this discussion because it was symptomatic of the spirit guiding young intellectuals of the middle class of that time. Certainly other reasons, particularly military ones, also helped to induce the Austrian government to issue an all but unacceptable ultimatum to Serbia. This was at the time when dueling was still in vogue in the circles of college students and officers. The appeal to the honor of the nation carried enough weight to override any hesitation and scruples that might have prevented our eighty-four-year-old emperor Franz Josef from signing the declaration of war against Serbia on July 28, 1914. What followed that fateful decision was a headlong succession of events which changed the political map of the world, in particular that of the very country which tried to defend its honor by going to war.

Though initially successful, the punitive campaign undertaken by Austria against Serbia kindled the First World War, which led to the complete defeat of the Austro-Hungarian monarchy. The empire was cut into eight fragments, seven of which were swallowed by neighbor states. What was left of Austria retained its independence, but survived in such a poor situation that twenty years later it was easy for Hitler to integrate it into his "Third Empire." But in 1918 the Hapsburg dynasty that had ruled Austria since 1273 was toppled and reduced to a powerless clan.

Its fall was preceded by the extinction of the family of the Czar and the ousting of the German Kaiser. Several Balkan kings shared the same fate, while communism got a foothold in Russia. From there Marxism-Leninism spread to other countries. Today the number of people under Communist rule exceeds one billion. Certainly this development results partly from the Second World War, but this in turn can be regarded as an offspring of the first one.

The two world wars in our century, which grew out of national vanity and military ambition, led to overall results that were unintended, unexpected, and most unwelcome to all who had advocated the "hard line." Historically, the most important outcome of the two wars was the spread of the theories of Marx and Lenin in worldwide application. This was exactly what the most ardent warmongers of 1914 and 1939 never wished to have happen. The man who had most reason to thank the militarists of 1914 for insisting upon strong measures against Serbia was Lenin, at that time a penniless emigrant in Switzerland without influence on any of the governments that decided on peace or war.

Thus, by comparing wars of different epochs, I learned another important rule. Although, of course, every war causes more loss than gain, more harm than good for both sides, there were cases in the past in which some instigators of a war were sufficiently satisfied afterward to discount the costs. *This is no longer true in our century.* Nearly all the people in power who favored one of the world wars and were involved in waging it had to suffer for their misdeeds either by loss of life, position, or fortune. None of them would ever have committed the insane crime if he had foreseen the consequences clearly enough.

Regarding future events, one can safely predict that any instigator of a third world war would have to repent his crime much earlier. The reason for this lies in the revolution of technology. Until the end of the nineteenth century, military experts seemed to be right in assuming that every progress in the destructive power of weapons would be compensated sooner or later by a corresponding progress of the means for defense—for instance, stronger guns, stronger armor—so that an equilibrium between offensive and defensive weapons could be maintained in the long run. The validity of this rule was shaken with the beginning of aerial warfare; it has become void since the advent of nuclear and thermonuclear weapons.

This is the field in which scientists are in a better situation than historians to foresee and foretell further developments. I do not mean that their brains are better developed than those of their colleagues, but they are equipped with the necessary information regarding facts of physics and chemistry which permit them to conclude what is possible and what is not.

Several times since 1913 I have had the opportunity to contradict and correct technical prognoses of politicians and journalists. During the Second World War, I was silenced, after Hitler's march into Austria, by being dismissed from my academic chair. The authorities felt that someone like me would be a danger to the military spirit of the German youth. But after the war I was reinstalled in my former position and had the opportunity of openly discussing the possibilities of using nuclear energy for peaceful and military purposes.

Thus the two nuclear bombs which in August of 1945 ended the Second World War did not come unexpectedly for some European physicists, including myself. Moreover, I happened to become a herald of the thermonuclear weapons. As early as 1929 another Vienna-born physicist, Fritz Houtermans, together with the American, Robert Atkinson, had suggested the idea, now generally accepted, that thermonuclear fusion reactions (that is, the buildup of heavier elements from lighter ones) might be the source of stellar energy. The scientists who worked on the atomic bomb at Los Alamos were quick to grasp the idea that such a fission bomb could be used as a detonator of a fusion bomb, which in turn might be made much more powerful than what they were constructing at that time.

This idea was near at hand for other inventive spirits and was therefore conceived almost simultaneously by physicists in other countries who had no access to the military secrets of the United States. Nor was any espionage necessary to arouse my interest in this matter. The official U.S. report on atomic energy wirtten by H. D. Smyth, issued late in 1945, contained enough information to make a physicist understand how the fission bomb worked. But it did not disclose anything about thermonuclear (or fusion) bombs. On the other hand, the tables of nuclear data published before the war contained sufficient information on the energy released by the fusion of hydrogen into helium or by other fusion processes. The study of all this inspired me in 1946 to write a book, *Die*

*Geschichte der Atombombe* ("The History of the Atomic Bomb")
in which I tried to widen the knowledge of the reader beyond the
officially released information to possible future developments of
nuclear weapons.

In Chapter 42 of this book I gave the first numerical data ever
published about the power-per-unit weight of hydrogen in a thermonuclear bomb and added the prediction that by the transition
from fission to fusion bombs, another jump to thousandfold more
destructive power could be foreseen. The book had no influence on
the decision of the Truman Administration to develop the bomb.
This was made when American scientists discovered that the Russians had tested an atom bomb in September 1949. The decision
was announced on January 31, 1950. Till that date all the work on
thermonuclear weapons was kept secret in the United States. During 1947, 1948, and 1949 about twenty-four thousand copies of my
book were sold in Austria and were mainly used in introductory
courses on nuclear physics in our colleges.

The only impact that my book had in the field of politics was to
help an American senator overcome an embarrassment. In the discussions on the loss of U.S. monopoly in the nuclear field, this gentleman was incautious enough to give hints of a possible American
superweapon some months before the secret was officially released.
For this he was severely criticized, and some opponents insisted he
should be accused of treason because he had disclosed to the Russians the idea of making a superbomb. By producing my book,
which long had been on sale in Austrian bookstores "right under
the nose of the Russians," the senator showed that anyone interested in the matter could obtain, for a few cents, more technical
information about the hydrogen bomb and its possibilities than
that disclosed in his talk or in the President's communication.

My forecast of 1946 regarding superweapons became true
when the first American megaton bomb exploded in November
1952. The Russian tests with even stronger (up to 57-megaton)

bombs followed. No further increase of the power of single bombs seems to be necessary or even desirable. But a big jump in means of delivery has been made since 1950. In addition to the bomber fleet, atom-powered submarines can be used for carrying Polaris rockets with thermonuclear warheads. Intercontinental ballistic missiles can deliver megaton bombs across the Atlantic. In case of an all-out war the total destructive capacity of all the bombs which any of the two superpowers could unload on its enemies' territory within a few hours is almost beyond imagination. Analyzing the chain of consequences of this entirely new state of world affairs, we find:

• There is no technical obstacle to either of the two superpowers' fully destroying the other one. ("Full destruction" of a nation means in this context the physical liquidation of the inhabitants of the big cities, destruction of the industrial centers, transport, water supply, and all kinds of power sources. In addition, wide areas of the bombed country would be heavily contaminated by the radioactive fallout.) The resultant damage would split the nation into a multitude of small islands without adequate means of intercommunication. The wretched survivors would be fully occupied with protecting the remnants of food from being stolen by refugees. They could not be expected to organize cooperation with survivors from other parts of the country.

• Because of improved protection of important military objects, the war machinery of the aggressor might speedily destroy a nation but could not at the same time annihilate the submarines and land-based missiles of its victim. In a nuclear war between the two superpowers, the aggressed state, though not able to avert its own destruction, will retain a sufficient retaliatory capacity to destroy its aggressor as well. Hence, every attempt to defeat one of the two superpowers by a kind of blitzkrieg would be suicidal.

• This fact is well known to the political leaders of both sides. They are seriously concerned not to escalate existing conflicts to the point of a general war. The risk and the cost of military engagements have risen so tremendously that no responsible statesman outside the Chinese wall would earnestly plan to widen either his territory or influence by means of a war. The position of the U.S.S.R. was formulated most clearly in a speech on disarmament and peaceful coexistence which former Soviet Premier Nikita Khrushchev delivered on July 2, 1960, in Vienna. He said, "One cannot drive a man into paradise with a cudgel nor a nation into communism by a war." In the same speech Mr. Khrushchev repeated the much-quoted intention of communism "to conquer the world," but made it clear that conquest cannot be realized in the nuclear age by a war, but by the victory of the better system, just as the technical achievements of our time (electricity, autos, film, radio, television) indeed have conquered the world.

In the same year the General Conference of the United Nations passed a resolution in which general and complete disarmament was declared to be the most urgent task of mankind. Never before 1960 did we seem that near to a world without war.

The three facts mentioned here—the overkill capacity of the superpowers, the hopeless prospect of defense in an all-out war, the general renunciation of military conquests—all these are logical consequences of the technical development. But since the beginning of the sixties an apparent paradox has made itself felt. In disregard of the facts listed here, the armaments race keeps on. The negotiations of the Geneva Disarmament Committee have been shifted to the sidetrack of test bans, pushing aside any mention of real disarmament. Attempts at international understanding are replaced by strict application of the rules of the "bible of Prussian militarism," written by von Clausewitz, which would have us think blindly the worst of our enemy's intentions.

Thus the necessity of keeping strong Western forces in Europe is based on the assumption that a strong NATO is the only means of preventing the Red Army from marching to the Atlantic. (We may call this fear complex "the Eastern bogey of the West.") The other side in turn argues that adequately armed Red troops of the Warsaw Pact are necessary security measures in view of the aggressive American imperialism and German "revanchism" ("Western bogey of the East").

Confronting these two bogeys we find this baffling fact: In spite of the persisting efforts of the United Nations and UNESCO to establish better international understanding, the reasons for spending tremendous sums on military purposes are quite incomprehensible for those against whom the weapons are aimed. The arguments of mistrust cannot but appear to them a slander and, moreover, grotesque nonsense. Here we have a good example of the infantile state of our civilization. Science is trying to probe into the mysteries of atomic nuclei, organic life, and the puzzling stellar objects at distances of billions of light years. But in reacting to alleged plans of neighbors on earth the authorities of most countries are behaving as if their knowledge of the potential enemy and its intentions and concerns were derived from oracles and fortune-tellers.

My harsh words against the people who overrate the danger threatening from a potential enemy do not mean that I consider them fools. Apart from the old habit in politics of being overcautious there are certain forces at work which tend to deepen the mutual mistrust. Their voices seem to be impressive enough to uphold the paradoxical situation of today.

To understand the paradox we must take into account the following sequence of events and situations:

1) The nations have built up their armed forces to protect their security.

2) The personnel of this instrument gain ever more importance and tend to grow autonomous.

3) The military profession of all countries is seriously threat-

ened by the plan of general disarmament. It is quite natural, therefore, that its spokesmen will try to prove the necessity of its existence. Thus, the majority of citizens who cannot study closely
enough the intentions of foreign statesmen are persuaded that the
freedom of the nation would be hopelessly lost unless it is defended
by adequately strong armed forces.

   I happened to observe a case in which the Austrian mass media
impeded better understanding of Khrushchev's efforts toward
peaceful coexistence. When he made his Vienna speech of 1960 in
which he declared that nations cannot be driven into communism
by a war, all Austrian papers printed full reports, particularly em-
phasizing his typical malicious remarks against the United States.
But, with one exception, all of them canceled the above-quoted
crucial point of his speech. It seemed to be worthwhile to test
whether this omission was made intentionally or just by chance.
Therefore, I wrote to Khrushchev in 1961 telling him that I regretted the deficient reports of his Vienna speech. I asked him to confirm in a letter to me his conviction that man cannot be driven into
communism by a war.

   His answer was a letter of eight typewritten pages which was
also published by Tass, the Soviet news agency, then printed in
nearly all papers of the Communist bloc and broadcast by its radio
stations. The above quoted sentence was duly repeated in this letter
and in all the reports of the Eastern mass media. The Austrian
papers carried reports, too. But in all of them, with the exception of
the Communist daily Die Volksstimme, the sentence that communism cannot be spread by a war was carefully left out.

   What we can learn from this incident is how easily a wrong
impression of a political antagonist can be given without a formal
lie and how this possibility is used in the propaganda against disarmament. The reports of Khrushchev's speech quite correctly
quoted those passages which the editors chose for publication. But

in omitting the most important part of his declaration, they hid the crucial point, namely, the urgent need of peaceful coexistence felt by the European Communist states. It is precisely the ultimate aim of these states, "to conquer the world by their better system," which is thwarted by the excessive load of armaments expenditure, and, therefore, they need total disarmament even more than do the democratic countries.

The trouble is that on both sides of the ideological frontier the tradition of military vigilance plus the influence of all those who are interested in maintaining military forces have succeeded in keeping alive the bogeys of aggressive and dangerous enemies. As a result of wrong information about the intentions of the other side a new attitude toward war and peace has crystallized today which might be called "neomilitarism." A neomilitarist is someone who is no longer aggressive himself and would not wish his own nation to invade a neighbor. Still, he believes in the aggressiveness of the others who, he feels, would not hesitate to attack a defenseless country.

The conception of neomilitarism does not imply anything unethical, but only lack of information. The majority of all people in East and West, though peaceful, are brought up as neomilitarists today, and as good conformist patriots they believe, and make others believe, in the bogeys haunting their country.

In the case of the two superpowers, the United States and the Soviet Union, there is no serious direct conflict of interests regarding possession of territories, natural resources, or markets. But tension exists because of the mutual suspicion. Therefore, the strategy of peace should differ entirely today from that of former times. Once it appeared necessary to leave no doubt that the country was strong enough to resist an aggressor. Today nobody doubts any longer the strength and determination of nuclear powers to resist. But all are badly suspect of being aggressive and tending to rob the others' freedom. Similar suspicions exist in the East against West Germany.

In such a political atmosphere we cannot expect a release of tension nor significant steps toward real disarmament. Hence, the United Nations should encourage its member states to start an enterprise which might lead to détente and can be undertaken with small expenditure. What we need is an International Campaign Against National Defamation, lending the opportunity to disprove slanderous accusations and to expel the bogeys. Such an antidefamation campaign could be carried out by frank and open discussions on problems which are of vital importance for the future of mankind but which, under the influence of neomilitarism, are shunned in conventional diplomatic talks. Such questions are: Why are we afraid of each other? What is your reason for lavishly wasting money and manpower for no other purpose than to prevent us from doing something which we recognize to be an international crime and would never do ourselves?

The UN members could, for instance, use specifically trained personnel in their embassies as "enlightenment attachés." They should be commissioned to discuss with all kinds of people, ranging from statesmen to the men in the street, the questions indicated above, and issue reports which should be publicized by all means of mass communication so that a great number of people will be enabled to understand why a country feels it is in a defensive position against an aggressive enemy. Another, more efficient method for enlightenment about peaceful intentions would be to arrange dialogues on the summit level on the same questions. Such discussions should be well prepared through correspondence between experts in order to collect and reject all essential arguments and counterarguments on both sides. It is only a condensed and well-edited final product which, preferably in form of a TV dialogue between heads of governments, should be given a maximum of publicity.

Summing up what I have learned from the history of the last two decades, but what most people have not yet properly understood, I find the following realities: Since 1945, science and the technology of warfare have changed so much that the net gain of any war will be negative for both sides. Therefore, all military plans are necessarily only defensive. In spite of this fact, more money than ever before in peacetime is spent for armament in anticipation of an attack from outside. More security than will ever be achieved by increasing armament could be gained by convincing potential enemies that one cannot think of striking first.

A successful international campaign against national defamation could remove the international misunderstanding breeding the bogeys. By doing so, it could pave the way to a world without war and thus yield the maximum of benefit to mankind at a minimum cost.


## Josef Hans Thirring

*In recent decades the voice of Austrian physicist Josef Hans Thirring has been heard throughout the world, pleading for restrained, rational approaches to the tinder of international disputes. Few men have better comprehended the horrors of thermonuclear warfare. In his book, The History of the Atomic Bomb, published in 1946—four years before President Truman announced the decision to produce the hydrogen bomb— Professor Thirring forecast the development of these weapons and revealed their characteristics and the potential of their destructive power. Professor Thirring was born in Vienna in 1888 and headed the department of theoretical physics at Vienna University for thirty years, both before and after World War II. During the war he was pensioned by the Nazis because of his antimilitarism. Since 1957 he has been vice president of the Austrian National Commission of UNESCO. From 1957 to 1963 he was a member of the Austrian Bundesrat. His books include Ideas of Einstein's Theory, Power Production, and Energy for Man.*

# WARREN WEAVER

## Confessions of a Scientist-Humanist

---

O BSERVATIONS, we have finally and painfully learned in science, depend upon the observer, and after each observation the observer is, perhaps by very little but nevertheless essentially, a different person. So I have to start by mentioning a few facts about my life.

My earliest curiosity was about how things are made and why they work. This led me by semantic error—my family and friends knowing the word "engineering" but being wholly vague about the word "science"—to my graduating from college with the degree of civil engineer. But it was during my sophomore year that the blazing beauty and power of differential and integral calculus were revealed by a great teacher, and I promptly knew that I wanted to move into mathematics and, eventually, into mathematical physics. So I went on to take a doctor's degree, and spent more than a dozen years teaching undergraduate mathematics to engineers, and the classical fields of mathematical physics to graduate students of physics.

Then came a reorienting. My friend and previous co-worker Max Mason had gone from the presidency of the University of Chicago to the Rockefeller Foundation, and he caused me to be invited to join that philanthropy as Director for the Natural Sciences. The phrase "natural sciences" there meant, in principle, "everything scientific except medicine"; however, it promptly began to mean, in operational terms, something different.

For, forced by the offer to think what a large philanthropic foundation ought to be doing, I rather suddenly realized that if such an agency were to have significant influence upon the development of science it ought not simply climb on a surfboard riding down a great wave that had been building for a century, and which was sweeping forward with majestic power—it ought to scan the horizon and try to help build a wave of the future.

Research in the physical sciences was, in 1932 when I faced this decision, moving forward with great vigor. The discouraged and complacent prediction of 1900 that there was nothing left to do but slightly to improve the accuracy of physical measurements had been blasted by Einstein, Planck, Bohr, and the genius of the "boy physicists" of the twenties. Relativity and quantum theory were leading to the beginnings of modern high-energy particle physics, and startling and beautiful new results were fairly bursting forth. The *Physical Review* changed from a thin monthly to a massively thick bi-monthly; and over the world dozens of new journals appeared.

All this was wonderful, was amazing, and was lovely. But this wave needed no special encouragement. Interconnections with technology and with defense were assuring massive support from industry and government. The problem with that wave was not to build it up—the real problem, when one considered nuclear energy, was to determine whether this wave of unleashed physical power was becoming a tidal wave that might engulf us.

There was discernible, however, another wave—one ready to swell. For centuries other able scientists had been concerned not with physical but rather with living nature. Its incredible variety and complication was such that for long, early periods little was possible beyond collection, description, and classification. Then observation became more penetrating, and scientists began to study the parts of living things, their actions and interactions, and the overall behavior of living organisms.

But variety and complication, and the lack of tools with which to deal with such variety and complication, limited progress. By 1932, however, when the problem of deciding on a new program in science faced the Rockefeller Foundation, one could see that the situation had essentially changed.

For the various physical sciences, notably chemistry and physics but also that nonphysical and essentially mental science, mathematics, had by then produced a whole array of new instruments, of new techniques of analysis, and of new general theories that promised to have the dexterity, precision, generality, and power to deal with the complex problems of living matter. It therefore seemed clear to me that the Rockefeller Foundation ought to concentrate upon developing modern experimental biology, or, more broadly and accurately, ought to concentrate upon financing the friendly invasion of the biological sciences by the physical sciences.

It seemed equally clear to me that I was no person to head such a program, since my training and experience had all been in the physical sciences. I was wholly fascinated by the physical sciences, and was very happy in the job I already had. But the officials of the Rockefeller Foundation persuaded me; and coming to this fork in the road, I chose the unexpected and strange turning.

As a result of this decision I spent twenty-eight years in the Rockefeller Foundation with a wholly new range of problems. I had to reorient myself scientifically by self-study of the various biological disciplines. As my responsibilites were enlarged to include the foundation's activities in agriculture and medicine, my contacts with scientists and with problems spread from its previous base in the United States and Europe to South America, India, and the Far East. The emphasis continued to be, broadly speaking, upon biological problems; and much of this work was rooted in the physical sciences.

Thus through the lucky fortune of my work I have had an opportunity to have unusually wide exposure to the different kinds of science and to different parts of the world. At the same time I have also been intensely interested in a lot of other things—in reading, in music, in gardening, in the general experiences of travel. For more than forty-five years I have been an ardent collector of Lewis Carroll, with special interest in the translations of *Alice in Wonderland* into nearly fifty languages. I have been confused, and on the whole bored, by my attempts to read political history, but have been fascinated to read intellectual history. I have a pleasant but rather dazed curiosity about formal philosophy, a subject which I disliked for many years, until I became sensible enough to realize that it profoundly differs from science in that its interest and value do not depend upon its making progress in the solution of the problems with which it is concerned. I have a deep and sustained interest in religion.

Out of all this good fortune of broad interests and exposure, what have I learned? I have a few assorted convictions, and a main conclusion.

Of the widely assorted convictions I will merely list as samples that childhood is usually an unhappy period (mine certainly was); that we do not take seriously enough the concerns, ideas, or abilities of children; that the central purpose of education should be to teach how to learn; that life's most important goals—such as happiness, to which I give a very high rating—must be attacked indirectly; that the luckiest persons are those who enjoy their work; that fun and gaiety are seriously important—solemnity, as Tristram Shandy reports a French wit to have said, being "a mysterious carriage of the body to cover defects of the mind"; that spelling is illogical, ridiculous, and unimportant; and that there is nothing worse than badly cooked vegetables, and nothing better than good cheese and Burgundy.

Turning from such trivia, the major thesis I will state is this, that as man's control of his environment has proceeded, giving him time to think and to make discoveries leading to further control, he has progressively uncovered more and more complication; but at the same time he has succeeded in discovering more and more unifying principles which accept the ever-increasing variety, but recognize an underlying unity. He has, in short, discovered the many and the one. Science has been a great leader in this process of revelation. But the process is by no means limited to science.

This view received a major scientific impetus when Copernicus, some four-and-a-half centuries ago, removed the ancient but unsupportable simplicity of a fixed and central earth resting at the center of a revolving painted dome. The special position of our earth was at one stroke destroyed, and we became one of the countless billions of stars. Man should at that moment have realized that his own supposed special position in creation was also subject to challenge.

Not long thereafter Galileo Galilei initiated the great series of theories that, while recognizing the wild variety with which objects can move, placed all these motions within the conceptual simplicity of the laws of dynamics. Starting with the pendulum and the falling feather and stone, he proved that the earth does indeed move; and his contemporary, Kepler, discovered the three laws that characterize the motions of all the planets. It has taken to the present to round out this ever-improving story, with a major contribution from Clark Maxwell—who captured in four short and universal equations the laws that are obeyed by electrical quantities—and with a still more recent improvement provided by quantum dynamics. All of this has brought about the present-day result that for all objects whatsoever, from the elementary particles which make up atoms to the stars which make up the galaxies, however complex and various their motions may be, all these are cases included within unifying laws of austere generality.

We will see in a moment that all matter is included within an even more widely embracing unity; but let us turn for a moment to the world of living things.

· ·

The singularity of man was shaken by Copernicus in a manner that we have fully recognized only recently when we became aware that there may well be billions of other cold stars in the universe with earthlike properties and perhaps with sentient inhabitants. But the great blow to man's illusion of singularity came, of course, with Darwin. With many details still and stimulatively lacking, the evidence is overwhelming that all living creatures are kin. It is relatively easy to grasp superficial aspects of this tremendous fact—indeed, as one sees recent moving pictures of the great apes it cannot be judged difficult to acknowledge our kinship to them. But as one looks at the almost incredible and indeed bizarre variety and complexity of the animal world—especially the inhabitants of the sea—it requires a real effort to appreciate the interconnections and the underlying unity.

The diversity, however, is a surface phenomenon. When one looks underneath and within, the universal unity again becomes apparent. We remember the name of Gregor Mendel, curious about the variety in the blossom colors of the peas in his monastery garden at Brünn. His revolutionary ideas about genetic mechanisms have cut through all of the surface diversity of the inheritance of characteristics. In its present-day formulation in molecular genetics, we recognize the universality of the basic structure of the genetic apparatus, the lovely spiral molecules that store genetic information and code the messages that, passed along by a second "messenger" molecule, guide the synthesis of proteins. The DNA differs in fine detail between you and me—which is, in fact, a reason why you are you and I am I. But the main architecture of the DNA is the same in a virus, a mollusk, a rose, or a man; and the code used for the genetic messages is universal for all living things.

So, inside, all living things have now become brothers. Indeed they are more profoundly similar than the comparisons of their gene mechanisms might suggest. For one of the striking univer-

salities of the whole biological kingdom is that not only the repro-
ductive mechanism but also the metabolic mechanisms are essentially the same in the cells of a lizard, an eagle, and a man—indeed,
in the single cell which constitutes all there is of an amoeba.
Thus the so-called Krebs or citric-acid cycle, within which are transformed the carbohydrates, fats, and proteins to furnish the chief
source of metabolic energy, occurs within the single cells of practically all creatures.

Because of this striking and lovely fact that the inner patterns
of life are closely similar in all forms, the biologist does not need
always to experiment upon man to learn about man. He may
choose convenient cases—neurospora for gene biochemistry, the
giant axon of the squid for nerve conduction, the gentle albino rat
for nutrition studies, the cat for a detailed study of visual patterns,
flatworms or pigeons or porpoises for investigating learning.

With the motions of all dead matter put into universal formu-
lae, and the revelation that all living things have deep common
traits, two further steps remained. One of these, at the moment, is
not completed; but no informed and responsible scientist doubts
that any gap will much longer remain between the world of dead
matter and the world of living matter.

That gap, previously so great, began suddenly to shrink in 1828
when the organic chemist F. Wöhler synthesized, from totally inorganic starting materials, a substance (urea) which is produced in
living bodies and which, it was formerly held, could be produced
only in a living body. By now chemists have synthesized thousands
of these "organic" compounds. Indeed such syntheses are so common that they go unnoticed unless the case is one of great complexity and difficulty, and the basis has been removed for a biologically
based distinction between "organic" and "inorganic" chemistry.

A much more important narrowing of the gap, however, results
from the fact that we are on the very verge of producing, in glass
dishes in the laboratory and starting from wholly dead matter, an

object which we will have to recognize as being alive. This object will presumably be a virus. These entities are known to share characteristic properties of both the inanimate and animate world. On the one hand they reproduce their kind; but on the other hand, as purified crystalline material they can be stored in a bottle indefinitely. The possibility of a laboratory-produced "living thing" is so tremendous, so awesome a fact, that some believe it better not to think about it.

There is further evidence of this closing of the gap between deadness and life. The last quarter-century has seen the birth and lusty development of a new hybrid science—molecular biology. It seeks to explain all biological phenomena in terms of the properties of molecules—that is to say, in terms of the laws of physics. I do not add "and of chemistry," for at this fundamental level the distinction between physics and chemistry is another instance of a variety which has become unimportant.

The triumphs of molecular biology have, to date, been primarily in genetics; but it is clear that a molecular biology of neurophysiology is about to evolve that will bring an explanation on the molecular level of memory, of learning, and indeed of the entire mind-brain-body relationship.

Although the living world holds the record for variety, with about 1,000,000 species and subspecies of plants and perhaps 2,500,000 of animals, nevertheless the world of inanimate objects is also complex. At present the physicist recognizes 104 basic kinds of elements, of which eighty-one are stable (hydrogen, helium, oxygen, carbon, iron, etc.), and twenty-three are radioactive (radium, thorium, etc.). The total count of nuclear species, including all the stable and unstable isotopes that are variants of the elements, is 1,511 at present, with about twenty additional ones being discovered each year.

Are there relations between these inanimate units out of which everything is built? Can one be transformed into or evolve into another? The answer depends upon whom you ask and when. The Greeks, the alchemists of the thirteenth century, Dr. William Prout in 1815–16, and modern physicists all say yes. A century ago any sober scientist would have said no, and would probably have scoffed at the questioner.

Indeed we now have a detailed and experimentally confirmed theory that explains how hydrogen, at the incredibly high temperatures within stars, "burns" to yield helium—and energy and more hydrogen as well, so that the process goes on and on. Three helium nuclei, in turn, can fuse to form carbon, with oxygen and helium nuclei as by-products. And so on and so on, the theory explaining, in good general agreement with the facts as far as we know them, the relative abundance in our universe of practically all the various physical elements. Thus, granting that details are still to be worked out, the physicists' theory of inorganic evolution is much more analytical and quantitative than the biologists' theory of organic evolution. The latter, for example, could not attempt to predict the equilibrium ratios between the total numbers of amoebae, ants, robins, chimps, and men.

Here again, then, is a story of the uncovering of tremendous variety and complexity—but the further discovery of the unifying relations that underlie and embrace all the complexity. The story, however, does not stop here, for there is one more major chapter.

That is the chapter which truly connects the dead world with the living world. The outlines of that chapter have as yet only been sketched. We have mentioned the initial clues of the synthesis of urea and the dual nature of viruses. But we have indeed seen the border between the living and the nonliving blur and become indistinct. Modern science is, in fact, now engaged in connecting the discovery of the prior act of the inorganic evolution of the elements with the second—and in our present view, culminating—act of the evolution of the living world. That is to say, science is now joining inorganic and organic evolution into a single grand pattern.

This joining is by no means complete at the moment, and even the partial results are still being debated. But there is direct evidence that in a primitive atmosphere of hydrogen, methane, ammonia, and water vapor an electric discharge can bring about the formation of several amino acids. These are substances which are the building blocks of protein, and proteins, as the word indicates, are the basic stuff of life. This story is only beginning to unfold, and much detail remains unexplored; but as always, the detail, confused at first, will fall into a pattern of overall simplicity.

Important as is this pageant of the discovery that the surface diversity of all nature is in fact superficial, being underlaid by an all-embracing unity, this is not all, for the materials and mechanics of life are not life. So, it seems to me, we should take still greater satisfaction in the evidence of the growing unification of the humane aspects of life. This even shows up in that most fractionated of all fields, world politics; for though we are still in the early stages of maturation which, tragically, may not occur soon enough, the mere fact of a world organization, the mere fact that favored nations are concerned about the ill-favored—this, we must remember in moments of discouragement, represents tremendous progress.

There is a sense of growing inner unity in the world of religion, with present-day ecumenical movements that would have been unbelievable even a half-century ago. The planet-wide worlds of art, of music, of literature, are unified as has never before been the case. Transport and communication bind us all together as never before. At times we resent the efficiency of communication, longing for the good old days when we did not know of the famines, plagues, riots, and insurrections that were torturing our fellow creatures. But as has been true in science, the complication must come to the surface and be recognized and faced before underlying unity can prevail.

The world of science has long been an internationalized world, and now that the true nature of science is more generally realized, science can join forces with the arts and humanities and with philosophy and religion. For we now know that science is motivated by curiosity, inspired by imagination, and based on faith. We know that it seeks increasing order, and does not pretend to deal with immutable truth. Magnificent as science is, and superbly useful as are its applications, we know that its apparent objectivity is only superficial, its pronouncements always open to revision. We know that, as is all art, it is culture-bound.

What then have I learned from a life spent chiefly in science, but also partly in the library and in the garden? It is that life is stimulatingly, deliciously complicated—but is all of one piece. We are built to appreciate variety, but to seek and recognize unity.

The variety of life cannot be disregarded. Variety is inevitable and desirable, but variety must be either resisted or accommodated and appreciated. To resist variety leads to sinful disaster. To recognize and tolerate variety and to penetrate it so as to discover the underlying unity is the common-good way of science, the arts, and religion.

When this way is pursued, what final lesson is then learned? It is that the ultimate unifying virtues are order, beauty, faith, and love. The emphasis in science is upon the first of these four words, slowly tapering off on the remaining three. The emphasis of religion, on the other hand, increases from first to last in this list, culminating on the final word. The arts and the humanities primarily emphasize the central two. But the underlying unity being what it is, all are concerned with all.

"All things," wrote Heraclitus, "come out of the one; and the one out of all things."


**Warren Weaver**

*Dr. Warren Weaver is an internationally famous administrator of large-scale, science-oriented research programs. Working through the Rockefeller and Alfred P. Sloan foundations, he has directed the administering* of millions of dollars in grants; the research done on these grants has made the U.S. preeminent in biology and medicine. One of his major beliefs is that "learning how to learn" is a basic step toward understanding and mastering our environment. He was born in Reedsburg, Wisconsin in 1894, obtained undergraduate and graduate degrees at the University of Wisconsin, and became chairman of Wisconsin's mathematics department. In addition to his connections with the Rockefeller and Sloan foundations, he is a member of the board of science consultants of the Sloan-Kettering Institute for Cancer Research. His books include Mathematical Theory of Communication (co-author), The Scientists Speak (editor), and Lady Luck—the Theory of Probability.

xx
# JOHN F. WHARTON

## Does Anyone Know Reality?

---

PERHAPS YOU were brought up, as I was, to believe in the endless possibilities of progress and in the ability of the individual to play a part in promoting it, and in the fact that the acquisition of knowledge gave the individual the power he needed for such a role. I still cling to this general view, even though world history during the past fifty years has done little to justify affirmative or rational approaches to critical problems. I confess that I came very close not long ago to abandoning the notion of personal relevance and responsibility. Modern science had something to do with it.

It struck me forcibly one day that modern science was pouring out knowledge, in the shape of discoveries, hypotheses, and tests, at a rate far surpassing my comprehension. Even the recent past was what Alice's Red Queen called a "slow sort of country"; by running fast one could get somewhere; now one has to run that fast to stay even with oneself, and twice as fast in order to get anywhere. I felt engulfed by a wave of the Scientific Future.

The effect was heightened by a talk with my daughter, a medical student. I asked casually what she thought of the following definition of science—"The systematized knowledge of the facts and laws of the material world, including both organic and inorganic matter."

My daughter said that it sounded fair enough; then, taking a deep breath, she suggested lovingly but firmly that I stop bothering myself with such matters, because I knew *nothing* of modern science. I felt this was a slight exaggeration, but I also recalled a small incident which tended to confirm it. I purchased a new book by Erwin Schrödinger, whose *What Is Life?* had fascinated me. Upon opening the new book, I discovered it consisted almost entirely of mathematical symbols. Not only were the equations unintelligible, *the symbols themselves were brand new and meaningless to me.*

Clearly, there was little scientific future for me. But, I realized, it was the people who did understand such symbols who were pouring out the new discoveries, who were making H-bombs, who were sending rockets to the moon. The world was seemingly becoming the domain of the expert in the Scientific Method. What could one such as I do to acquire the knowledge necessary to contribute to human progress?

I was of an age where I could flirt with the great American Circe—retirement—and I was tempted. I found great appeal in the notion of sitting on the sidelines and watching a game which, true, I would understand less and less, but would still remain fascinating. Subconsciously I knew that retirement à *l'Américaine* was likely to be the beginning of a short end, but it looked alluring. However, some phantom Mercury handed me the protective white flower just in time. It happened thus.

I chanced upon a succinct statement of the Scientific Method and how it became the Great Tool of research after Galileo, Kepler, and Newton launched modern science on its triumphant career. In using this tool the scientist observes data, makes a hypothesis that certain results will follow certain causes, and tests the hypothesis under controlled circumstances. If the results follow, the hypothesis is deemed to be proved. For example, Einstein observed the behavior of a beam of light; he hypothesized that it traveled in a curve; pictures of an eclipse were taken, and the plates recorded a curve. I noted that the Method began and ended with observation; without something to observe, it is admittedly inoperable.

I noted one other point. There was no explanation of what, to me, was the most important factor—Einstein's inspired guess. What produced that? And wouldn't it have been just as true if there had been no cameras capable of space photography? If so, couldn't there be many truths for which there could be no scientific proof at all? And isn't the *inspired* guess the basis of increasing human knowledge?

I broke off this train of thought in order to keep an engagement at an art museum where a loan exhibit was showing the painting which Gauguin considered his greatest work—the one which he entitled *Whence come we, what are we, whither go we?* Both the painting and the title struck me as masterpieces. For you cannot answer those three questions without starting a whole train of other profound questions—is life meaningless, or divinely purposeful, or something in between; is there a God; is there a soul; is the soul immortal; are we punished or rewarded in a hereafter for our acts on earth; is there a goal to which our actions *should be* directed? Gauguin's searching-eyed women brought home sharply the fact that for six thousand years men and women had been asking these questions, and for the same six thousand years a series of priests, philosophers, and politicians had been on hand, ready and willing— but never fully able—to offer completely satisfying answers.

It suddenly crossed my mind that not one of these answers was the result of the Scientific Method. They have all been guesses— hopefully inspired—for which no proofs were available. Yet the answers which did become widely accepted have had, and still have today, a greater impact on human behavior and human happiness than all the scientific discoveries put together. For the accepted answers have had, and still have, such a tremendous influence in shaping human conduct that one might well say that they are today determining whether the fruits of science will be used to produce the Apostle John's new heaven and new earth or to blow several hundred million people to bits.

The more I thought about it, the more extraordinary it all became. It is *not* facts but our beliefs about facts which control our actions. It also occurred to me that once an unscientific hypothesis is accepted—for example, personal immortality—the true believers will support it with a devotion and sacrifice seldom accorded to any scientific thesis. Galileo bowed to the Pope; St. Peter did not bow to Caesar.

All very strange, I thought. In any event it became clear to me that science does not dominate the world. There still is plenty of room for the unscientific thinker. Indeed, in the present state of human evolution, he might be more important than the greatest scientific discoverers. If only one man knew the secret of atomic energy, we would admit readily the immensity of his power. But consider the possibility of one man's having the secret of making *all* people believe what he wishes them to believe? *That* would dwarf all other powers, for good or evil. Consider two minor examples— the almost psychotic George Fox's convincing the English people to abolish slavery; the truly psychotic Adolf Hitler's convincing millions of sober Germans that they belonged to a master race entitled to wreak vengeance and torture on helpless people whom they considered inferiors.

People forget; hence they fall into error. Most thinking today on the subject of force, for example, is incredibly shallow. People seem to think that men who can make and deliver atomic bombs are dangerous. Actually, it is the men who have the secret of controlling the beliefs of the bomb-makers and bomb-droppers who have the power. People state, ponderously, that a totalitarian regime cannot be overthrown because the rulers have all the force; they forget that these rulers only have it so long as they can control the thinking of the force-wielders.

I do not believe any one man will discover such an all-embracing secret as the control of thought on a universal scale, but I have come to the conclusion that groups of thinkers might, today, begin to get a better understanding of it. If they do, it will be the result of inspired guesses which a nonscientist may well make. When I arrived at this point in my thinking, my intellectual enthusiasm returned; my despair evaporated; I dropped all thought of retirement; I decided to become one of such a group. Perhaps we would be "reaching for the unreachable star," but I determined to pursue the question of what makes people believe what they do believe—particularly what they take on faith.

Of course, this is not a brand new quest. Many thinkers have given it consideration before. But certain possible new elements are present today.

For one thing, the nonscientist can obtain great aid from the scientist, *if* the latter is willing to join with him in the quest. Scientists are loath to do this. They follow quite literally the injunction to render to Caesar the things that are Caesar's; they usually stop there, and cast a jaundiced eye on any attempt to render to God the things that are God's. But, clearly, some beliefs come from the double impact of environmental sensations on our five senses—a process which is within the scientist's domain—and also from endosomatic stimuli which, as yet, are so mysterious that an unscientific thinker's inspired guess may prove the first clue to understanding.

A *possible* new element in the quest came to my attention in a curious way. Out of the blue I received a call from a man named Arthur Arshawsky, better known as Artie Shaw, the famous bandleader. He is no longer interested in the music game, and the express purpose of his call was to ask me to discuss some motion picture problems. However, when we met he opened the conversation by urging me to read a little-known book by G. N. M. Tyrrell entitled *Homo Faber*. I had read it under the English title, *Man the Maker*—a fact which surprised Mr. Shaw, but only increased his enthusiasm to a point which led me to reread it. It presents a startling hypothesis.

Mr. Tyrrell's thesis, if I understand him correctly, holds that primitive man (*Homo faber*) was almost entirely governed by what we now call the Old Brain—although Tyrrell does not use this term —the seat of the instincts. He had very little cortex, the seat of intellect and creativity. The Old Brain resists creativity; it wants no change; it is the greatest of all No-no-no personalities. It wants a simple, easily understood world; it resists advances in knowledge. But the cortex grew; Man became *Homo sapiens* as well as *Homo faber*. As the cortex evolved into a stronger and stronger organ, it demanded more and more knowledge, of itself and of its environment, although the *Homo faber* in us tried to hold it back. Today, Tyrrell seems to argue, the cortex has evolved to a point in many human beings where it will consider some startling hypotheses— whether, for example, the world recognizable by the five senses is the whole world.

That proposition is too far a country for our present travels, but it contains a simpler hypothesis which would make a good starting point for our quest: Human beings can communicate with one another—and hence influence one another—by methods which seem to lie outside the five senses. If this is true, it may have a tremendous impact on the problem of controlling man's beliefs.

In one way, this is not such a surprising thesis. Clearly, animals communicate with one another in ways that are completely mysterious to us. Why should not human beings have similar capacities? Would this not explain, for example, the mysterious phenomenon of leadership? Think of the impact of John F. Kennedy on the American people; was it accomplished simply by his looks, words, and deeds? Wasn't there *something* more?

Tyrrell discusses extrasensory perception at some length. He is amazed by the refusal of the scientific priesthood to so much as look at the evidence—which, he insists, would certainly be studied if it were in any other field. He thinks this is a clear case of the *Homo faber* in us being so terrified of the possibility that it will not let us investigate. Certainly the idea of a group of people on earth who are able to communicate with one another by seemingly miraculous means *is* frightening. Bernard Shaw touched on this point in his play, *Back to Methuselah*.

The modern abstract arts are an interesting example of combining sensual and supersensual communication. Sir Herbert Read has described the appeal of abstract art with his usual lucidity and directness:

The [modern] artist becomes a man gifted with the capacity to project symbols from his subconscious which are of general validity—that is to say, they are symbols which other people might project if they had the capacity, and which, when projected to them, they can immediately accept. This act of acceptance replaces the feeling of pleasure which is the reaction in the case of a normal work of art.

Incidentally, I have never experienced extrasensory powers in myself, and my own subconscious has never responded in the way Sir Herbert describes. Indeed, as I saw many friends reveling in abstract art, I began to feel almost ashamed of myself and to ask despairingly, "Why *doesn't* my subconscious respond?" I felt like the hero of Ionesco's *Rhinoceros*, who asks unhappily at one point why *his* skin doesn't turn into a leather hide. Yet the fact that extrasensory communication is not for everyone does not prove its nonexistence.

But ESP and abstract art are only two of many new elements around. If one will glance through the small-circulation journals, he will find gropings here, there, and everywhere. I have met personally two men who are studying the possible impact of cosmic forces on human behavior. There are still plenty of thinkers around. Some are undoubtedly crackpots, but some will prove to be important voices crying in the wilderness.

Just consider: In my childhood my teachers taught that the molecule was the smallest particle of matter. I still remember their saying that if a drop of water was magnified to the size of the earth, the molecules would look like tennis balls. They did also say that some theoreticians were talking of something the Greeks called an atom, but we pupils should remember the tennis balls. From there, in one lifetime, we have gone to electrons, neutrons, protons, and supersensual physical forces. Would it be surprising if we began to discover supersensual psychic forces?

One further new element to spur this quest should be mentioned. It is the threat of human annihilation. If necessity is the mother of invention, fear can be the progenitor of discovery. Certainly this threat will speed up the search.

All things considered, there has never been such an exciting time in human history. It *is* possible to progress to a better world. And when one realizes the importance of the nonscientific thinker, despair at one's incompetence vanishes. Everyone can participate in the quest, and may accomplish something. After all, it was not an astronomer, nor even a mathematician, who introduced to Renaissance man the idea that the sun is one of many stars; it was simply a thinker. I do not profess to be another Giordano Bruno, but I can still hope to contribute some small something to the sum of human happiness and dignity.

## John F. Wharton

*John F. Wharton, prominent New York attorney and public citizen, has made noteworthy contributions to the worlds of public affairs, publishing, and the arts. Born in Newark, New Jersey, in 1894, he is a graduate of Williams College and Columbia Law. He has served as board chairman of SR; a director and general counsel of Field Enterprises, Inc., World Book, Parade magazine, Simon and Schuster, and Pocket Books; vice president and a governing trustee of the American Ballet Theatre; and trustee of other cultural organizations. He is credited with devising the form of limited partnership used for financing most Broadway plays since World War II, and because of his vast knowledge of the theater* was chosen to be consultant-director of the Legitimate Theatre Industry Exploratory Committee to assist theatergoers and theater interests in solving various long-standing problems. Recently Mr. Wharton has begun work on his autobiography. His books include This Road to Recovery, Earning a Living, and The Explorations of George Burton.